Stereotyping and Social

B

Stereotyping and
Social Reality

Penelope J. Oakes,
S. Alexander Haslam and
John C. Turner

BLACKWELL
Oxford UK & Cambridge USA

First published 1994

Blackwell Publishers
108 Cowley Road
Oxford OX4 1JF
UK

238 Main Street
Cambridge, Massachusetts 02142
USA

British Library Cataloguing in Publication Data

A CIP catalogue record for this book is available from the British Library.

Library of Congress Cataloging-in-Publication Data

Oakes, Penelope J.
Stereotyping and social reality / Penelope J. Oakes, S. Alexander Haslam, and John C. Turner.
p. cm.
Includes bibliographical references and index.
ISBN 0-631-18871-1 (alk. paper). — ISBN 0-631-18872-X (pbk.: alk. paper)
1. Stereotype (Psychology) 2. Social psychology. I. Haslam, S. Alexander.
II. Turner, John C., 1947– . III. Title.
HM291.022 1994
302—dc20
93-22846
CIP

ISBN 0-631-18871-1

Typeset in 10 on 12 pt Sabon
by Best-set Typesetter Ltd., Hong Kong

Printed in Great Britain

This book is printed on acid-free paper

Contents

8 Politics, Prejudice and Myth in the Study of Stereotypes

List of Figures

List of Tables

The Authors

Penelope J. Oakes, S. Alexander Haslam and John C. Turner are, respectively, Lecturer in Social Psychology, Postdoctoral Research Fellow, and Professor of Psychology (Head of Department) in the Department of Psychology, The Australian National University, Canberra, Australia.

Preface and Acknowledgements

Stereotyping has fascinated social psychologists for over seventy years, but our relationship with the topic has always been slightly ambivalent. We can see that stereotyping is a crucial part of everyday adaptation to the social environment, yet insist that it is a distortion of reality, that it represents a failure to appreciate the way people *really* are – unique, differentiated, disparate individuals. This view is also widespread outside our science. The idea of stereotyping as it appears in the general media or in common parlance is almost always framed negatively, with a message of tired, old, unimaginative images (stereotypes) substituting for the reality of living, breathing, dynamic individuality.

When it really took hold in the late 1970s, the cognitive approach to stereotyping bid fair to change this image of the process. Stereotyping was seen as normal, rational, it served positive ends. But the issue of the relationship between stereotyping and reality has never been confronted head-on in the cognitive literature as this has concentrated on the relationship between stereotyping and *cognition*. As a result, ideas of distortion, oversimplification and overgeneralization have survived intact. In this book we ask the question straightforwardly – what is the relationship between stereotyping and social reality? – and find that a new type of social cognitive analysis is necessary before we can answer it to our satisfaction.

We decided to write a book on stereotyping in 1988, but the work that has culminated in this particular book began in the late 1970s in Bristol, England, when John Turner began to develop self-categorization theory (Turner, Hogg, Oakes, Reicher and Wetherell, 1987). The theory provides the essential building blocks of the analysis of stereotyping presented here, but it was during the 1980s and early 1990s that the analysis was slowly worked out. Whilst each of us has made distinctive contributions to that analysis, the book has emerged very much as a joint effort and we all take responsibility for the whole.

Of course, self-categorization theory has continued to develop since 1987 (e.g. Turner, 1991; Turner, Oakes, Haslam and McGarty, in press), and we see this book as very much a part of that process of development – we hope it will be seen as moving the theory forward as much as it clearly draws upon it. In a sense, the book stands as something of a *test* of the theory. The social group and social categorization are the core of the theory, and they are at the heart of social stereotyping. We feel that the ability of a self-categorization analysis to synthesize issues in the stereotyping literature was crucial for the theory, and we hope that it will prove fruitful for the field as a whole.

We would like to acknowledge the special intellectual and personal debt we owe to Henri Tajfel. His legacy is apparent throughout the book. The ideas of Solomon Asch and Muzafer Sherif have also influenced us profoundly, ideas which we feel have been relatively neglected by stereotyping researchers to the detriment of theoretical development within the area.

Many colleagues and friends have contributed to the ideas expressed here as they have developed over nearly fifteen years. In particular, we thank Craig McGarty for lively discussions (sometimes arguments!) and for insights into illusory correlation (chapter 7), and categorization and social judgement. Our thanks also to Steve Reicher, Russell Spears, Bernd Simon, Jacques-Philippe Leyens, Vincent Yzerbyt, Barbara David, Margaret Wetherell, Miles Hewstone, Michael Hogg, Lyndon Brooks, Brett Hayes, Susan Morris, Karen Hutchinson and Mary Carse, and to Patricia Brown, Diana Grace and Kate Reynolds for the hours they put in compiling the index. Alison Mudditt and Alison Truefitt at Blackwells have provided invaluable support throughout.

Alex Haslam thanks the Commonwealth Scholarship and Fellowship Plan for financial support while he was completing his PhD (1986–90). The Australian Research Council has funded projects on 'Social influences on cognition' (1991–93) and 'Social stereotyping and the perception of ingroup and outgroup homogeneity' (1993–95) which continue to assist the development of ideas presented in this book.

Finally, we would like to express our love and thanks to Catherine Haslam, Jane Turner and Isobel Turner, three people who are very important to us. They put up with the absent-mindedness, highs and lows, and general unpredictability that book writing seems to bring out in even the most well-adjusted partners and parents.

Prologue

This book is a whole with closely interdependent parts – a gestalt. The gestalt is held together by the theme of the relationship between stereotyping and reality, and by the fact that each part represents a necessary step towards the realization of the main goal, the presentation of a new analysis of social stereotyping. The book is not 'just a text', or 'just a review', or 'just a research monograph' – it is aiming to be all three, combining thorough review with the development of new ideas and presentation of new research, in a format and style aimed at advanced undergraduate students as well as postgraduates, researchers and teachers.

It may be helpful if we place the parts of the gestalt in context at this point. Following the general introduction and overview in chapter 1, chapters 2 and 3 are review chapters, covering the early and then cognitive approaches to stereotyping respectively. Chapter 4 is also partly review, as it discusses the tradition of social identity research and ideas which must be seen as part of the social psychological literature relevant to stereotyping. But chapter 4 is also where presentation of our own analysis begins, with an outline of self-categorization theory – the basis on which we have reassessed social stereotyping. Chapter 4 ends with a summary of how the basic ideas of the theory can contribute to a new understanding of stereotyping, and chapters 5, 6, 7 and 8 develop and extend these ideas, applying them explicitly to issues and themes which dominate the stereotyping literature. Whilst new material is reviewed in chapters 5 and 6 (largely from the categorization and social judgement literatures) the main aim of the chapters from 5 onwards is to elaborate the self-categorization analysis of stereotyping. Chapters 5–7 focus primarily on cognitive aspects of stereotyping consistent with the current emphasis in social psychology and the validity issue is discussed in that context. In chapter 8 the discussion of stereotype validity is broadened to include social aspects. As well as the cognitive form of stereotypes, their social content must also be considered in terms of both psychological and social validity. The latter distinction is, we believe, crucial for unravelling the issue of stereotype validity.

In summary, the book flows from straight review through to critical comment and presentation of our alternative analysis. Although individual chapters can be read in isolation (particularly 2, 3 and 4), each is part of, and has grown from, the integrated analysis which the book as a whole seeks to advance.

1

Introduction: The Social Psychology of Stereotyping

This book is about the social psychology of stereotyping. Stereotyping is the process of ascribing characteristics to people on the basis of their group memberships. Suppose, for example, we believe that 'women are emotional', that 'men are aggressive' or that 'white South Africans are racist', these are stereotypical beliefs and the perception of individuals as emotional, aggressive or racist *because* we have identified them as members of the relevant social groups is stereotyping. The collection of attributes believed to define or characterize the members of a social group is a stereotype. The stereotypes of one group *shared* by the members of another group are usefully referred to as *social* stereotypes (Tajfel, 1981a).

The way that we behave towards other people and our feelings about them very much depend upon the social groups to which they belong. Whether it is desirable or not, we hold beliefs about social groups and these beliefs influence our interaction with people identified as members. Think, for example, of your everyday interactions with a librarian, a doctor or a policewoman, and of interactions between Catholics and Protestants in Northern Ireland, Serbs and Croats in the former Yugoslavia, Israelis and Palestinians in the Middle East, and so on. This book is about the psychology of such beliefs, or more precisely about how and why we perceive people as members of social categories. Under what conditions do we categorize people as members of groups rather than as unique individuals, what determines how we characterize such groups, and when are these stereotypes applied to particular individuals?

Group-based interactions of the type alluded to above are ubiquitous – the process of dealing with people in terms of the groups to which they belong appears to be indispensable. However, it is often claimed that this process can lead to the misrepresentation of people's true characteristics.

This argument has two parts. First, it is suggested that when we deal with individuals in terms of their group membership, we typically treat them as if they were more similar to some people (members of the same group) and more different from others (members of different groups) than they *really are*. Second, it is proposed that group-based perception is contaminated by discriminatory values – we tend to believe that the groups to which we belong are better than those to which we don't. On these grounds stereotyping has been characterized as, at best, a process of simplification which serves to make reality manageable and, at worst, a pathological vehicle for prejudice and ill-treatment.

Social psychologists who seek to understand stereotyping are thus presented with an apparent paradox. On the one hand, it is clear that groups are a part of social reality, that important aspects of our lives depend upon them. On the other, many argue that group-based perception is a distortion of reality. This book seeks to make sense of this paradox. In it our aim is to explore the relationship between stereotyping and features of the social world. We shall confront a range of questions that have been central to previous research on this topic. Why do we so often characterize people in terms of their group memberships rather than in terms of their qualities as differentiated individuals? Is this done to deny individuality, or to facilitate prejudice, or to make dealing with people cognitively less demanding? In what sense, if any, are these characterizations deficient? Are stereotypes wrong because (and to the extent that) they are the manifestation of defective psychological processes?

In the past almost all researchers have assumed at the outset that stereotyping *is* deficient and then channelled their efforts into identifying the psychological basis of that deficiency. This approach (and the theme of deficiency) has been central to the study of stereotyping since the properties of stereotypes were first remarked upon by Walter Lippman in 1922. We shall provide an alternative theoretical perspective and argue that this assumption is unwarranted.

A Historical Overview of Stereotyping Research

Lippman (1922) initiated formal enquiry into stereotyping with the publication of his book *Public Opinion*. The attraction of this work has been enduring, primarily because it identified a number of features of stereotypes and stereotyping that were to form the basis of subsequent understanding.

In *Public Opinion* stereotypes were characterized as being selective, self-fulfilling and ethnocentric, ideas summed up in the claim that they 'constitute a very partial and inadequate way of representing the world', the word 'partial' here conveying the double sense of incomplete and biased (p. 72). Other apparent shortcomings were also noted. Stereotypes were understood to be defences which justify individuals' own positions and blind spots which preclude objective, balanced reasoning. They were seen to be rigid in the sense of being both 'obdurate to education or criticism' and insensitive to changes in reality (p. 65). They presented overgeneralized, exaggerated images which overlooked variability and denied individuality.

Not surprisingly, Lippman disapproved of stereotyping, commenting that if one wants to see the world *as it really is* 'there is no shortcut through, and no substitute for, an individualized understanding' (p. 59). At the same time though, he argued that stereotyping fulfilled a necessary function in allowing the individual to interact with a world too complex ever to represent in all its detail: 'the need of economizing attention is so inevitable, that the abandonment of all stereotypes for a wholly innocent approach to experience would impoverish human life' (p. 60). We shall see that this tension between, on the one hand, the apparent necessity of the processes underlying stereotyping and, on the other, rejection of their outcome persists in many modern accounts.

The first significant social psychological research into stereotypes was conducted by Katz and Braly (1933, 1935) some ten years after the publication of *Public Opinion*. The intention of this work was to examine the link between stereotypes and prejudice (i.e., *unjustified* negative reactions to an outgroup). This was achieved by administering a checklist to students at Princeton University which required them to assign five traits from a list of 84 to various racial groups. The findings revealed a high degree of consensus in subjects' stereotypic images. For example, 75 per cent of students characterized Negroes as lazy. Katz and Braly argued that this degree of agreement could not arise from students' personal knowledge of the groups which they described. Thus they contended that stereotypes are public fictions which arise from prejudicial influences 'with scarcely any factual basis' (p. 288). This view was later summarized by Katz and Schanck (1938, p. 89):

> The essential secret of the matter is that through the stereotype, or collec-
> tive representation, man sees an identity in nature, or in society, where
> none exists. The stereotype is an undiscriminating construct which assimi-
> lates varying types of experience into the same pattern on the basis
> of a minor resemblance or a fallacious similarity . . . The corollary of this

process is that men will hold absurd and contradictory views, since stereotypes are not governed by the sharpness of inclusion and exclusion of scientific concepts.

Although they were made long before stereotyping was properly understood as a product of categorization (see below), these comments speak to the fundamental issues which must be addressed in exploring the relationship between stereotyping and reality: the nature of categories (both social categories and general categories, such as scientific concepts), and the nature of reality, especially (for our purposes) social reality. Having considered chapters 4 to 8 the reader might like to return to, and perhaps re-evaluate, Katz and Schanck's statement.

As a consequence of Katz and Braly's work, the study of stereotypes became strongly associated with attempts to understand prejudice. Furthermore, because the checklist methodology which they employed became widely accepted as an appropriate research tool, these authors also shaped the nature of that research. Early empirical investigations were almost solely concerned with issues of stereotype *content* (Brigham, 1971).

The theme of error and bias persisted through this work, although some researchers became aware that the nature of apparent error was more subtle than had originally been supposed. For example, Mace (1943) saw stereotypes as 'quasi-pathological' but at the same time argued that in them 'the interplay of cognitive and emotional factors serves, as in a caricature, both to reveal and distort essential truths' (p. 29). This emerging 'kernel of truth' hypothesis gained strength from a number of studies showing that stereotypes were quite sensitive to changes in international relations brought about by World War II (e.g., Buchanan, 1951; Meenes, 1943). The idea of a stereotypical kernel of truth stands as one of the few attempts to resolve the fundamental paradox elaborated in the introductory paragraphs above. Its advocates proposed that while stereotypes failed to encompass individual differences, they nonetheless encapsulated some important features of group reality (e.g., see Vinacke, 1949, p. 284).

In the 1950s two distinct trends are discernible in stereotyping research, each elaborating one aspect of the dilemma at the heart of the kernel of truth debate. The majority of researchers continued to concentrate on the deficiencies of stereotyping (e.g., Bogardus, 1950; Hayakawa, 1950; Klineberg, 1950, 1951) while others began to question the assumptions which underpinned this traditional position (e.g., Laviolette and Silvert, 1951). This latter perspective was favoured by Asch (1952) who argued that in a great many situations the behaviour of individuals (e.g., members of audiences, committees, families, armies) *is* determined by their group membership and that representing people in terms of these group memberships (i.e., stereotyping) could thus be important in the representation of social reality. In his words: 'it is wrong to assume that we can best achieve a correct view of a person by ignoring his group relations' (p. 238). Sherif and his colleagues (e.g., 1967) argued that stereotypes serve to reflect the reality of *intergroup relations*. He provided convincing evidence of this in his famous boys' camp studies in which the content of the stereotypes held by rival groups became more favourable as relations between those groups became more cooperative.

Related ideas were presented by Fishman (1956) and Vinacke (1956, 1957). Fishman argued that stereotypes were valid to the extent that they served to reflect the nature of interaction between stereotyped and stereo-typing groups (p. 60), while Vinacke suggested that stereotypes were representations of authentic high-level conceptual relationships between individuals (i.e., social groupings; 1957, p. 239). The radical implication of all this work was that stereotypes were by nature neither irrational nor 'bad'.

These ideas could have provoked a major reconceptualization of stereotyping. Unfortunately their development, like that of the field as a whole, was limited by the reliance of mainstream stereotyping research upon a methodology (the Katz–Braly checklist) which became associated with issues of content alone and thus tended to draw attention away from the analysis of *psychological processes*. Partly for this reason, the exploration of other social psychological issues exerted a strong influence on the understanding of stereotyping. Primarily, theories of *prejudice* were seen to be relevant to stereotyping because many workers assumed that these phenomena were virtually interchangeable (e.g., Katz and Braly, 1935, p. 191; see Ashmore and Del Boca, 1981; Gardner, 1991). These theories typically incorporated a negative conceptualization of both stereotypes and stereotyping. For example, in their classic work *The Authoritarian Personality*, Adorno, Frenkel-Brunswik, Levinson and Sanford (1950) argued that stereotyping was a product of cognitive processes specific to intolerant people (authoritarians). Research in this tradition took the form of attempts to describe the aetiology of particular personality traits (e.g., intolerance of ambiguity, mental rigidity and narrow-mindedness) which were seen to characterize this type of person and account for the undesirable features of stereotypes.

However, not all research which approached stereotyping as an aspect of prejudice followed this line. Notably, in writing *The Nature of Prejudice*, Gordon Allport (1954) discussed the extent to which the *categorization process* (i.e., the cognitive grouping of individual objects as

identical, interchangeable) was involved in prejudice. Whilst he emphasized that categorization was essential to 'orderly living' (p. 20; cf.
Lippman, 1922), and noted many of its subtle features (in particular, its
general flexibility and responsiveness to the changing definition of
ingroups and outgroups), he continued to regard stereotypes as deficient
because they exaggerated the properties of the categories with which they
were associated and stood in the way of differentiated thinking. Moreover, in his discussion of these issues Allport maintained a clear distinction between the rational and irrational use of categories as associated
with the behaviour of tolerant and prejudiced people respectively.
Allport thus took a crucial theoretical step forward in suggesting that
prejudice might be a product of *normal* processes, but his analysis
contained an inherent contradiction. It suggested that the processes of
categorization implicated in stereotyping were essentially rational (cf.
Asch, 1952; Vinacke, 1957) but that their rationality was nonetheless
contingent upon the character of the individual stereotyper (cf. Adorno
et al., 1950; see Billig, 1985).

The spirit of uneasy compromise epitomized by Allport's analysis
prevailed for the best part of two decades, during which time research
interest in stereotyping steadily declined. The state of theoretical impasse
was then breached, and interest rekindled, by Henri Tajfel's (1969)
account of the 'Cognitive Aspects of Prejudice'.

Unlike G. Allport, Tajfel's primary background was not in the study
of prejudice. His work emerged from the study of judgement in the 'New
Look' tradition of the 1940s and 1950s. One of the central aims of this
type of work had been to look at the way in which psychological
processes were functionally affected by social factors. In the early 1960s
Tajfel conducted studies which looked at processes of *accentuation*, i.e.
the exaggeration of both *differences between* and *similarities within*
categories (Tajfel and Wilkes, 1963a). He reported results implying that
such accentuation could be induced simply by presenting cues which
encouraged subjects to perceive individual stimuli (lines of different
length) in terms of categories (long or short). In his 1969 paper Tajfel
spelled out the implications of these findings in the claim that:

> Without the introduction of variables of a social or emotional nature they
> present the essential features of social stereotypes: the subjective accentua-
> tion of differences in *relevant dimensions* between classes of stimuli, and
> their subjective reduction within each class. (pp. 84–5)

The distinctive legacy of this work, as identified by Tajfel himself, was 'to
stress the importance of the adaptive cognitive functioning of man in the
causation of prejudice' (1969, p. 96).

Tajfel thus reconceptualized stereotyping as the product of explicitly normal cognitive processes *common to all individuals*, although he too maintained the view that stereotypes themselves were deficient in being rigid and neglecting individual differences. His contribution is widely acknowledged as being revolutionary (e.g., see Ashmore and Del Boca, 1981; Hamilton, 1981c, p. 335; Stroebe and Insko, 1989). This revolution had several ramifications. First, researchers moved away from the analysis of stereotype content to explore the stereotyping *process* in its own right. Second, attempts to explain stereotyping became concerned with normal cognitive functioning rather than pathology. Third, and as a consequence of both these changes, the Katz–Braly checklist was replaced by the more formal methodology of experimental psychology. Fourth and finally, these developments led to a massive increase in stereotyping research (see Ashmore and Del Boca, 1981).

The breadth of stereotyping research carried out from a social cognitive perspective has been considerable. In particular, the movement gathered momentum in North America where the aim has been 'to push the cognitive analysis as far as it could go' (Hamilton and Trolier, 1986, p. 153; see also Hamilton, 1981c, p. 347; Ashmore and Del Boca, 1981, p. 31). The basis of this 'push' has been to seek out and examine cognitive processes responsible for particular features of stereotyping. Research has followed Lippman, G. Allport and Tajfel in suggesting that these processes fulfil the necessary function of rendering the stimulus world less complex. However, it is argued that the perceiver sometimes has to sacrifice accuracy for efficiency, as these processes (or shortcuts) can introduce perceptual error, bias and distortion. Stereotyping is understood to be an example of such distortion, a 'necessary evil' arising from the fact that the ideal situation – in which all perception is based on individualized case information – is ruled out by the inherent limitations of human mental functioning.

Although the last fifteen years of stereotyping research has been dominated by the cognitive perspective, it has not been without its critics. One clear problem is that as the cognitive analysis has progressed, important issues of actual stereotype *content*, central to the area in the 1940s and 1950s, have slipped from social psychologists' agenda. This point was recently made by Hoffman and Hurst (1990) who suggest that an unwillingness to confront the question of the relationship between stereotyping and reality may be contributing to the move away from content:

> The content origin issue has been a much more difficult problem to conceptualize satisfactorily within the information-processing paradigm in social psychology. Stereotypes belong to a class of 'schemas' that, in general, are

thought to have as their goal the representation of external reality (even though they may achieve only a selective or simplified version of this reality). In the case of stereotypes, however, this is tantamount to saying that they contain at least a kernel of truth – a position that social psychology has, understandably, been somewhat reluctant to embrace. (p. 197)

Is it the case that to conceptualize a stereotype as, in any sense, a 'representation of external reality' one has to adopt some variant of the kernel of truth approach, as it has been outlined by stereotyping researchers (see chapter 2)? We shall discuss this in detail in later chapters. Again, the reader might like to keep this issue in mind as our argument unfolds through this book.

Other commentators have also criticized aspects of the cognitive analysis. In fact one of the most prominent of these was Tajfel himself. In his 1981 paper 'Social Stereotypes and Social Groups' he argued that, as it had progressed empirically, so the social cognitive movement had retreated theoretically by overlooking the social (i.e., group-based) determinants of cognition. This critique was based on Tajfel's own research into and analysis of intergroup relations, as outlined in the *social identity theory* developed by Tajfel and Turner (Tajfel, 1972; Turner, 1975a; Tajfel and Turner, 1979, 1986). Social identity theory adopted the intergroup perspective of Sherif, arguing that prejudice and discrimination were not problems of individual attitudes but of intergroup behaviour. It assumed that images of own and other groups were held in common by individuals as members of social groups and reflected the character of intergroup relations. Individuals derived social identities from their group memberships and compared ingroup with outgroup to evaluate themselves in terms of these identities. The ethnocentric aspect of stereotyping and intergroup behaviour could be traced in part to a general motive to differentiate the ingroup positively from the outgroup, arising from the role of intergroup relations in self-definition.

Table 1.1 summarizes what we see as the major milestones in the study of social stereotyping up to Tajfel (1981a). Whilst personality theories of the type advanced by Adorno et al. have now more or less disappeared from the stereotyping scene, research into both intergroup relations (following Sherif and Tajfel) and individual cognition (following G. Allport and Tajfel) is still active and crucial. In the 1981 paper Tajfel tried to begin a process of rapprochement between the hitherto rather disparate cognitive (individual) and intergroup (social) traditions in the area, having himself been closely involved in both. In some ways this

Table 1.1 Historical developments in the study of social stereotyping

Key publications	Conceptualization of stereotypes	Focus of empirical work
Lippman (1922)	Rigid, over-simplified and selective, but necessary for simplification	—
Katz and Braly (1933)	Unjustified and contradictory fictions	Description of the content of various stereotypes
Adorno et al. (1950)	Erroneous products of pathological personality	Study of authoritarian and non-authoritarian individuals
G. Allport (1954)	Based on rational process of categorization, but rationality contingent on individual's nature	—
Sherif (1967)	Products of intergroup relations	Examining the effects of changing social relations
Tajfel (1969)	Based on rational processes of categorization common to all	Analysis of processes of accentuation
Hamilton (1981a)	Products of generalized and necessary cognitive processes that inadvertently produce error	Identification of various cognitive biases
Tajfel (1981a)	Shared products shaped by group membership and intergroup relations	Demonstrating the contribution of groups and values to the stereotyping process

book can be seen as a continuation of that effort. Broadly speaking, we aim to elaborate the argument that in order to understand the psychology of group phenomena (like stereotyping) it is necessary to examine the ways in which cognition both mediates and *is mediated by* individuals' group memberships and social relationships (see Tajfel, 1979, 1981b; Turner and Oakes, 1986). In these terms, processes of perception and cognition are *social* psychological, not merely because they involve the processing of information about people, but because they are the psychological products of an interaction between mind and society. In this book we focus these ideas on the issue of stereo-typing, and in so doing aim to achieve a better understanding of the role of this fascinating process in the individual's adaptation to the social environment.

An Overview of the Chapters

As we have said, the central task of this book is to investigate the dynamic relationship between stereotyping and reality. In order to pursue this goal it is necessary to provide a thorough review of previous research to put this issue in full context and to survey the array of potential responses to it. Thus we seek to draw a large net over the stereotyping literature rather than confine our analysis to recent (social cognitive) developments. Accordingly, chapter 2 reviews the many approaches to stereotyping and prejudice that preceded Tajfel's 1969 paper.

Chapters 3 and 4 both take Tajfel's 1969 paper as their starting point. Chapter 3 discusses the large body of research inspired by the social cognitive analysis of stereotyping. Here we examine work that identifies a range of cognitive mechanisms (shortcuts or biases) which are offered as explanations for various stereotyping effects. Rather than emphasize the role of cognition in determining social phenomena, chapter 4 explores the role of group life in shaping cognition. This alternative approach is central to the work of social identity theorists and has been elaborated more recently in Turner's (1985) self-categorization theory, discussed in some detail in chapter 4.

The process of categorization emerges from chapters 3 and 4 as critical in the explanation of stereotyping, yet disagreement about the role of categorization in social perception is also apparent. Chapters 5 and 6 focus on this disagreement, with chapter 5 examining the purpose of categorization, and chapter 6 its outcome. More specifically, chapter 5 asks whether categorization functions primarily to reduce the amount of information entering the cognitive system. This idea is the cornerstone of current cognitive analyses of stereotyping. We argue, in contrast, that the purpose of categorization is to *elaborate* rather than simplify perceptual input, and that this is *incompatible* with the idea that it is an information-reduction mechanism. After a general discussion of the functioning of categorization in person perception, the conditions under which social categories become salient (the essential first step in stereotyping) are formalized, leading to the claim that this occurs where given categories fit (and enable us to make sense of) the content and structure of people's actions, in interaction with the relative accessibility of categories in the perceiver's repertoire. Further implications of and evidence for this reconceptualization are presented in chapter 6, where the outcome of categorization is examined in detail, and it is argued that stereotypic *accentuation* can be seen as a veridical reflection of the social categorical features of stimuli across changing contexts.

Chapter 7 elaborates upon the theoretical implications of this analysis for two specific and important issues in current stereotyping literature: the representation of groups and stereotype formation. In particular, we present explanations of the phenomena of intragroup homogeneity (e.g., Quattrone and Jones, 1980) and illusory correlation (e.g., Hamilton and Gifford, 1976). Finally, chapter 8 summarizes and discusses the main points of our analysis in relation to the issue of stereotype validity. It considers not only whether the cognitive aspects of stereotyping represent 'prejudice' but also the psychological and social validity of stereotype content. One point to emerge here is that while the prevailing approach to stereotyping tends to emphasize the limitations of human cognition, our own work points to its general fitness. In these terms (social) cognition is seen not as an impediment to the perception of reality, but rather as the means by which its richness can be fully apprehended.

Suggested Further Reading and References

Here, and at that end of each chapter, we provide a list of readings which we think will enhance your appreciation of the issues that we have discussed. While we do not always agree with their content, where possible we have chosen readings which present clear arguments and convey enthusiasm for the issues in question.

Good historical overviews of stereotyping research are provided by Stroebe and Insko (1989) and Ashmore and Del Boca (1981). Readings dealing with more specific topics are recommended in the chapters that follow, but it is still hard to find better general, non-technical introductions to the area as a whole and the questions it raises than are provided in the books by Lippman (1922) and G. Allport (1954).

Allport, G. W. (1954) *The Nature of Prejudice.* Cambridge, MA: Addison Wesley.
Ashmore, R. D. and Del Boca, F. K. (1981) Conceptual approaches to stereotypes and stereotyping. In D. L. Hamilton (Ed.), *Cognitive processes in stereotyping and intergroup behaviour.* Hillsdale, NJ: Erlbaum. pp. 1–35.
Lippman, W. (1922) *Public opinion.* New York: Harcourt Brace.
Stroebe, W. and Insko, C. A. (1989) Stereotype, prejudice, and discrimination: Changing conceptions in theory and research. In D. Bar-Tal, C. F. Graumann, A. W. Kruglanski and W. Stroebe (Eds), *Stereotyping and prejudice: Changing conceptions.* New York and London: Springer Verlag. pp. 3–34.

2

Early Approaches to Stereotypes and Prejudice

The aim of this chapter is to review early approaches to the study of stereotypes and stereotyping. We shall examine the various strands of research which led up to the elaboration of a social cognitive approach to stereotyping.

The first research papers to discuss issues related to stereotypes were of three main types: those which, after Katz and Braly (1933), simply used checklists to ascertain the content of particular stereotypes held by various groups; those which attempted to establish the factual basis of stereotypes; and those which, after Lippman (1922), offered a broad theoretical analysis of the subject. Although these different approaches are not mutually exclusive, this chapter is structured around the development of each.

The Analysis of Stereotype Content

As suggested in our introductory chapter, the pattern of early stereotyping research was established by Katz and Braly's (1933) study of the 'Racial Stereotypes of One Hundred College Students'. Their subjects, one hundred Princeton students, were asked to read through a list of eighty-four adjectives and to 'select those which seem to you typical of the Germans'. The subjects' task was to write down as many of the adjectives as necessary to 'characterize these people adequately'. They could add adjectives of their own if they found those provided inadequate. Each subject repeated this procedure ten times, characterizing first Germans, then Italians, Negroes, the Irish, the English, Jews, Americans, the Chinese, the Japanese and Turks. Finally, the subjects were asked to go back over their lists and, for each group, mark with an 'x' the five adjectives 'which seem to you the most typical of the race in question'.

Table 2.1 presents the ten stereotypes elicited by Katz and Braly, and it can be seen from this that there was a high degree of consensus among subjects in the assignment of particular traits to groups (as revealed in the overall index of stereotype uniformity). This consensus was apparent in

Table 2.1 Stereotypes revealed by Katz and Braly's (1933) study: traits applied to different national groups by 100 Princeton students, the percentage of students endorsing each, and level of stereotype uniformity (U)

	%	U		%	U
Italians		6.9	*English*		7.0
artistic	53		sportsmanlike	53	
impulsive	44		intelligent	46	
passionate	37		conventional	34	
quick-tempered	35		tradition-loving	31	
musical	32		conservative	30	
imaginative	30				
Negroes		4.6	*Jews*		5.5
superstitious	84		shrewd	79	
lazy	75		mercenary	49	
happy-go-lucky	38		industrious	48	
ignorant	38		grasping	34	
Germans		5.0	*Irish*		8.5
scientifically-minded	78		pugnacious	45	
industrious	65		quick-tempered	39	
stolid	44		witty	38	
intelligent	32		honest	32	
Americans		8.8	*Japanese*		10.9
industrious	48		intelligent	45	
intelligent	47		industrious	43	
materialistic	33				
ambitious	33				
Turks		15.9	*Chinese*		12.0
cruel	47		superstitious	34	

Table only includes traits assigned by at least 30 per cent of subjects.

The index of uniformity (U) is the number of traits needed to include 50 per cent of subjects' assignments; where $U_{max} = 2.5$ and $U_{min} = 42$ (i.e., a lower number indicates greater uniformity).

(Adapted from Katz and Braly, 1933, tables 1 and 2)

the assignment of traits both to their national ingroup (Americans) and to the various outgroups. Katz and Braly argued that in the latter case consensus could not arise from subjects' personal experience of the groups concerned. Rather, it reflected the existence of 'public attitudes' about racial groups, which were as important as 'private prejudice' in the development of racism. In a subsequent study (Katz and Braly, 1935) sixty-five subjects (with no knowledge of the previous experiment, or the idea that the traits were in any way related to racial groups) rated the 84 traits in terms of their 'desirability . . . in friends and associates' (p. 183). Using the stereotypes elicited in 1933, the overall favourability of the traits used to characterize each of the ten groups was then calculated, and the groups rank ordered accordingly. A further sixty subjects were explicitly asked to rank order the ten groups in terms of 'your preference for association with their members' (p. 185).

These two rank orderings were highly similar. Katz and Braly considered two possible interpretations of this finding. It could indicate that prejudice (as reflected in the explicitly group-based ordering) is 'a response to the actual characteristics of races', implying that the stereotypes were in some sense true, e.g., that Negroes, as a group, really were superstitious, lazy, etc. and this was why subjects disliked them (cf. 1933, p. 289). On the other hand, and in Katz and Braly's opinion, it could reflect the fact that prejudice was not a single, specific emotional reaction to a racial category (cf. G. Allport, 1954), but was represented within a stereotype which included beliefs about and evaluations of typical characteristics as well as emotional responses. Thus:

> The student, for example, not only has a prejudice against the word Turk, but holds the belief that the Turk is cruel, physically dirty and sensual, and has a low opinion of these traits. This whole complex is his racial attitude and can be called out by the stimulus of the race name. This does not mean, of course, that it is justified. None of these ideas and attitudes need be based . . . upon the true characteristics of Turks. But the prejudice is strongly bolstered by the rationalizations concerning the Turkish character. In other words, prejudice does not exist toward an empty race name, but toward a race name which represents an imaginary individual of nasty character. (1935, p. 190)

For Katz and Braly, prejudice and stereotypes were inextricably linked, the latter providing 'information' about groups to bolster the prejudiced emotional reaction. This position, which became widely accepted, was summarized by Katz and Schanck (1938) in the claim that 'collective representations are the reason for the difficulty men have in understanding other cultures' (p. 89).

Thus Katz and Braly presented a clear analysis of the way in which a stereotyping process contributed to racial prejudice. They comment, in the introduction to their 1935 paper, that the psychological investigation of prejudice should be concerned with 'the *basic mechanisms* . . . the common factors and *processes* underlying all prejudice' (p. 183, emphasis added). It seems somewhat unjust that their methodology has attracted so much blame for what has been seen as an early obsession with content to the exclusion of process (e.g. Brigham, 1971; Ashmore and Del Boca, 1981).

Further research in the tradition of Katz and Braly's work sought to elaborate their analysis of the fundamentally problematic nature of stereotypes. One potential deficiency upon which checklist methodology threw particular light was that of *rigidity*. The view that stereotypes were rigid had been central to Lippman's work and was emphasized by a number of later researchers (e.g., Kerr, 1943; Mace, 1943; Zawadzki, 1942). Indeed, this belief is reflected in the etymology of the word 'stereotype' – the Greek word *stereos* meaning 'solid' or 'firm'. The term was initially used in the printing trade where a stereotype is a cast-metal plate used to make repeated copies of the same text. The manner in which this meaning was instilled into common social psychological opinion is exemplified by Rokeach's (1948) statement that:

> It is not necessary to go far beyond common experience to convince ourselves that there is probably nothing more resistant to change than stereotypic attitudes towards outgroups. (p. 259)

In fact, studies using the Katz–Braly checklist produced very little support for this position. Most of these studies dealt with the degree to which stereotype content was affected by international conflict. Thus Meenes (1943) found that the Second World War led to substantial changes in the content of a number of stereotypes held by American students (those concerning Chinese, Japanese, Germans, Turks and Italians). As we might expect, images of groups with which America came into conflict became less favourable (e.g., Germans were seen as cruel and treacherous rather than progressive). More strikingly, stereotypes of the Japanese and Chinese were reversed – the Japanese were seen as sly, treacherous and deceitful whereas formerly they had been portrayed as artistic and progressive, while over the same period the Chinese came to be characterized as reserved and courteous rather than sly, conventional and treacherous (p. 333).

Seago (1947) measured American-held stereotypes of Americans, Germans, Japanese and Negroes each year from 1941 to 1945. She found that the stereotype of the Japanese was subject to considerable change over this period – becoming much less favourable after the attack upon Pearl Harbour (cf. Meenes, 1943). Similarly, the stereotype of Germans incorporated the traits 'aggressive' and 'cruel' for the first time in 1942 and 'arrogant' in 1943 (cf. Dudycha, 1942). Stereotypes relating to Americans and Negroes were relatively stable over the five-year period and were actually very similar to those elicited around ten years earlier by Katz and Braly (1933).

From similar findings Buchanan (1951) concluded that stereotypes 'may be more flexible than is often assumed' (p. 526). He found that Americans' stereotypes of Russians changed markedly between 1942 and 1948 in the context of deteriorating post-war relations, such that Russians came to be perceived as less brave and hardworking but considerably more cruel and conceited. Prothro and Melikian (1955) adopted a similar position with respect to findings from a study conducted at the University of Beirut. This examined changes in Arab students' stereotypes as a result of an increased American presence in the city. No alterations in the representations of groups other than Americans were observed, but stereotypes of this group changed considerably, subjects now seeing Americans as sociable and superficial as well as endorsing some previously assigned traits (e.g., 'rich', 'industrial') more consensually. Considering this finding in the context of arguments that stereotypes might contain at least a kernel of truth (see below), Prothro and Melikian suggested that stereotype content 'constitutes a kind of socio-psychological truth' in appearing to reflect the realities of intergroup relations (p. 9).

Sinha and Upadhyaya (1960) looked at some of the ethnic stereotypes held by Indian students across a period of eleven months in 1959, during which time a border dispute arose between India and China. As in Prothro and Melikian's study, only 'meagre' changes were apparent in the stereotypes of groups not involved in the border dispute. However, the Chinese who had formerly been perceived as artistic, religious, industrious, friendly, progressive and honest, were now attributed the characteristics 'aggressive', 'cheat', 'selfish', 'war-monger' and 'cruel'. Note, though, that Sinha and Upadhyaya took the absence of widespread stereotype change as evidence for the rigidity of stereotypes, commenting 'the Sino-Indian border dispute has not substantially affected the stereotypes of university students ... Thus group stereotypes are not easily modified. It requires unusual local or world events to modify them' (p. 35). This latter sentiment reflected the views previously expressed by Harding, Kutner, Proshansky and Chein (1954, p. 1024) in their influential review of 'Prejudice and Ethnic Relations'.

Irrespective of particular researchers' interpretations of their findings, the above studies all demonstrate that change in stereotype content is *selective* rather than indiscriminate. This general view was endorsed by Karlins, Coffman and Walters (1969; see also Hartsough and Fontana, 1970) following their analysis of changes in the stereotypes held by three generations of college students. They used the same methodology as Katz and Braly (1933) and Gilbert (1951), and explicitly compared their findings with the results of the earlier studies. Karlins and his colleagues observed 'major changes' in stereotype content over these generations. The stereotype of Japanese, for example, changed from 'intelligent', 'industrious' and 'progressive' in 1933, to 'imitative', 'sly' and 'extremely nationalistic' as a result of World War II (cf. Meenes, 1943; Seago, 1947) and back to yet stronger emphasis of 'industrious' and 'ambitious' in 1969. Karlins et al. concluded that such change 'provides a clear case of stereotypes responding to the currents of history and world events' (p. 7).

Summarizing all the above studies it appears that, where it is observed, stereotype change is a product of specific alterations in intergroup relations (Sherif, 1967). As a corollary, where relations over time are characterized by stability, there is little or no change in stereotype content. As Fishman (1956) argued, if stereotypes serve to reflect or rationalize intergroup relations it is unreasonable to *expect* them to change where all other elements of the relations between groups are unaltered. This argument would explain why Seago (1947), Prothro and Melikian (1955) and Sinha and Upadhyaya (1960) found no evidence of change in their subjects' stereotypes of groups that were incidental to particular conflicts.

Further support for the view that stereotypes change in response to *particular* alterations in reality was provided by a series of studies conducted by Diab (1963a, 1963b). Again using the Katz–Braly paradigm, he found that stereotype content differed significantly according to the number and types of groups to which Arab–Moslem students at the University of Beirut assigned traits. In a preliminary study, Diab (1963a) noted that Americans were described more positively (e.g., as 'democratic' rather than 'superficial') when characterized at the same time as six rather than twelve other groups and immediately after Russians rather than Germans. Stereotypes of the French and English also changed as a function of this manipulation, becoming less positive when they were judged immediately after (and hence contrasted with) Algerians and Egyptians respectively.

In Diab's second study (1963b) the effect of this type of contextual manipulation was even clearer. In one condition subjects assigned traits to a range of thirteen groups, and in a second condition to only five of these, four of which were 'low-anchor' (i.e., unpopular) groups. Diab found that the French were portrayed in considerably more favourable terms in the second condition (as, amongst other things, sociable, artistic, cultured, and democratic) than in the first (where they were depicted as base, selfish, materialistic and mean). The stereotypes of some of the low-anchor groups were also more favourable in the second condition than had been the case in the first. Negroes, for example, were now character-ized *inter alia* as fun-loving, strong and courageous rather than down-trodden, ignorant and backward. These studies thus draw attention to another aspect of the sensitivity of stereotypes to the specific context of their production (cf. Diab, 1962). Not only do they change as a conse-quence of particular social events which disturb intergroup relations (e.g., war), but they are also affected by the overall context in which those events and relations are perceived – in this case, the number and nature of the comparison groups which define individuals' frames of reference.

Looking over these studies of stereotype content, it can be seen that although researchers set out to advance the analysis of stereotype *defi-ciency* their findings led them down a somewhat different path. Diab's studies, for example, suggest that stereotypes are not the result of indis-criminate, fixed prejudices but are context-dependent statements about intergroup relations that can be influenced by a complex set of intergroup comparisons. These early studies of content can be seen as sending some fairly clear messages about process (for example, that stereotyping is a process that is comparative and contextually variable). Nonetheless, a growing number of researchers argued that attention to content-related issues had led to a descriptive rather than an explanatory stance and had thus hindered genuine theoretical advance (e.g., Brigham, 1971; Fishman, 1956; Gardner, 1973; Taylor and Aboud, 1973).

Methodological dissatisfaction with the checklist also increased. Ehrlich and Rinehart (1965) argued that the Katz–Braly paradigm was 'biased in the direction of displaying greater prejudice and intergroup hostility than may exist' after finding that subjects completing checklists assigned nearly three times more traits to groups than those using an open-ended format (p. 574). The stereotypes of the former subjects also exhibited a corresponding increase in consensuality. This criticism ech-oed aspects of a view expressed by Eysenck and Crown (1948, p. 36) that checklist methodology forced subjects to make stereotypic judgements and that responses elicited by this means might thus 'be merely the last resort of a subject driven into a neurotic choice situation ("I don't know the answer – I must give an answer")'.

On the other hand, Sigall and Page (1971) compared subjects' ratings of Americans and Negroes under standard checklist and 'bogus pipeline' conditions. In the latter, subjects were informed that the experimenter had a foolproof physiological measure of attitude, a form of 'lie detector'. It was found that in this bogus pipeline condition the American stereotype was more favourable and the Negro stereotype more unfavourable than in standard conditions, i.e. ingroup bias increased. Sigall and Page 'elected to interpret the [bogus pipeline] results . . . as relatively distortion-free, as more honest and as 'truer' than rating-condition responses' (p. 254), which would suggest that, in general, checklist studies may under- rather than overestimate stereotyping and prejudice.

It is worth pointing out that although researchers identified some weaknesses associated with the checklist methodology, the intention was not to dismiss completely the contribution which had been made by research employing the Katz–Braly paradigm. Ehrlich and Rinehart, for example, emphasized the importance of the analysis of stereotype content 'to the development of a general theory of intergroup behaviour', stating 'we know of no argument or evidence that invalidates a check list as a research technique' (pp. 573, 574). None the less, as workers moved away from considerations of stereotype content in the 1970s, the advances made by research in this tradition were easily overlooked.

Attempts to Establish the Factual Basis of Stereotypes: The Kernel of Truth Debate

Central to Lippman's (1922) characterization of stereotypes was the view that they misrepresented reality and were distorted by the prejudices of the stereotyper. As research into stereotyping began, one of its first goals was to test this claim against the alternative hypothesis that stereotypes were based on fact and thus had a 'kernel of truth'. Indeed, this test was central to the stereotyping debate throughout the 1940s and 50s (see Fishman, 1956; Klineberg, 1951; Schoenfeld, 1942).

Experiments seeking to provide this test were in fact carried out by Rice (1926–7) and Litterer (1933) prior to Katz and Braly's (1933) more famous work. Both showed that subjects could match photographs with 'social types' and were prepared to make personality attributions on the basis of this matching process, a practice which easily led to error if the match was incorrect. To use one of Rice's examples, a photograph of a person who was actually a Soviet envoy but who had 'a wing collar, van Dyke beard and moustache' might be matched with the label 'United

States senator'. He would then be rated as more intelligent than when correctly identified (p. 269). On this basis stereotypes were characterized in the title of Rice's paper as 'A Source of Error in Judging Human Character'. In a conceptually similar study, Razran (1950) showed that the ethnic labeling of photographs of women (by attaching bogus last-names) significantly affected ratings of the women's character. For example, a woman was perceived to be more intelligent and ambitious, but less likeable and entertaining, when she was said to be called Rabinowitz (and thus assumed to be Jewish) than when cues to her ethnic group membership were absent.

Other results were similarly reported as evidence of the distorting influence of stereotypes. In a commonly cited study, LaPiere (1936) sought, amongst other things, to compare the stereotype of Armenian immigrants held by Californians with 'objective fact'. It was found that despite their reputation for lawlessness, Armenians, who represented 6 per cent of the population in the community studied, appeared in only 1.5 per cent of court cases brought by the police.

An analysis by Shrieke (1936) of stereotypic images of the Chinese in California during the latter half of the nineteenth century, revealed that during the time of post-Civil War prosperity the Chinese were popularly represented as thrifty, sober, tractable, inoffensive and law-abiding, but that as a result of the ensuing depression (1869–73) they came to be seen as clannish, dangerous, criminal, secretive, debased and servile (p. 11). Several workers (e.g., Klineberg, 1950, 1951; Harding et al., 1954) later interpreted these findings as evidence of the inaccuracy of stereotypes, arguing that it was unlikely the Chinese themselves actually underwent any corresponding change in character (although refer to the previous section for a different way of looking at these findings). In another commonly cited study, Hartley (1946) asked subjects to evaluate three fictitious groups ('Danireans', 'Pireans' and 'Wallonians') on a modified social distance scale (after Bogardus, 1933). Their willingness to do so, together with the fact that these ratings correlated strongly with individuals' evaluations of Jews (an outgroup), was taken as further evidence for the claim that stereotypes and prejudice can have an extremely weak factual basis.

A similar conclusion was reached by Fernberger (1948) from the results of a study in which he asked subjects to fill in the blanks in a 'once upon a time'-type story by attributing behaviours to either male or female actors, or to leave a blank if neither seemed appropriate. These behaviours were strongly related to prevailing gender-based beliefs (e.g., the actor 'talked too much', 'did not like to fight', 'gave up more freedom'), but in a thorough rejection of the utility of stereotyping

Fernberger asserted that 'the perfect score, from the psychological point of view is zero (no spaces filled)' (p. 97). Indeed he tried to encourage this response by giving the subjects a lecture on the fictional nature of sex differences shortly before the experiment, and presenting the option of leaving blanks in capitals and underlined! In spite of this, subjects were still prepared to make the gender assignments, and did so with considerable consensus.

The conclusion generally drawn from findings such as these was that the factual basis of stereotypes was negligible, if not non-existent. Schoenfeld (1942) remarked 'to the extent that a stereotype corresponds to objective facts, it is not a stereotype at all' (p. 12). In a similar vein, Klineberg (1951) opened a discussion of 'the meaning of stereotypes' by commenting that 'they may occasionally contain some truth, but if they do so, it appears to be largely by chance' (p. 505). In an even more scathing analysis, Zawadzki (1942) commented:

> The stereotype as a concept of what is a typical member of a group is a very poor device in thinking . . . [T]raits are selected, not because they are actually most often found among members of the group, but because they serve best the malicious intent of ridiculing or discrediting the group. (p. 130)

In line with these conclusions Fishman (1956) observed in a major review of the field that 'the oldest and still the most widely ascribed attribute of stereotypes is their alleged content of error and distortion' (p. 26).

Having converged on this view by the middle of the century, researchers turned their minds to ways of counteracting this aspect of stereotype deficiency. A widely accepted solution was to ascertain the *objective* truth about particular groups of people. Thus Klineberg (1951) suggested that '*every* stereotype must be examined in order to determine its relation to objective reality' (p. 51). Even more adventurously, Bogardus (1950) advocated the collection and dissemination of 'sociotypes' which, in contrast to stereotypes, would be 'socially representative and sociologically valid', having a basis in 'empirically-tested data', 'objective method' and the avoidance of 'value judgements' (pp. 286–291). Similarly, Fishman (1956) presented a research plan to 'compare the facts revealed by *the science of national character* with the views of the *popular-science of national character*, of which stereotyping . . . is the outstanding example' (p. 30; see also Duijker and Frijda, 1960).

In the 1960s a number of studies were conducted which attempted to establish the validity of stereotypes using 'objective' methods such as these. Interestingly, the results of these studies failed in any simple way to endorse received views of stereotype inaccuracy. For example, Schuman (1966) focused on the veridicality of two traits ('pious' and 'money-loving') that represented part of the stereotype of people from one particular district in East Pakistan. These were chosen because they could be compared with appropriate survey interview data, whereas many stereotypic attributions (e.g., 'brave', 'shrewd') 'are probably not measurable at all by ordinary interview methods' (p. 433). Schuman's general conclusion was that certain stereotypic attributions (here 'pious') may have validity, but that others (here 'money-loving') may be factually invalid. This finding led Schuman to the general hypothesis that stereotypes are more likely to be accurate when they are favourable and concern groups that change relatively little over a long period of time.

Adopting a slightly different strategy, Abate and Berrien (1967) addressed the problem of stereotype validation through comparison of the self- and other-stereotypes of Japanese and Americans with self-reports of preferences gathered by administering the Edwards Personal Preference Schedule (EPPS). The EPPS was supposed to 'provide an approximation of the target's real characteristics' (p. 435). Surprisingly perhaps, the main finding to emerge from the study was a low correspondence between the EPPS responses and subjects' self-stereotypes. One implication of this might be that peoples' stereotypes of outgroups are more accurate than their self-stereotypes. Alternatively, the findings could reflect personal, idiosyncratic self-images (EPPS scores) co-existing with quite *distinct* views of the self as a member of a national ingroup. In any event, the assessment of stereotype validity was proving more difficult than anticipated.

Vinacke (1949) used evidence of the correspondence between stereotypes of a group and that group's own stereotype to argue that 'stereotypes . . . consist, at least in part, of actual characteristics of the group described' (p. 285; see also Bogardus, 1950). Triandis and Vassiliou (1967) picked up on this point, and also suggested that this correspondence would increase as contact between groups increased, i.e. that contact would produce more accurate intergroup images (Campbell, 1967, p. 821; Saenger and Flowerman, 1954). They found that increased contact with Greeks resulted in the self-stereotype of Americans becoming more favourable, while Americans' stereotype of Greeks became less favourable. Conversely, high contact Greek groups appeared to have more favourable stereotypes of Americans than those with low contact. So, as Americans came to be seen by Greeks as 'systematic, hardworking and practical', Greeks became portrayed by Americans as 'unsystematic, lazy and theoretical' (p. 320). Discussing these developing images, Triandis and Vassiliou suggested that 'there is a "kernel of truth" in most stereotypes when they are elicited from people who have firsthand knowledge of the group being stereotyped' (p. 324).

Although the kernel of truth debate was far from resolved by studies like those of Schuman (1966), Abate and Berrien (1967), and Triandis and Vassiliou (1967), interest in the issue of stereotype accuracy had declined by the end of that decade. As suggested in the previous chapter, this decline is partly attributable to the increased interest in issues of psychological process brought about by the emergence of the cognitive approach to stereotyping. However, it is also clear that there were problems inherent in both the issue itself and the way it was tackled by researchers (Hoffman and Hurst, 1990). A number of these were the focus of articles written in the 1970s (in particular, see M. Mackie, 1973; Perkins, 1979).

First, the view that interviews and self-report measures – which provide detailed information about individuals – are *necessarily* more accurate than generalized stereotypic images (Abate and Berrien, 1967; Nettler, 1961; Schuman, 1966) may be seen to derive from the individualistic premise that the truth about people is to be found in their individuality rather than in their group memberships (cf. Asch, 1952; see chapter 4). We might also ask just how 'objective' studies like those discussed above really were. The assertion that the championed methods of sociology or 'the science of national character' are 'value-free' seems particularly questionable. At best, these endeavours simply reach conclusions on the basis of a different set of values and assumptions to those of the layperson, and when researchers suggest that a particular research strategy is objective they appear to mean only that the results associated with its deployment are acceptable to them (M. Mackie, 1973). Accordingly, while certain workers have suggested that increased contact is correlated with stereotype accuracy, this view is less popular where it is apparent that unfavourable aspects of stereotypes are resistant to or enhanced by contact. This argument was not used by Mussen (1950), for example, who found that children's stereotyped statements about Negroes became more negative over the course of a summer camp.

Similarly, the argument that convergence of ingroup and outgroup stereotypes implies factual validity becomes more controversial where a given group assigns unfavourable traits to itself. Bayton (1941) naturally pointed to the insidious influence of propaganda rather than stereotype accuracy in explaining agreement among Negro and white college students on the stereotype of the Negro as superstitious, lazy, happy-go-lucky, ostentatious and loud. Indeed, in a review of the literature, Cauthen, Robinson and Krauss (1971) identified the phenomenon where 'the member of any minority group may accept and behave in terms of the stereotype that helps to maintain [their minority status]' as one of the major problems associated with stereotyping (p. 117).

Tajfel (1972) made observations similar to these in a discussion of the role of values in social categorization. Reviewing studies of stereotyped reactions to speakers with different accents (Cheyne, 1970; Lambert, Hodgson, Gardner and Fillenbaum, 1960), he argued that similarity between a group's self-stereotype and the stereotype of that group held by others is a reflection only of a *shared* understanding of social reality. Cheyne found that Scottish and English subjects both rated English speakers as more wealthy, prestigious and intelligent than Scots. This, Tajfel suggested, simply indicated that the socio-economic advantages of the English were important for both groups. Indeed, a consensual stereotypic image did not emerge here anyway. Generally the Scottish subjects enhanced the intergroup differences more than the English, a finding which Tajfel attributed to the greater self-referential significance of socio-economic differences for the Scots. Also, as was the case for Triandis and Vassiliou's (1967) Greek subjects (whose stereotype of Americans contained within it the image of 'well-oiled work horses'), the value connotations of the Scots' image of the economically successful outgroup may have rendered the *specific content* of the stereotype less flattering than that group's self-stereotype (see also Vinacke, 1949 pp. 285–287).

Two points emerge from the work reviewed in this section. First, some of the methods of reality measurement which have been adopted to examine the factual basis of stereotypes are value-laden. Second, hard-and-fast methods of establishing stereotype accuracy have proved elusive. Thus perhaps the most significant message to be gleaned from the research into the kernel of truth issue is that it is the social values of the researcher which largely determine both the perceived accuracy of stereotypes and the perceived appropriateness of any measure of accuracy in a given context.

Theoretical Approaches to Stereotyping and Prejudice

Early theoretical advance in the study of stereotyping was constrained by the fact that stereotyping was typically equated with prejudice (e.g., Ehrlich, 1962; Kerr, 1943). Stereotyping itself tended to be of only secondary interest to most researchers, but a number of different explanations were developed within theories of prejudice. As a consequence of this, stereotyping was typically characterized as irrational and invalid since prejudice itself was commonly understood in these terms. G. Allport (1954), for example, defined prejudice as 'thinking ill of others without sufficient warrant' (p. 6).

In the 1940s and 1950s a large number of theories of prejudice were developed, fuelled by researchers' desire to understand the psychological basis of the atrocities committed in the Second World War. Several of these were influenced by psychoanalytic theory, incorporating the idea that prejudice was a product of hostility and frustration displaced or projected onto scapegoats. For example, Dollard, Doob, Miller, Mowrer and Sears (1939) argued that intergroup hostility and aggression arose from a necessary outpouring of built-up psychic energy produced by frustration. In the case of Nazi anti-Semitism, it was argued that this derived from the displacement of aggression caused by frustration with ingroup members (Germans) onto an outgroup (Jews). Similarly, Williams (1947) delineated a general process whereby the prejudiced individual displaced frustrations felt against those with power over him or her onto highly visible and vulnerable others. Other workers sought to explain why only *particular* groups are victimized in this manner. Projection theorists (e.g., Ichheiser, 1947) suggested that targets were chosen because they displayed some characteristic which prejudiced individuals saw in themselves and disapproved of, or wanted to draw attention away from.

Within this psychoanalytic tradition the most influential work was presented by Adorno et al. (1950) in *The Authoritarian Personality*. These researchers administered a range of psychometric tests and interview schedules to subjects and identified a number of distinctive patterns of cognition that appeared to differentiate between potentially prejudiced subjects (authoritarians) and more tolerant others. The thought processes of the prejudiced person were characterized by intolerance of ambiguity, rigidity, concreteness (poor abstract reasoning) and overgeneralization. Within this framework the evolution and manifestations of the personality type were more roundly described as follows:

A basically hierarchical, authoritarian, exploitive parent–child relationship . . . culminate[s] in a political philosophy and social outlook which has no room for anything but a desperate clinging to what appears to be strong and a disdainful rejection of whatever is relegated to the bottom. The inherent dramatization likewise extends from the parent–child dichotomy to the dichotomous conception of sex roles and moral values as well as the dichotomous handling of social relations as manifested especially in the formation of stereotypes and of ingroup–outgroup cleavages. (p. 971)

This portrayal stands in contrast to descriptions of the liberal (non-authoritarian) type, of which the following is an example:

> By virtue of the greater integration of his instinctual life [he] becomes a more creative and sublimated individual. He is thus more flexible and less likely to form stereotyped opinions about others. (Frenkel-Brunswik, 1948, p. 306)

In terms of this theory stereotyping was an aspect of an inferior way of representing the world, and one peculiar to certain individuals.

However, this approach to both stereotyping and prejudice has been questioned by a number of researchers (for reviews see R. Brown, 1965; Stroebe and Insko, 1989). For example, on the basis of a reappraisal of Adorno et al.'s data, Billig (1978, 1985) suggested that authoritarians, as much as liberals, were unwilling to endorse rigid statements and that both groups of subjects made similarly-structured categorical statements about outgroups. This, indeed, has been seen by many workers as the principal shortcoming of the personality structure and dynamics approach – that it explains phenomena that are in fact common to large numbers of people in terms of experiences and processes unique to the individual (e.g., R. Brown, 1965; Milner, 1981, pp. 105–7; Sherif, 1967, p. 13).

Alternative theories of prejudice focused upon the manner in which the psychology of the individual was affected by his or her place within a broader social system. Muzafer Sherif formulated his theory of intergroup conflict on the basis of field studies of the behaviour of boys at summer camps. These studies (conducted with Carolyn Sherif and other colleagues in 1949, 1953 and 1954; summarized in Sherif, 1967) found that when boys were divided into different groups and those groups then competed for goals that only one could attain, they engaged in 'hostile and aggressive deeds' and developed consonant stereotypic attitudes (1967, p. 85). This intergroup hostility arose between normal, healthy youngsters in the absence of physical, economic, historical or personal differences (indeed, the division into groups cut across pre-existing friendships). Sherif's theory thus asserted that prejudice and stereotyping were best understood simply as products of realistic *competition* between social groups arising from a conflict of interests. As he put it:

> Intergroup hostility arises from conflicts over vital interests and changes when the groups are directed towards superordinate goals. Apparently, both hatred and friendship are characteristically human, depending upon

man's relationship to his groups and their position vis à vis others. (1967, p. 153)

Sherif's field studies, like the research reviewed in the first section of this chapter, also supported the conclusion that 'stereotyped images of other groups change following altered relationships with those group- ings' (1967, p. 25). The boys involved in his summer camps quickly developed highly negative stereotypes of the other group during intergroup conflict, but these images became much more positive after some sustained intergroup cooperation (e.g. 1967, p. 90). Sherif took the line that stereotypes were not in themselves deficient but served merely to reflect ongoing relations between groups. In doing this they were highly flexible:

> The choice and the salience of particular attributes . . . reflect the stance of our own group in past and/or current relationships with the particular group in question. Both the generalized and vague descriptive character of the attributes and their *singular point of view* make the search for 'kernels of truth' in stereotypes unrewarding. (1967, p. 37, emphasis added)

In other words, Sherif argued that a stereotype held by a group represents an intergroup relationship from that group's point of view. This is the function served by stereotypes and it is unreasonable, and unfruitful, to abstract them from this context in order to establish some abstract, 'objective' validity.

On the basis of similar considerations, a small number of researchers (notably, Asch, 1952; Fishman, 1956; Laviolette and Silvert, 1951; Vinacke, 1956, 1957) attempted to present theoretical approaches to stereotyping that were removed from the analysis of prejudice. A com- mon thread running through these contributions was the idea that stereo- types were shaped by group memberships and were a response to intergroup relations. Laviolette and Silvert (1951) thus argued that stereotypes were rationalizations which enable the stereotyper 'to man- age his interpersonal and group relations' and to 'express . . . his group identifications' (pp. 259–60). Like Sherif, these authors challenged the view that stereotypes were necessarily a product of deficient thinking and argued instead that:

> They are in their functioning a product of social differences. Their clarity, generality, intensity and perseverance will depend on the relative degree of continuity and rate of change which characterizes the whole of the social system of which they are a partial product. (p. 261)

In a complex and wide-ranging paper, Fishman (1956) also contended that stereotypes are a product of intergroup relations, stereotype content reflecting, in part, the 'the unique relationships arising out of the interaction of the two groups' (p. 60). Fishman saw stereotypes as social norms, developed within groups and used under conditions of 'high group-saliency', i.e. when the stereotyping group was influencing individual perceptions and responses. However, running through Fishman's strongly group-oriented analysis is an insistence that stereotyping is the product of faulty, *irrational* processes (e.g., p. 43, p. 59). Indeed, he discusses the doctrine of suggestibility and suggests that stereotyping is the result of individuals succumbing to powers of suggestion wielded by groups with which they identify. In order to remain members in good standing, individuals use stereotypes, choosing the 'abandonment of accuracy for the sake of personal safety and stability' (p. 44). Nonetheless, Fishman did not reject stereotype *content* as necessarily and wholly false – the faulty process could throw up a valid product, and proper scientific methods should be used to assess the validity of stereotype content. Overall, Fishman's paper represents an uneasy compromise between a recognition of the 'group-relatedness' of stereotypes and an insistence upon their irrationality, the fact that they 'by-pass that capacity for making objective and analytic judgements which man does possess' (p. 59; cf. Tajfel, 1969).

In contrast, Asch (1952) and Vinacke (1956) rejected the 'faulty process' view. In particular, both took exception to the argument that stereotypes were necessarily deficient simply because they treated people as identical members of a class rather than as unique entities. Asch argued that in a great number of situations individuals *do* behave as members of groups and that groups (e.g., football teams, infantry platoons) have distinct psychological properties:

> Group-properties are the forms that the inter-related activities of individuals take, not simply the actions of separate individuals. A flying wedge of policemen has a quality of power or threat that is a direct consequence of its organization. A picket line in front of a plant has a quality of unity that is a product of its organization. In each of these instances the group-property cannot be rediscovered in the individuals taken singly. (1952, p. 225)

Whilst aware of 'the fundamental fact that we do not have identical experiences with two different persons', he thus proposed that in order to be able to represent the true properties of other people it is sometimes necessary to stereotype them – that is, to 'categorize them under one rubric and therefore regard them *as if they were identical*' (p. 231, emphasis added). Asch summarized this argument as follows:

> Observing the distortions that follow from merging individuals with their groups, some have counseled that it is misleading to judge persons in terms of group relations and that the canons of objectivity require of us to understand persons first and foremost as individuals. It is correct to urge that we should strive to see persons in their uniqueness. But it is wrong to assume that we can best achieve a correct view of a person by ignoring his group relations . . . If there are group forces and if they exert effects, we should understand them to understand individuals. (p. 238)

We shall consider consider the significance of Asch's ideas about the importance of the group in more detail in chapter 4.

Vinacke (1949) reported a study in which students at the University of Hawaii were asked to characterize eight groups (Japanese, Chinese, 'Haole' (Caucasians), Koreans, Filipinos, Hawaiians, Samoans, and Negroes). Six groups were represented in the subject sample (all the above except Samoans and Negroes), as Vinacke was particularly interested in 'the two-way nature of the stereotyping process' (p. 287), the fact that the stereotyper is also stereotyped. He found that the different subject groups tended to agree on essential aspects of group images (e.g. there was strong agreement that the Hawaiians were musical, easy-going, friendly, etc.), but also noted that 'two groups scarcely ever characterize any other group exactly alike' (p. 276). (Haoles, for example, were much more likely than other groups to see Hawaiians as expressive). He commented on 'the complexity of stereotyping as an intergroup phenomenon' (p. 290), and argued strongly for the validity of stereotyping, together with the need to consider stereotyping and prejudice as separate (though possibly related) phenomena.

These arguments were developed further in his 1957 paper, 'Stereotypes as Social Concepts'. Here it was proposed that people could be defined and, moreover, were capable of acting, in terms of different levels in a hierarchical system. Thus, we need to be able to represent others in terms of broad-based concepts high up in a hierarchy (e.g., as Oriental or Caucasian), or in terms of narrowly-defined concepts lower down that hierarchy (e.g., as a friend or neighbour). Vinacke's central point was that just as it is appropriate in certain circumstances to recognize the high-level conceptual relationship between a soup spoon and other pieces of cutlery, even though at a lower level the former is still specialized for eating soup, so it is sometimes appropriate to respond to particular individuals in terms of their group memberships. He argued:

The fact is that traits represented in stereotypes depend solely upon properties which a group of people agree are typical of a class, just as is the case,
in practice, for classes of other objects. In this sense, the properties of
stereotypes have a social reality, regardless of whether objective measurement would support them or not. (p. 239)

In conclusion, Vinacke proposed that there is nothing inherently 'bad' in
stereotyping, any more than in forming concepts of any kind (p. 241).

The views of Sherif, Asch and Vinacke, similar in several respects,
represented a potentially new approach to stereotyping. First, they disagreed with the analysis of stereotyping as an aspect of prejudice since this
encouraged the characterization of stereotyping as irrational. Second,
and for much the same reason, they argued that attempts to establish the
factual basis of stereotypes were misguided and unhelpful. It was claimed
that the psychological processes of stereotyping could not be presumed to
be deficient simply because the content of stereotypes was inaccurate (as
was implied by most research which tackled the kernel of truth issue).
The fact that stereotypes can be wrong, it was argued, does not necessarily imply that they are underpinned by a faulty process, just as perceptual
illusions (e.g., movement after-effects) are not necessarily indicative of
poor visual processing (Asch, 1952, p. 232; Sherif, 1967, p. 27; cf.
Fishman, 1956).

An important step towards a psychological approach to prejudice
more consistent with this new perspective was presented by G. Allport
(1954). As suggested in the previous chapter, Allport's work built upon
Lippman's claim that the categorization processes involved in stereotyping were an important aspect of general cognitive functioning. He argued
that

The human mind must think with the aid of categories . . . Once formed
categories are the basis for normal prejudgement. We cannot possibly
avoid this process. Orderly living depends upon it. (p. 20)

The principal advance made by Allport was to examine closely features
of this categorization process as it was related to the functioning of the
individual. He proposed that prejudice was facilitated by an association
between categorization and differences in value, and that 'the most
important categories a man has are his own personal values' (p. 24). The
primary source of these values was identified as individuals' memberships
in various ingroups. It was argued that prejudice is typically determined
by a process of categorizing others in relation to categories associated
with the self: while people and objects associated with ingroup categories

are customarily liked, those associated with outgroups are, in certain circumstances, rejected.

Allport's analysis of categorization noted the manner in which ingroup categories changed in response to changing contexts:

> Not only do the strength and definition of ingroups change over the years in a given culture, but a single individual, too, may have occasion at one time to affirm one group loyalty and at a different time another ... [I]ngroup memberships are not permanently fixed. For certain purposes an individual may affirm one category of membership, for other purposes a slightly larger category. (1954, p. 35)

In this sense, categorization was understood as a dynamic, flexible process. However, Allport still attempted to maintain a clear distinction between the rational and irrational use of categories as associated with the behaviour of tolerant rather than prejudiced people. In a similar manner to Adorno et al. (1950), he argued that 'the cognitive processes of prejudiced people are *in general* different from the cognitive processes of tolerant people' (p. 175). As he saw it, prejudiced people were those disposed to make extremely simple dichotomous judgements – for example, that ingroups are good and outgroups bad (p. 174).

Because it was founded upon this inherently contradictory analysis of categorization, Gordon Allport's approach to stereotyping sat uncomfortably between the received view that stereotypes were deficient and the suggestion of other workers that they might represent important social realities. He maintained the view that stereotypes were faulty because they typically presented simplistic judgements that were undifferentiated and exaggerated but also saw that they were sensitive to the social realities of relations between groups. Although Allport's analysis did not embrace all aspects of stereotyping as understood by researchers such as Asch and Sherif, it nevertheless pointed to the possibility of examining the psychological processes of stereotyping as an aspect of *normal* cognitive functioning. When this possibility was explored in more detail by Tajfel in his 1969 paper 'Cognitive Aspects of Prejudice' its impact was revolutionary.

Overview

We have seen in this chapter that early approaches to stereotyping were limited by a number of factors. In particular, theoretical advance was hindered by reliance on checklist methodology (Brigham, 1971, 1973; Gardner, 1973; C. McCauley and Stitt, 1978; C. McCauley, Stitt and Segal, 1980) and the failure to distinguish either between stereotyping and prejudice or between the issues of faulty content and faulty process (Asch, 1952). Accordingly, whilst researchers did try to face up to the major issues, such as stereotype validity, they tended to frame them in ways that rendered them intractable (e.g., the kernel of truth debate). For the analysis of stereotypes and stereotyping to advance there was a pressing need for research which integrated a well-defined empirical research strategy with a coherent theoretical analysis of psychological process (Asch, 1952; Brigham, 1971).

Yet in spite of these problems the work reviewed above conveys a breadth and richness absent from much of the later research. These early researchers were motivated by a desire to explore the powerful and distinctive properties of representations that were widely shared by members of large-scale groups and which arose (and needed to be understood) in the context of intergroup relations (e.g. between nations in World War II). Although often overlooked, it is this concern with stereotyping as a *group*-based phenomenon that perhaps represents the most significant legacy of early stereotyping research.

Suggested Further Reading and References

One of the best features of early stereotyping papers was that researchers were concerned to address the big questions (e.g., concerning stereotype validity and the relationship between stereotyping and prejudice) and rarely hedged their bets. For this reason, the commonly-cited papers by Fishman (1956), and Katz and Braly (1933) make interesting reading, but it is worth looking up some of the less well-known material too. Klineberg (1951) and Richter (1956) lauch vehement attacks on stereotyping, but Laviolette and Silvert (1951) and Vinacke (1957) provide some convincing defence. For research demonstrating that stereotypes are products of intergroup relations, read the fascinating account of stereotyping in the summer camp studies in Sherif (1967, especially chapters 2 and 5).

Fishman, J. A. (1956) An examination of the process and function of social stereotyping. *Journal of Social Psychology*, 43, 27–64.

Katz, D. and Braly, K. (1933) Racial stereotypes of one hundred college students. *Journal of Abnormal and Social Psychology*, 28, 280–290.

Klineberg, O. (1951) The scientific study of national stereotypes. *International Social Science Bulletin*, 3, 505–515.

Laviolette, F. and Silvert, K. H. (1951) A theory of stereotypes. *Social Forces, 29,* 257–262.

Richter, M. N. (1956) The conceptual mechanism of stereotyping. *American Sociological Review, 21,* 568–571.

Sherif, M. (1967) *Group conflict and co-operation: Their social psychology.* London: Routledge and Kegan Paul.

Vinacke, W. E. (1957) Stereotypes as social concepts. *Journal of Social Psychology, 46,* 229–243.

3

Stereotyping as Information Processing Error: The Cognitive Emphasis

In his 1969 article, 'Cognitive Aspects of Prejudice', Tajfel rejected prevailing accounts which considered prejudice and stereotyping to be irrational, pathological phenomena. He argued powerfully for an approach based on people's 'capacity to modify [their] behaviour as a function of the way in which [they] perceive and understand a situation' (p. 80), that is, a *cognitive* approach.

Tajfel noted that intergroup processes are at the heart of 'the flux of social change' (p. 92):

> Much of what happens to us is related to the activites of groups to which we do or do not belong; and the changing relations between these groups require constant readjustments of our understanding of what happens and constant causal attributions about the why and the how of the changing conditions of our life (p. 81).

These attributions, he argued, were based on three cognitive processess: categorization, assimilation, and the search for coherence. Categorization provided 'the mould which gives shape to intergroup attitudes' (p. 91), the assimilation of social values and norms contributed to their content, and the search for coherence in an ever-changing social landscape produced a tendency to explain group behaviour in terms of 'inherent' group characteristics (cf. Hoffman and Hurst, 1990). Whilst the discussion of intergroup attribution has also been highly influential (e.g. see Hewstone and Jaspars, 1984), it was Tajfel's discussion of categorization that transformed the social psychology of stereotyping. He argued that:

> Stereotypes arise from a process of categorization. They introduce simplicity and order where there is complexity and nearly random variation. They can help us to cope only if fuzzy differences between groups are transmuted

into clear ones, or new differences created where none exist ... in each relevant situation we shall achieve as much stereotyped simplification as we can without doing unnecessary violence to the facts. (p. 82)

As we have seen, other writers (most notably, G. Allport) had recognized that categorization was implicated in stereotyping and prejudice. Uniquely, Tajfel turned to the issue from a background of research on judgement processes, which had included the investigation of categorization effects (e.g., Tajfel, 1957, 1959, Tajfel and Wilkes, 1963a). Thus he brought to the social psychology of stereotyping a more precise understanding of the perceptual and cognitive functioning of categorization and, importantly, clear empirical evidence that it could 'be responsible ... for biases in judgements of individuals belonging to various human groups' (1969, p. 85).

The seminal study was carried out by Tajfel and Wilkes (1963a). Three groups of subjects were presented with a series of eight lines differing from each other in length by a constant ratio. In one 'classified' condition the four shorter lines were labelled 'A' and the four longer 'B' while in an 'unclassified' condition no labels were presented and in a 'random' condition there was no predictable relationship between the length of line and the label attached to it. It was found that when reporting the length of lines, subjects in the classified group, and these subjects alone, accentuated the difference between the two classes of lines by exaggerating the difference between the shortest of the longer four and the longest of the shorter four. As can be seen in table 3.1, subjects

Table 3.1 Accentuation of interstimulus differences in the context of a superimposed classification

Stimulus	Class	Actual length (cms)	Actual difference between adjacent stimuli	Judged difference between adjacent stimuli	Ratio of judged over actual difference
1	A	16.2	0.8	1.1	1.4
2	A	17.0	0.9	0.8	0.9
3	A	17.9	0.9	1.2	1.3
4	A	18.8	0.9	1.9	2.1
5	B	19.7	1.0	1.3	1.3
6	B	20.7	1.0	1.1	1.1
7	B	21.7	1.1	1.9	1.7
8	B	22.8			

Judged differences are averaged across two experimental sessions.
(Adapted from Tajfel and Wilkes, 1963a, table 2)

judged this difference to be more than twice what it actually was. There was also some evidence to suggest that subjects in the classified condition minimized the differences between lines within each of the two classes.

The following principle emerged from this study:

> When a classification is correlated with a continuous dimension, there will be a tendency to exaggerate the differences on *that* dimension between items which fall into distinct classes, and to minimize these differences within each of the classes. (Tajfel, 1969, p. 83)

Tajfel conceives of this as a distortion of perception: stimuli are being perceived as more similar and different than they really are, than they would appear to be if the perceiver made more effort, or took 'a closer look' (see Tajfel, 1972).

The next step was to demonstrate how these categorization effects might account for some of the features of social stereotypes. If, for example, having white or black skin was thought to be *correlated* with certain personal characteristics (e.g., laziness, intelligence), then in terms of those characteristics members of one racial category would be seen as both very similar to each other and very different from members of the other category. Distinct and exaggerated stereotypes of each group would emerge (e.g., representing blacks as lazy and whites as industrious, blacks as stupid and whites as intelligent).

As a manifestation of emotional pathology stereotyping had been intriguing but isolated, an interesting oddity unrelated to other topics in person perception research. As a product of normal cognitive functioning it moved into the mainstream of social psychology. The constraining checklist methodology could be exchanged for experimental studies of categorization and other cognitive processes. Rather than simply catalogue stereotype content, the new goal was to uncover the mechanisms of thought responsible for social stereotypes, to examine 'their general structure and function' (Tajfel, 1969, p. 82).

During the latter part of the 1970s and through the 1980s the study of social cognition was dominated by ideas about the *limited capacity* of the information processing system (Fiske and S. Taylor, 1991). Whilst the emphasis was on the efficiency of human cognition, rationality was nonetheless seen as 'bounded' by capacity limitations, making selective and therefore potentially 'biased' information processing strategies necessary. In an overview of social cognition research, S. Taylor (1981b) dubbed this period the age of the 'cognitive miser', conveying the idea that dealing with capacity limitations (rather than seeking consistency or following logical strategies, as in earlier work) was seen as the driving force in human information processing.

It was very much in this context that Tajfel's categorization analysis of stereotyping was discussed and elaborated by researchers interested in stereotyping and group processes, and became so widely influential. The strong emphasis on errors and biases which characterized the early cognitive miser period (see Fiske and S. Taylor, 1991) fitted well with the enduring conceptualization of stereotyping as an erroneous and biased (because overgeneralized and exaggerated) form of person perception. It was still considered to be erroneous and biased, but this was now explained as an inevitable, if unfortunate, outcome of information processing strategies designed to cope with limited capacity (e.g., Fiske and Neuberg, 1990, p. 14). Stereotyping was understood to be the product of 'certain flaws in the way in which we process information about other people' (R. Jones, 1982, p. 41).

This chapter reviews the substantial empirical advances in our understanding of stereotyping achieved by social cognition researchers. Our aim is to provide a general overview of this now sizeable literature rather than a comprehensive review. The theoretical and metatheoretical implications of the cognitive miser analysis will be discussed in more detail in chapter 5.

Categorization: The Basic Effects

Whilst a number of information processing mechanisms have been identified as contributing to stereotyping (e.g., attention to distinctive stimuli, confirmatory biases in memory; see below), categorization is seen as crucial. As Hamilton and Trolier (1986) put it, 'the basis for all stereotyping is the differential perception of groups. Without such differentiation between groups, stereotyping cannot occur' (p. 134). Categorization is believed to produce two basic, relatively automatic effects: the distortion of perception such that intragroup similarity and intergroup difference are accentuated, and evaluative and behavioural discrimination favouring the ingroup. Both are considered fundamental to stereotyping.

The Accentuation of Similarity and Difference

That stereotyping involves an unwarranted homogenization of individuals within groups has long been considered its definitive characteristic. A dictionary of psychological terms provides this example of stereotyping:

'the perception of "bankers" – *in general and without discrimination* – as *invariably* cold-hearted in business dealings' (English and English, 1959, p. 523, emphasis added; see also Aronson, 1972, p. 172). Early research demonstrated that perceivers, especially prejudiced perceivers, sometimes had considerable difficulty distinguishing between members of an outgroup (Malpass and Kravitz, 1969; Secord, 1959; Secord, Bevan and Katz, 1956). The latter paper also found a significant exaggeration of the *difference* between blacks and whites in skin colour and other physiognomic characteristics associated with race amongst prejudiced subjects (see also Pettigrew, G. Allport and Barnett, 1958; Seeleman, 1940). Much of the appeal of Tajfel's categorization analysis stemmed from the fact that the accentuation effects he identified provided such a simple and elegant explanation of these perceptual distortions: the accentuation of similarity within and difference between categories occurred as an automatic product of the categorization process itself. Not surprisingly, there have been many attempts to verify the existence of these effects, and to demonstrate their relevance to the explanation of stereotyping (for reviews see Doise, 1978; Deschamps, 1984; Eiser and Stroebe, 1972; McGarty and Penny, 1988; Wilder, 1986). Some of the most interesting findings relevant to accentuation effects have emerged from research on social judgement, which will be discussed in chapter 6. Here we review studies more directly focused on stereotyping and social group membership.

In one early study Tajfel, Sheikh and Gardner (1964) asked Canadian subjects to describe two Indians and two Canadians after listening to separate live interviews with each. As Tajfel's analysis predicted, it was found that subjects minimized differences between the two stimulus persons in each racial group but only with respect to traits that were relevant to the stereotype of each.

Doise (1978) remarked that as the group members rated by Tajfel et al.'s subjects were physically present during the rating task the findings might have reflected a real similarity between the representatives of each group on stereotyped dimensions, rather than a distortion of similarity due to categorization (see also Wilder, 1981, p. 218). Against this interpretation, two studies reported by Doise and his colleagues (see Doise, 1978) suggested that the accentuation observed was a genuine product of the categorization process. Doise and Deschamps asked ten-year-old boys and girls to describe members of one gender group either with or without the knowledge that they would later describe members of the other group. It was found that both intracategory similarity and intercategory difference were accentuated where the subjects were led to anticipate the description of both groups (see also Doise and Sinclair,

1973). Doise, Deschamps and Meyer (1978) asked Swiss subjects to describe the three linguistic groups found in Switzerland (German, French and Italian speaking). In some conditions a national outgroup replaced one of these Swiss groups (i.e., Germans from Germany, French from France, or Italians from Italy). With the introduction of this international categorization intragroup differences between the two Swiss groups were reduced (see also Capozza and Nanni, 1986).

Wilder has reported a programme of research investigating categorization effects (see Wilder, 1981, 1986, for reviews) which provides consistent evidence of accentuated intergroup difference and intragroup similarity. In one study (Allen and Wilder, 1979) subjects were divided into two groups ostensibly on the basis of their preference for paintings by Klee or Kandinsky but in fact randomly (after Tajfel, Flament, Billig and Bundy, 1971, Experiment 2). Before being assigned to a group each subject completed a questionnaire assessing their opinions on various issues, some relevant and some irrelevant to art (the apparent basis for categorization). Following group assignment they completed the questionnaire again, this time as they thought another ingroup (or outgroup) member would complete it. These second ratings indicated that ingroup members' opinions were expected to be more similar to the subject's than outgroup members', and not only on art-related issues. A subsequent study (reported in Wilder, 1981, p. 227) extended this finding with evidence that categorized subjects were better able to recall information which described their similarities to the ingroup and their difference from the outgroup. Wilder has also demonstrated that, given a choice, subjects prefer to be exposed to information confirming intragroup similarity and intergroup dissimilarity (Wilder and Allen, 1978). He concludes that, in a variety of ways, 'persons act to maintain differences between cognitive categories' (1981, p. 228). Similarly, in a recent investigation of category learning, Krueger and Rothbart (1990) present evidence that 'the learning of category information is biased toward intercategory separation' (p. 658).

Using a different paradigm, Wilder (1978a) asked subjects to read a summary of a legal dispute presented as the opinion of a person who was either in a single group, in one of two groups, or one of an aggregate of unrelated individuals. Subjects then had to predict the opinions of another person in the same group, a person in the other of the two groups, or another of the individuals in the aggregate. As expected, it was found that subjects in the single group condition assumed significant similarity between the opinion they had heard and the opinion they predicted; little similarity was assumed in the other two conditions, where no shared category membership was involved. In a later study (Wilder, 1984) subjects predicted the similarity of their own opinions to those of others in an ingroup/outgroup condition, an ingroup only condition, and an ungrouped condition. The relevance of the opinion topics to the basis for categorization was also manipulated. As predicted, on topics relevant to the categorization, subjects perceived themselves as most similar to ingroup others in the intergroup condition, and least similar to outgroup others in the intergroup condition, with the other conditions falling between these two. Wilder comments: 'the presence of an outgroup accentuated perceived belief similarity with the ingroup' (p. 327; see also Wilder and Shapiro, 1984).

Taylor (1981a; Taylor, Fiske, Etcoff and Ruderman, 1978) presents a categorization analysis of stereotyping which integrates Tajfel's accentuation hypothesis with some other ideas about how the categorization process might work in person perception. The latter will be considered presently, but for the moment we shall focus on Taylor et al.'s first two experiments which provide evidence of accentuation effects. A carefully controlled tape–slide presentation of three black men and three white men discussing a publicity campaign for a play was prepared. After viewing this, subjects were given a list of all the suggestions made during the discussion and asked to recall which speaker had made which suggestion. Results indicated a significantly higher inter-race than intra-race error rate, that is subjects were fairly good at remembering whether a black or a white speaker had made a given suggestion, but were much less able to make accurate distinctions within the racial categories. A second experiment employing gender rather than race as the basis for categorization replicated the error rate findings, which Taylor et al. interpret as evidence for the accentuation effects of the categorization process. A number of more recent experiments using this error rate measure have provided further evidence of the pervasiveness of accentuation effects (see Frable and Bem, 1985; Hewstone, Hantzi and Johnston, 1991; Jackson and Hymes, 1985; Miller, 1986; Stangor, Lynch, Duan and Glass, 1992; S. Taylor and Falcone, 1982; Walker and Antaki, 1986).

There is, then, considerable evidence that categorization can affect judgement in the way Tajfel suggested. We should note, however, that not all studies investigating categorization always find the accentuation effects predicted. The effects are *variable*, depending in part upon the contextual salience or meaningfulness of the categorization (see McGarty and Penny, 1988; McGarty and Turner, 1992). Returning to accentuation effects in 1981, Tajfel noted that some more recent applications of his earlier findings to stereotyping had failed to incorporate two important aspects of his analysis. First, he had predicted accentuation only on dimensions relevant to the division into categories, an idea supported by some studies cited above (e.g., Tajfel et al., 1964; Wilder, 1984) but not by the results of Allen and Wilder (1979; see also Acorn, Hamilton and Sherman, 1988). Second, he felt that 'the crucial role played in stereotypes by value differentials associated with social categorizations' (1981a, p. 151) was being ignored in the push to construct cognitive analyses. In the next section we discuss the development of a further aspect of Tajfel's work in which the 'value added' aspects of social categorization become apparent.

Categorization and Ingroup Bias

One of the most intriguing consequences of categorization is that the mere division of people into groups leads to . . . discrimination in favour of ingroup members and against outgroup members (Stephan, 1985, p. 613).

As we saw in the previous chapter stereotyping has often been considered in close association with prejudice, which is partly why stereotypes are rarely seen as neutral (over)generalizations but rather as highly evaluative, more specifically as ethnocentric (e.g., R. Brown, 1965, p. 181). They tend to denigrate outgroups. The categorization analysis of stereotyping became even more powerful when Tajfel produced evidence suggesting that categorization processes alone might be responsible for ingroup bias.

Tajfel and his colleagues (Tajfel et al., 1971) had originally set out to discover the minimal conditions under which intergroup discrimination would occur. To do this they decided to begin with experiments in which the most rudimentary, seemingly meaningless ingroup/outgroup division was introduced, in order to establish a 'no discrimination' baseline. They planned to incorporate other variables cumulatively and thereby establish the *necessary* preconditions for ingroup favouritism (Tajfel, 1978a, pp. 10–11).

In their first studies young schoolboys were assigned to two groups. The subjects believed that this assignment was made on the basis of fairly trivial criteria (their estimation of the number of dots on a screen, or their preference for the abstract painters Klee and Kandinsky) but in fact it was random. There was no social interaction at all either between or within the groups; indeed, subjects did not even know who was in their group and who was in the other group as membership was anonymous. The groups were neither positively nor negatively interdependent, they

Table 3.2 Example of a booklet page in a minimal group study

These numbers are rewards for

| member no. 74 of Klee Group: | 25 23 21 19 17 15 13 11 9 7 5 3 1 |
| member no. 44 of Kandinsky Group: | 19 18 17 16 15 14 13 12 11 10 9 8 7 |

Please fill in below details of the column you have just chosen:

	Amount
Reward for member 74 of Klee group	—
Reward for member 44 of Kandinsky group	—

Subjects choose one column from each matrix. Thus a subject choosing the first column in the above matrix would be allocating 25 points to the Klee group member and 19 points to the Kandinsky group member.

(From Tajfel et al., 1971, table 7, reprinted by permission of John Wiley and Sons, Ltd.)

had no history of hostility, and members' self-interest was not linked to their group membership. The groups were truly 'minimal', simply perceptual or cognitive categories.

Once divided into these minimal groups the subjects were asked to allocate rewards (points signifying amounts of money) to individuals who were identified only by a code number and their group membership. The individuals to whom points were awarded never included the subject himself. Rewards were allocated using a matrix format similar to that presented in table 3.2.

Findings from the first study indicated that even these most minimal of conditions were sufficient to produce ingroup bias: subjects tended to assign more money to individuals who were members of the same group as themselves. In a second study the reward matrices were designed to reveal specific strategies the subjects might use to divide the points between recipients. The strategies of interest were (a) maximum joint profit (giving the greatest total reward to the two recipients), (b) maximum ingroup profit, (c) maximum difference in favour of an ingroup member, and (d) fairness. For example, using the matrix in table 3.2, a subject in the Kandinsky group can achieve both maximum joint profit and maximum ingroup profit by choosing towards the left hand end of the matrix. Fairness is represented in the middle, and maximum difference towards the right hand end.

Perhaps more surprising than the initial findings, this second experiment revealed a strong influence of maximum difference on subjects' matrix choices. They sacrificed absolute ingroup gain (i.e., maximum ingroup profit and maximum joint profit) in order to ensure *relative* ingroup gain.

A number of further experiments replicated, clarified and elaborated the basic findings. For example, Billig and Tajfel (1973) conducted one study which established *categorization*, rather than subjects' perceived personal similarity to other ingroup members, as the crucial factor determining ingroup bias. Doise, Csepeli, Dann, Gouge, Larsen and Ostell (1972) demonstrated that intergroup discrimination in the allocation of rewards extended to stereotypic representations. In a minimal group procedure subjects were asked to describe the two groups on a number of evaluative dimensions. As anticipated, it was found that stereotypic representations of the outgroup were less favourable than those of the ingroup (see also Brewer and Silver, 1978). Similarly, Howard and Rothbart (1980, Experiment 1) divided subjects into groups on the basis of a dot estimation task, then gave them a list of positive and negative traits to be assigned to ingroup and outgroup members. As predicted, more positive than negative traits were assigned to the ingroup, and evaluative ratings of the ingroup were significantly more favourable than those of the outgroup. This tendency also appears to operate in memory; Kanungo and Dutta (1966; Dutta, Kanungo and Freibergs, 1972; cf. Hymes, 1986) report that subjects were able to remember more desirable information about their own group (e.g., English Canadians) and more undesirable information about an outgroup (e.g., French Canadians).

As Stephan (1985, p. 613) comments, it appears that virtually any basis for categorization can lay the foundations for ingroup favouritism. Perdue, Dovidio, Gurtman and Tyler (1990) demonstrate that simply using collective pronouns such as *we*, *us*, and *ours* or *they*, *them*, and *theirs* is sufficient to engender ingroup bias. In their first experiment, for example, nonsense syllables unobtrusively paired with terms such as *we* were rated as more pleasant than those associated with terms like *they*. Relating the development of ingroup bias to the spread of communicable diseases, Perdue et al. conclude that 'ingroup and outgroup associated words may function as linguistic vectors that establish an evaluative predisposition toward targets previously uninfected by prejudice' (1990, p. 482).

Discussions of the relationship between categorization and ingroup bias have included evidence that variables which affect the current psychological significance of categorization, or category *salience*, are important determinants of bias (e.g., Abrams, 1985; Brewer, 1979; Oakes, 1987; Turner, 1975a, 1981; Worchel, 1979). For example, findings that collective rather than individual encounters between group members are more likely to be characterized by bias (e.g., Doise and Sinclair, 1973; Dustin and Davis, 1970) have been interpreted as evidence of a salience effect. Similarly, the ability of intergroup conflict to heighten bias has also been accounted for as an effect of the increasing salience of the relevant categorization (e.g., Dion, 1979, p. 218; Turner, 1981, p. 74).

As a corollary to this argument, several writers have suggested that bias may be reduced through interventions which reduce the salience of category boundaries (e.g., Turner, 1981; Wilder, 1986; Worchel, 1979). For example, Wilder (1978b) demonstrated that the presence of one dissenting outgroup member individuated perceptions of the group (i.e., members were seen more as separate individuals, less as a coherent group) and significantly reduced bias. More recently, Gaertner, Mann, Murrell and Dovidio (1989) divided sessions of six subjects into two three-person groups, which then took part in a group decision-making exercise. In one condition the two-group configuration was maintained, but in the other two conditions subjects were induced to 'recategorize' as either one superordinate group or as separate individuals. As predicted, both these recategorizations reduced ingroup bias relative to the two-groups condition. Interestingly, the separate individuals manipulation reduced bias through a decrease in the attraction of former ingroup members, whereas the one-group condition produced an increase in the attraction of former outgroup members, and considerably higher attraction towards all participants than the individual condition. The interaction in the one-group condition was also rated as more friendly, cooperative, trusting and close than it was in the separate individuals condition.

Several explanations of the relationship between categorization and ingroup bias have been offered (e.g., see Wilder, 1986), the most prominent of which is social identity theory (Tajfel and Turner, 1986), to be discussed in the next chapter. However, it was the straightforward message that intergroup discrimination can be 'a direct product of the categorization process' (Wilder, 1981, p. 228; see Messick and D. Mackie, 1989, p. 59) that took hold in the rapidly developing cognitive approach to stereotyping. It appeared that the mere categorization of the self and others in group-based terms was sufficient to induce discriminatory behaviour of the sort typically identified with stereotyping. In a sense, this allowed the cognitive approach to develop without losing sight of its roots in ideas that stereotyping was closely, perhaps inevitably, linked with unjustified prejudice and irrationality.

Investigation of these basic effects of categorization clearly laid a firm foundation upon which a more general cognitive analysis of stereotyping could be built. Both the perceptual distortion and the evaluative bias seen as so symptomatic of stereotyping appeared to be accounted for in cognitive terms. Whilst categorization and its basic effects remained central to the cognitive analysis, researchers went on to identify a number of other apparent errors or biases in information processing which seemed to account for certain features of stereotyping. We shall begin our review of this work with the issue of stereotype formation; can information processing mechanisms help explain why stereotypes form at all, and why they take the specific form that they do?

The Formation of Social Stereotypes

The major attempt to explain stereotype formation from a cognitive perspective rests on the identification of a cognitive bias called *illusory correlation*. First investigated by Chapman and Chapman (1967), illusory correlation refers to a tendency to perceive a relationship between two variables where none actually exists. This was applied to stereotyping by Hamilton and Gifford (1976), who focused specifically on the case where the co-occurrence of distinctive stimulus events produces an erroneous inference that they are correlated. The assumption is that distinctive (i.e., numerically infrequent) stimuli are perceptually 'salient', they automatically attract enhanced attention and thus become more available in memory (e.g., see S. Taylor and Fiske, 1978; note that we used the term 'salience' in a different sense, to refer to current psychological significance rather than perceptual prominence, in the preceding section; see Oakes, 1987, pp. 118–19). Co-occurring distinctive events should attract particular attention, and especially efficient encoding of the fact that they occurred together, even if this was in fact quite accidental (e.g., Hamilton and Gifford, 1976, p. 393). They thus become cognitively correlated. Hamilton argues that, under appropriate circumstances, this general information processing bias can:

> Effect . . . the *development* of stereotypes by contributing to the *initial* perception of intergroup differences. More specifically, the illusory correlation bias results in the differential perception of groups that have been described by evaluatively equivalent information. Once this differentiation has been made, these groups become meaningful social categories in the perceiver's head, and these cognitive categories can then be the basis for further biases in the information processing about these groups in the future' (Hamilton and Sherman, 1989, pp. 75–76).

In the original study linking the illusory correlation bias with stereotyping, Hamilton and Gifford (1976, Experiment 1) presented subjects with 39 statements describing behaviours of varying desirability per-

Table 3.3 Evidence of illusory correlation in group assignment and frequency estimation tasks

Statement type	Actual number	Number assigned to groups	Estimated number
Desirable Group A	18	17.5	17.1
Undesirable Group A	8	5.8	8.9
Desirable Group B	9	9.5	7.3
Undesirable Group B	4	6.2	5.7

The pattern of results suggests that subjects overassign distinctive statements to the minority group (i.e., undesirable statements to Group B) and overestimate the number of those statements.

(From Hamilton and Gifford, 1976, table 1)

formed by members of two groups, A and B (e.g., 'John, a member of Group A visited a friend sick in hospital'). There were twice as many statements about Group A members (thus making Group A the 'majority' and Group B the distinctive 'minority') but for both groups the ratio of desirable to undesirable behaviours was the same – either 9:4 (Experiment 1) or 4:8 (Experiment 2). Thus in Experiment 1 Group B and undesirable behaviours were both distinctive, but not correlated, and in Experiment 2 Group B and desirable behaviours shared uncorrelated distinctiveness. It was found (a) that subjects subsequently overestimated the incidence of distinctive behaviours performed by the distinctive group (as illustrated by the data in table 3.3), and (b) that this effect also influenced subjects' representation of that group as desirable or undesirable. Subjects thus appeared to form an illusory correlation between the distinctive group and the distinctive behaviour, resulting in 'unwarranted differential perception of two social groups' (Hamilton and Sherman, 1989, p. 62).

Hamilton and Gifford drew explicit attention to the potential correspondence between the information conditions created in their experiments and those found in many real world contexts. They suggested, for example, that for residents of many small towns in the American Midwest Catholics are numerically distinctive. If negative or strongly disapproved behaviour is also infrequently encountered, the stage is set for a negative stereotype of Catholics to develop on 'a purely cognitive basis' (1976, p. 406).

Since 1976, Hamilton and Gifford's findings have been replicated a number of times (e.g., Acorn et al., 1988; Hamilton, Dugan and Trolier, 1985; R. Jones, Scott, Solernou, Noble, Fiala and Miller, 1977; Kim and

Baron, 1988; Sanbonmatsu, Sherman and Hamilton, 1987; Spears, van der Pligt and Eiser, 1985, 1986) leading Hamilton and Sherman to conclude that 'the illusory correlation in group perception is a quite reliable phenomenon' (1989, p. 69; see also Mullen and Johnson, 1990). There have, however, been some reported deviations from the expected pattern. Spears et al. (1985, 1986), using attitudes to nuclear power (pro or anti) and the towns from which they emanated (large or small) as stimulus materials, did not find an illusory correlation effect where the minority attitude position differed from the subjects' own. Sanbonmatsu, Shavitt, Sherman and Roskos-Ewoldsen (1987) found that when the minority category was the self it was associated with the *more* frequent behaviour type, and Pryor (1986) failed to replicate the illusory correlation effect with subjects given impression formation instructions.

Further, Stroebe and Insko (1989, p. 26) prefer to limit the robustness of the effect to cases where the stimulus groups are laboratory-based and have no prior meaning. This caution seems warranted in the context of demonstrations that the illusory correlation is weakened or eliminated where the stimulus groups have meaning for the subjects. For example, McArthur and Friedman (1980) conducted experiments conceptually similar to those of Hamilton and Gifford (1976) but the stimulus groups were identified as composed of blacks or whites, males or females, young people or old (rather than just Group A or B). Illusory correlation effects were only evident where the infrequently observed group performed acts that were associatively linked to that group (i.e., consistent with pre-existing stereotypic beliefs). Thus, for example, subjects' responses revealed no illusory correlation effect where an ingroup minority (e.g., whites) performed undesirable behaviours. Along similar lines, Schaller and Maass (1989) found that in conditions where subjects believed that they were members of the minority group (B), the tendency to overrepresent negative behaviours performed by members of that group was completely overridden by an ingroup favouritism effect.

Taken together, these deviations from the basic pattern of illusory correlation between infrequent characteristics and infrequent groups must throw some doubt on Hamilton's interpretation of it as an outcome of relatively automatic mechanisms of selective attention (cf. Hamilton and Sherman, 1989). Fiedler (1991) concludes that '. . . the notion of distinctiveness-based illusory correlation is difficult to defend in view of the available evidence' (p. 35), and offers an alternative cognitive interpretation of the relevant data, based on hypothesized selective 'information loss' that occurs when information of varying frequencies is processed. E. R. Smith (1991) has reproduced the effect with a computer simulation of memory storage and information aggregation that involves no distinctiveness-based encoding or retrieval biases. The force of his analysis derives from the fact that in the standard Hamilton and Gifford paradigm the difference between positive and negative behaviours is greater for Group A $(18 - 8 = 10)$ than for Group B $(9 - 4 = 5)$. Smith concludes that 'unbiased memory processes alone can explain the basic effect' (p. 120).

Moreover, the results reported by McArthur and Friedman (1980) and Schaller and Maass (1989) suggest that, whatever its specific character, the cognitive process of forming illusory correlations can be influenced by social factors, such that illusory correlations do not form where they would contradict an established social stereotype, or result in negative evaluations of the ingroup (see Schaller and Maass, 1989, p. 718; Stroebe and Insko, 1989, pp. 25–28). In summary, it appears that both the specific cognitive basis of the effect, and its potential mediation by social factors, require clarification. We shall discuss the illusory correlation further in chapter 7.

In sharp contrast with Hamilton et al.'s message that stereotype formation can proceed in the absence of relevant correlations, Eagly and her colleagues have presented a social structural theory of stereotype development, arguing that stereotypes stem from and accurately represent *social-structural relationships* (Eagly and Wood, 1982; Eagly and Steffen, 1984; Eagly and Kite, 1987). Thus, 'the . . . cause of gender stereotyping is the differing distributions of women and men into social roles' (Eagly and Steffen, 1984, p. 752). Specifically, Eagly and Steffen address the stereotype of women as communal (i.e., selfless, concerned with others, wanting to be at one with others) and men as agentic (self-assertive, motivated to master their environment), suggesting that it is an *actual* correlation in society between the homemaker (communal) / employed (agentic) variable and gender that creates the gender stereotype. In support of this they present evidence (1984, Experiment 3) that, whilst women were perceived as more communal and less agentic than men when no role information was provided, *all* homemakers (whether male or female) were perceived as equally and highly communal, and *all* employees as highly agentic. Eagly is not, however, arguing that stereotypes are necessarily valid representations of individuals, as the stereotypic inference is based on exposure to a display of attributes limited by social role demands. How these relate to the 'true' attributes of individuals (e.g., do the role distributions arise from the fact that women 'really are' more communal than men?) is an issue on which Eagly remains noncommittal (e.g., see Eagly and Steffen, 1984, pp. 751–752). She is only prepared to say that the content of gender stereotypes is explicable in terms of the current role distribution, whatever the basis for that distribution.

However Hoffman and Hurst (1990), in an interesting recent paper which also considers the development of gender stereotypes, are more forthright. They argue that although gender stereotypes may have developed in response to certain social structural realities, they are not valid representations of the characteristics of men and women. They are 'explanatory *fictions* that rationalize and make sense of the sexual division of labor' (p. 199, emphasis added) and are not dependent on or necessarily related to gender-based differences in personality (i.e., 'real' differences). Hoffman and Hurst suggest that Eagly's emphasis on the simple observation of the relationship between gender and roles cannot explain why the relevant images come to characterize males and females *in general*. 'Why do we have *gender* stereotypes in addition to homemaker and breadwinner stereotypes?', they ask (p. 198). Their answer is that stereotypes develop as explanations or rationalizations of the division of labour, rather than simply 'summary abstractions' about it. Generalization occurs because the explanations developed tend to make reference to inherent, natural differences between males and females, for example 'Women care for the children, and understandably so – they are *by nature* kinder, gentler, and more sensitive than men' (p. 199, emphasis added) – if it is women's nature to care for children, then of course they will all do it.

The paper reports two studies testing these ideas. In the first subjects were told about two fictional groups from a distant planet, Ackmians and Orinthians. These groups were presented as either separate species (biological condition) or distinct subcultures (nonbiological condition), living together in social collectives. The roles of 'city worker' and 'childraiser' were also introduced, as was the idea that there was no gender on this planet: any individual could produce offspring with any other (except that in the biological condition it had to be a member of the same species). Subjects read individual descriptions of fifteen members of each category. Half of the time twelve Orinthians were city workers and three were child raisers, with these frequencies reversed for Ackmians, and in the other half of the description sets the Ackmians were predominantly city workers while more Orinthians raised children. The descriptions took the form, 'Dolack, an Ackmian who raises children, is outspoken, compassionate, and reliable' (p. 200), designed to each include one agentic (e.g., outspoken), one communal (e.g., compassionate) and one neutral (e.g., reliable) trait. Thus, there was no correlation between the targets' personalities and either their category membership or their role. In addition, half of the subjects were explicitly requested to *explain* the observed category–role correlation. The main response measures assessed stereotyping of Ackmians and Orinthians (both with and without the city worker or child raiser role specified) on agentic and communal dimensions.

It was found, as predicted, that Ackmians and Orinthians were stereotyped as communal or agentic depending on the correlation between category membership and child raising or working in the city. This category stereotyping still occurred when a target's role was specified, attesting to the power of the stereotype to generalize (cf. Eagly and Steffen, 1984). Stereotyping increased in strength when the basis for the categorization was supposedly biological, and when subjects had been asked to explain the role difference. Seventy-two per cent of subjects had given personality-based explanations, e.g., 'The Ackmians are more self-confident and forceful, therefore better suited for working in the city' (p. 202; recall that no group *was* more forceful, etc.). Hoffman and Hurst ruled out possible contamination of their results by implicit association with current gender stereotypes through analysis of post-experimental inquiries (only 12 per cent of subjects made any reference to gender), and with a second study which replicated the first using roles with no association to familiar human categories. They conclude that:

Stereotype formation of the kind at issue here is not purely an information processing phenomenon ... role-based category stereotypes originate in a rationalization process that operates by positing intrinsic differences between the categories in question. (p. 206)

They also point to the relevance of their analysis for social categorizations other than gender, e.g., the idea that the stereotype of American Blacks (as lazy, stupid, etc.) arose to justify slavery, and persists to rationalize lower socio-economic status (see also G. Allport, 1954; Stephan and Rosenfield, 1982).

There are, then, two distinct current approaches to the formation of social stereotypes, one emphasizing cognitive processing and illusory correlation, the other social structure and actual correlation between role demands and category membership. However, both of these analyses tend to emphasize bias and the distorting properties of stereotypes. For Hamilton the bias is inherent in a cognitive system which has to be selective. For Hoffman and Hurst (and less clearly for Eagly) the bias is socially produced, through a division of labour long since obsolete but continuing through inertia and now justified through stereotypes (see Hoffman and Hurst, 1990, p. 207). In both cases, stereotypes fail to represent any 'true' characteristics of the people to whom they are applied.

One current exception to this overall approach to stereotype formation tests a hypothesis consistent with ideas and data to be presented in later chapters. Ford and Stangor (1992) have recently reported studies which demonstrate that subjects are sensitive to attributes which best *differentiate* between groups in a stereotype formation task. Information about both the central tendency and variability of groups on different attributes contributed to the formation of highly 'diagnostic' stereotypes, ones which maximized differentiation between the two categories (see Rosch, 1978; Turner, 1985; Turner et al., 1987, and chapters 4–6). For example, subjects told about the friendliness and intelligence of two groups formed stereotypes in which friendliness was more salient where that attribute differentiated more strongly between categories. In contrast, intelligence dominated stereotypes where that was the more differentiating dimension. Ford and Stangor conclude that

> The formation of social stereotypes is not always driven by cognitive errors, biases, and heuristics, but may at least in some cases be driven by a goal of accurately assessing real intergoup differences . . . we assume, consistent with the 'kernel of truth' hypothesis (e.g., Allport, 1954) that there are real differences between groups and that detection of those differences . . . plays an important role in stereotype formation. (1992, p. 365)

Thus, unlike Hoffman and Hurst (p. 197), Ford and Stangor are prepared to embrace the kernel of truth perspective as a basis from which to argue for stereotypes as (at least partially) founded on reality rather than distortion. Again, we need to ask ourselves whether the kernel of truth idea is the only way forward in this context – we shall return to this question in chapter 8.

Issues of Category Representation: Levels, Prototypes, Exemplars and Relative Homogeneity

Whilst the research just discussed tries to determine how groups come to be represented in terms of specific characteristics (why people think Blacks are lazy, for example), social cognition researchers have also become interested in much more general issues of category representation: whatever its specific character, how is social category information represented in memory? In simple terms, this research asks 'what, cognitively speaking, *is* a stereotype?' Is it a fairly complete listing of all the characteristics expected of members of a given category, does it include information about every category member encountered, or is it a rather more abstract summary of what category members might be like? As well as these questions about the internal nature of individual social categories, researchers have addressed the structure of the category system as a whole, the way in which different categories relate to each other.

Of course, such questions are not only of interest to students of social categorization. Within cognitive psychology, the 'Roschian revolution' (Neisser, 1987a, p. vii) of the 1970s introduced some key new ideas to the analysis of category structure and representation. As is now well known, Rosch challenged the classical view of category representation with her ideas about, and evidence of, extensive *variation* in category structure. She and her colleagues (e.g., Rosch, 1978; Rosch, Mervis, Gray, Johnson and Boyes-Braem, 1976) found that, *within* categories, members vary in their typicality, e.g., robins are seen as more typical of the category 'bird' than are ostriches. This lead to the idea of a category *prototype* (a best example of the category) and the argument that category membership requires a certain level of similarity to the prototype rather than a full, necessary set of attributes, as in the classical view. Further, comparisons *between* categories reveal that they vary in their relative inclusiveness, e.g., 'dalmatian', 'dog', 'animal', 'living thing' are categories of increasing inclusiveness. Those at a higher level are called superordinate, compared to lower-level categories known as subordinate. Around the middle of the hierarchy of inclusiveness is the *basic* level (e.g., 'dog', 'car', 'chair', 'tree') at which, it is argued, most perceptual activity takes place (Mervis and Rosch, 1981). These ideas have been very influential in cognitive analyses of categorization (e.g., Neisser, 1987a; E. E. Smith and Medin, 1981; see chapter 5), and soon found their way into social cognition (e.g., Cantor and Mischel, 1979) and the social psychology of stereotyping (e.g., Brewer, Dull and Lui, 1981; Deaux and Lewis, 1984; Deaux, Winton, Crowley and Lewis, 1985).

A good illustration of the straightforward application of Rosch's ideas to stereotyping is the work of Brewer and her colleagues (Brewer et al., 1981; Brewer and Lui, 1984; Lui and Brewer, 1983). Brewer et al. (1981) explicitly conceptualized 'stereotypes as prototypes', and investigated the processing of information about the elderly in a series of studies. In the first experiment it was found that photographs of elderly people were naturally clustered into sub-categories (e.g., the 'grandmother' or 'senior citizen' type). It was also found (Experiment 2) that subjects presented with highly prototypical instances of these categories displayed more coherent clustering than those subjects presented with relatively non-prototypical examples. In a third experiment, Brewer et al. (1981) used the prototypes 'grandmother', 'senior citizen' and 'young woman' to test for effects of prototypicality on the processing and recall of relevant information. They found that category-consistent information was processed faster and recalled better than inconsistent information, and that recall errors within categories were considerably greater than those between categories (see S. Taylor et al., 1978, above).

Brewer et al. conclude from this pattern of results (specifically, from the swifter processing and better recall of consistent information) that social information is naturally structured in terms of 'basic' level sub-categories. This argument has since been elaborated by Andersen and Klatzky (1987; Andersen, Klatzky and Murray, 1990) who suggest that social information is typically processed at this basic (social stereotypic) level since, like the basic level identified in Rosch's work, 'it is more vivid and easier to visualize . . . [and] should always be more predictive and robust' than individual trait-type information (1987, p. 244).

However, it has also been suggested that social perception is strongly influenced by *generic categories* such as gender, race and age which are activated more or less automatically at the beginning of the impression formation process (Brewer, 1988; Brewer and Lui, 1989; Fiske and Neuberg, 1990; Hewstone, Hantzi and Johnston, 1991). The idea that perceivers tend to be reluctant to elaborate impressions beyond this point (because of capacity limitations) features in impression formation models outlined by both Brewer (1988) and Fiske (Fiske and Neuberg, 1990). Thus, both superordinate categories (e.g., gender) and sub-types (e.g., 'grandmother-type') have been identified as 'basic' to (in the sense of most influential in) social perception. On the other hand, Messick and D. Mackie (1989; following Turner, 1985) recently concluded (from evidence of social-contextual variation in the hierarchical relationship between categories) that 'no basic level of categorization exists for social stimuli' (p. 53). They also suggest that, far from being a fixed, stable image of the 'best' category member, social category prototypes may be contextually variable, depending in part on the intergroup comparison being made (Turner et al., 1987; see chapter 4). As Messick and D. Mackie put it, 'the attributes thought to be prototypical of university professors may be different depending on whether they are compared to research scientists or high school teachers' (1989, p. 52). Rosch herself had cautioned against any reification of the protoype concept, stressing that it was *judgements of prototypicality* that mattered, and that to imagine any fixed prototype was to reintroduce the classical, all-or-nothing approach in a subtly different form (Rosch, 1978; see Barsalou, 1987, Beck, C. McCauley, Segal and Hershey, 1988, and Dunning, Perie and Story, 1991, for evidence of variation in category prototypes).

Prototype-based models of category representation are not the only ones on offer. Researchers in both general and social cognition have presented evidence of subjects' ability to make estimates of *category variability* (the range of stimuli allowed membership) in support of *exemplar-based* models of representation (e.g., Hintzman, 1986; Linville, Salovey and Fischer, 1986; Linville, Fischer and Salovey, 1989; E. E. Smith and Medin, 1981; E. R. Smith and Zarate, 1992). For example, Linville and colleagues assume that people represent categories (e.g., 'politicians') in terms of separate descriptions of category exemplars. These may be individual category members ('Ronald Reagan') or category subtypes ('right-wing Republicans'). Membership decisions are based on similarity to retrieved exemplars rather than an abstract prototype, and more general judgements about the category, such as estimates of its homogeneity, also depend on assessments of exemplar information. To complicate matters further, *mixed* or *dual storage* models of category representation have also been proposed (e.g., Judd and Park, 1988; Park and Hastie, 1987), in which information both summarizing (i.e., prototypical) and specifying (i.e., exemplar) category members is stored. For example, Judd and Park suggest that abstracted information about such factors as a group's overall homogeneity is represented in memory together with exemplar descriptions.

The 'prototype vs. exemplar controversy' (Schneider, 1991, p. 534) has perhaps been most closely argued in relation to the *outgroup homogeneity* effect. This refers to the tendency to perceive greater intragroup similarity within outgroups than within ingroups. In an early demonstration of the effect, Linville and E. Jones (1980, Experiment 3) found that white subjects, asked to sort forty traits into coherent groups, produced more groups when asked to think about white males (an ingroup) while they were doing the task than when they were asked to think about black males (an outgroup). Linville and E. Jones (1980) interpreted this finding as evidence that ingroup 'schemas' are more differentiated than outgroup ones because we interact with more ingroup members. This produces a 'rich background of experience' (p. 691) of the ingroup which necessitates a fairly complex representation (see also Quattrone and E. Jones, 1980). In comparison, our experience of outgroups is less extensive and less varied, producing relatively simple representations.

This outgroup homogeneity effect has been demonstrated using various conceptualizations and measures of homogeneity, and with both real and minimal groups (Brewer et al. 1981; Brewer and Lui, 1984; E. Jones, Wood and Quattrone, 1981; Linville, 1982; Park and Rothbart, 1982; Quattrone and E. Jones, 1980; Wilder, 1984). For example, Park and Rothbart (1982) asked male and female subjects to estimate the proportion of males and females who would endorse each of fifty-four attitudinal and behavioural items. The items varied in both relevance to sex stereotypes and favourability. As predicted, opposite-sex estimates were more sex-stereotypical than same-sex estimates: for example, men's estimate of the proportion of women endorsing stereotypic items was higher than women's estimate of the same proportion. Favourability did not affect this pattern: the outgroup was stereotyped more than the ingroup on favourable just as much as on unfavourable items.

Reviewers of the relevant evidence have concluded that outgroup homogeneity is 'a robust phenomenon of social perception' (Quattrone, 1986, p. 34; see also Linville et al., 1986; Mullen and Hu, 1989; Park, Judd and Ryan, 1991; Wilder, 1986), but the explanations proffered have been almost as varied as the methods used to demonstrate the effect (e.g., Quattrone, 1986; Wilder 1986, pp. 308–309). There is, however, a degree of consensus that it is a matter of 'understanding how the cognitive representations of ingroups and outgroups differ' (Messick and D. Mackie, 1989, p. 55), and both the exemplar-based and the mixed model of category representation claim superiority in this regard.

As part of their multiple exemplar model of category representation, Linville and her colleagues (Linville et al., 1986, 1989) offer an elaboration of the earlier Linville and E. Jones (1980) schema-based analysis of outgroup homogeneity. Their differential familiarity hypothesis holds that the perceived differentiation (probability of distinguishing between category members in terms of a given attribute) and variability (range of attribute values represented in the category) of a category representation depend on familiarity with individual category members. Thus, ingroup category representations will reflect greater differentiation and variability than outgroup categories because perceivers tend to be more familiar with the ingroup than the outgroup.

The hypothesis that familiarity increases perceived category differentiation and variability was tested in a natural experiment (Linville et al., 1989, Experiment 4) tracing the development of a classroom group. Measures of perceived differentiation and variability were taken at the beginning, the midpoint and towards the end of semester in a class of fifty-six students in an introductory psychology class. As predicted, linear trends indicated increases in both differentiation and variability in individuals' representations of the group over this time period. Linville et al. claim clear support for the differential familiarity hypothesis from both this experiment and from a computer simulation of the multiple exemplar model. In summary, then, they are arguing that it is differences in familiarity with in- and outgroup members which produce richer exemplar-based representations of the former than the latter, and hence the generalized judgement of outgroups as more homogeneous.

Judd and Park (1988; Park and Judd, 1990), on the other hand, apply their dual storage model of category representation to the explanation of outgroup homogeneity. They argue that both exemplar information of the type discussed by Linville and abstract information about the group's overall homogeneity should contribute to variability judgements. However, in practice, and for a variety of reasons including lack of elaborated contact with the outgroup (Park and Rothbart, 1982), greater awareness of ingroup subgroups (Park, Ryan and Judd, 1992) and of the individuality of ingroup members, including oneself (Judd and Park, 1988), and motivations to represent the ingroup more accurately (Judd, Ryan and Park, 1991), exemplar-level information is used *less* for outgroup than for ingroup judgements. This accounts for the observed effect.

Judd and Park (1988) pitted their model against Linville et al.'s in a modified minimal group procedure which (a) controlled the number of in- and outgroup exemplars encountered, and the kind of information known about them, (b) included a manipulation of group membership salience (anticipated competition versus cooperation), and (c) required judgements and recall of individual information about in- and outgroup members as well as group-level homogeneity judgements. They found that, with equal information about both groups (i.e., no difference in 'familiarity') an outgroup homogeneity effect did appear, but only when the group boundary was salient (i.e., with anticipated competition but not with anticipated cooperation), and only on group-level variability judgements (i.e., those requiring a rating of the group as a whole). Measures of the perceived variability of individual group members showed no outgroup homogeneity effect. Judd and Park conclude that Linville's exemplar model cannot account for their results, as the effect observed is clearly not mediated by differences in information about exemplars (see also E. Jones et al., 1981; Park and Rothbart, 1982). However, Linville et al. (1989) and Ostrom and Sedikides (1988) counterattack, pointing out, for example, that even in Judd and Park's minimal group design, the exemplar information about in- and outgroups is not balanced because the ingroup includes the self, 'likely to be mentally represented by more exemplars than are other individuals' (Linville et al., 1989, p. 185). They thus cast doubt on the ability of Judd and Park's design to distinguish between the two models. Linville et al. also suggest that differential familiarity is not, in fact, crucial to their model. They only wish to argue that differential familiarity is sufficient to produce the outgroup homogeneity effect. It is not necessary, 'not the only cause of outgroup homogeneity' (p. 185). Other factors, such as motivational pressures towards making distinctions within the ingroup (cf. Judd et al., 1991), can, they argue, be incorporated in their exemplar model without damage to its basic assumptions.

While this argument over the cognitive representational basis of the effect has continued, other researchers, influenced by the tradition of research into social identity (Tajfel and Turner, 1986; see chapter 4), have approached the issue from a more group-oriented perspective. This work has provided evidence which suggests that outgroup homogeneity might be rather less of a 'universal law' than had been assumed (see Simon, 1992, p. 23). Simon and R. J. Brown (1987) assessed perceptions of homogeneity amongst experimentally created minorities and non-minorities. They found that whilst non-minority members followed the usual pattern of judging the outgroup to be more homogeneous than the ingroup, minorities assumed more ingroup than outgroup homogeneity (an ingroup homogeneity effect; see also Simon and Pettigrew, 1990). Simon and Mummendey (1991) argued, and demonstrated, that with no explicit information about relative group size subjects assumed their group was in the majority, and produced the outgroup homogeneity effect. With explicit information that the groups were of equal size the outgroup homogeneity effect disappeared.

An interesting study by Kelly (1989) assessed perceptions of the homogeneity of the British Labour and Conservative parties amongst Labour Party supporters. The category-relevance of the judgement dimension emerged as an important influence in this study. An outgroup homogeneity effect was found on irrelevant personality dimensions, whereas judgements on highly relevant issue dimensions (e.g., higher welfare spending, private health care) produced an ingroup homogeneity effect.

Simon (1992) reports a test of the hypothesis that ingroup homogeneity effects will occur on typical ingroup attributes, outgroup homogeneity effects on typical outgroup attributes. Subjects were categorized, ostensibly on the basis of artistic preferences, into either a minority or majority group. The homogeneity measure was subjects' frequency distributions of group members on a seven-point scale assessing liking for certain paintings. Frequency distributions for both the ingroup and the outgroup in relation to both the ingroup-preferred and the outgroup-preferred artist were obtained. As predicted, an ingroup homogeneity effect was found for ingroup-preferred paintings, and a non-significant trend indicated an outgroup homogeneity effect for the outgroup-preferred paintings. This effect was not qualified by the minority/majority status of the groups.

Simon, Glassner-Bayerl and Stratenwerth (1991) hypothesized that a strong social stereotype about relative group homogeneity could also influence group members' judgements. Specifically, they predicted that both gay and straight men would be aware of, and use in their judgements, the stereotypical belief that gay men are more homogeneous as a group than straight men. As predicted, on group-relevant dimensions the straight subjects evidenced outgroup homogeneity, the gay subjects ingroup homogeneity.

Simon suggests that his accumulated findings of ingroup homogeneity, and the conditions under which they occurred, are problematic for both the Linville and the Judd and Park models. He argues that perceptions of group homogeneity are socially mediated, 'not an invariable cognitive output of the human "hardware" ' (1992, p. 18), and that static models of category representation cannot account for the influence of social-contextual variables (such as minority/majority status; widely shared stereotypes) on the perception of homogeneity (see chapters 4 and 7). His own 'egocentric categorization' model will be outlined and discussed in chapter 7.

In summary, there are both arguments and evidence within this research literature suggesting that judgements of prototypicality, the 'level' at which social categorization occurs, and perceptions of in- and outgroup homogeneity are all highly context-dependent. Perhaps the explanatory focus needs to shift from category representation to the functioning of the categorization *process* before an adequate and heuristic account of variability in levels of categorization, issues of prototypicality, and homogeneity effects can be achieved. We shall return to these issues in chapters 4 and 7.

The Biasing of Encoding and Recall by Social Categories

As we noted in chapter 2, the idea that stereotypes resist change, that they stubbornly persist in the face of contradiction, has been a constant of the past seventy years of stereotyping research. A cognitive explanation of this tendency appeared to come to hand with evidence that social categories biased the encoding and retrieval of information in the direction of their own confirmation (see Neuberg, in press, for a review). Thus, Hamilton (1979, p. 80) concluded that 'a stereotype's persistence ... is a natural consequence of the biases inherent in its employment.'

Early evidence consistent with this conclusion comes from a classic study by Duncan (1976) which manipulated the race (black/white) of both the perpetrator and the victim of an 'ambiguous shove'. The shove tended to be seen as fooling around when perpetrated by a white actor, but as violent behaviour when perpetrated by a black actor, particularly when the victim was white (see also G. Allport and Postman, 1947; Sagar and Schofield, 1980). The black actor's behaviour was interpreted and encoded in a way which confirmed a stereotype of blacks as 'impulsive and given to crimes and violence' (Duncan, 1976, p. 591).

Findings from a number of studies suggest that individuals structure their intake of information from the environment such that it will tend to confirm rather than disconfirm expectancies, including stereotypic expectancies (e.g., Ickes, Patterson, Rajecki and Tanford, 1982; Major, Cozzarelli, Testa and McFarlin, 1988). Perhaps best known in this area is research by Snyder and his colleagues (see Snyder, 1984, and in press, for reviews). Typical of this work is a study by Snyder and Gangestad (1982, cited in Snyder 1984, pp. 276–277) in which subjects were given one of four hypotheses about endomorphs and ectomorphs (e.g., '*endo*morphs tend to be relaxed and sociable rather than restrained and anxious', or '*ecto*morphs tend to be relaxed and sociable ...') and asked to test this hypothesis by recalling relevant information about people they knew. Subjects' reports selectively focused on confirming examples.

Snyder has also reported evidence that individuals' interaction strategies tend to elicit behaviour from others which confirms a stereotypic expectancy (Rosenthal, 1974). For example, Snyder and Swann (1978) gave subjects the expectation that a person with whom they were about to interact, with a view to ascertaining their personality, was prototypically either an extravert or an intravert. From a list of potential questions provided by the experimenter, subjects with the former expectation selected items like, 'What would you do if you wanted to liven things up at a party?', whereas a subject expecting an introvert might ask, 'What factors make it hard for you to really open up to people?' Thus, subjects selectively asked questions likely to produce confirmation rather than disconfirmation of their expectancy, and indeed their interviewing technique did this. Snyder and Swann report that the targets' behaviour was constrained by these questioning strategies such that those expected to be extraverts did present themselves as more extravert than those expected to be intraverts, a difference detected by naive judges who were presented with only the targets' responses (see also Snyder, Tanke and Berscheid,

1977; Word, Zanna and Cooper, 1974). Snyder argues that stereotypic expectancies not only bias the encoding of information, they become 'self-fulfilling prophecies', biasing the actual behaviour of their targets towards their own verification (see Snyder 1981a, b).

The fact that stereotypes *can* produce their own confirmation in this way by no means implies that they always do so. This has been the emphasis of recent commentaries, some reviewers suggesting that the expectancy confirmation processes identified by Snyder and others are fairly insignificant outside the laboratory (e.g., Jussim, 1986, 1991). Others have developed models which identify mediating variables responsible for expectancy confirmation under some conditions, disconfirmation under others. For example Hilton and Darley (1991) distinguish between 'assessment sets' (where interaction goals focus on impression formation) and 'action sets' (where management of the behavioural interaction is the priority), predicting that confirmation processes are much more likely in the latter. Where perceivers are motivated to form *accurate* impressions, confirmation processes are expected to be minimized (see also Stangor and Ford, 1992). Similarly, Neuberg (in press) emphasizes motivational influences on expectancy confirmation, noting in particular the role of capacity limitations in determining whether or not the perceiver can pursue certain goals. Capacity limitations also set confirmation processes as the 'default' response when resources are scarce. Finally, Snyder (in press) presents a functional analysis, identifying various purposes expectancy confirmation and disconfirmation can serve for both perceiver and target, and using these to predict when each process is more likely. Thus, the earlier emphasis on the power of stereotypes to produce their own confirmation has been exchanged for a more complex view which recognizes the status of both perceiver and target as active agents of social influence.

Further evidence indicates that social categories can influence *recall* of information, and initial conclusions were that this also worked more or less automatically to bolster stereotype validity (e.g., Hamilton, 1979). Relevant findings were reported by Zadny and Gerard (1974). In one of their experiments the academic major of a target was manipulated (e.g., chemistry, psychology, music) and found to affect memory for information associated with the target. Specifically, information consistent with the major was best recalled, for example a preponderance of science classes, titles of science books, carrying a slide rule tended to be recalled for a chemistry major. Similarly, Cohen (1981) showed subjects a video of a woman identifed as either a librarian or a waitress. At recall they tended to remember information consistent with the ascribed identity,

Retrieval of social info
expectancies + lab.

e.g., that the 'librarian' had worn glasses, or that the 'waitress' had been drinking beer.

Snyder and Uranowitz (1978) gave subjects a biography of a woman, 'Betty K.', which detailed her childhood, early home life, education, social life in high school and college, choice of profession, etc. A week later they returned to complete a recall test, but were first informed either that Betty was now living with another woman in a lesbian relationship, or that she was now living with her husband in a heterosexual relationship. This information significantly affected the details of Betty's life recalled by subjects. For example, those in the lesbian condition tended to remember that she had never had a steady boyfriend in high school (though not that she'd had many dates in college), while those who believed she was married recalled her relationship with a man in college (but not that it was a friendship rather than a romance).

This effect has also been demonstrated with expectancies about groups generated in the laboratory, rather than pre-existing stereotypes. Rothbart, Evans and Fulero (1979) presented subjects with a set of fifty statements each describing the behaviour of a different man. Twenty of these behaviours related to friendliness (seventeen were friendly, three non-friendly) and a further twenty related to intelligence (seventeen described intelligent behaviour, three non-intelligent). The remaining ten behaviours were unrelated to friendliness or intelligence. Subjects were told that the group of targets was intelligent or that they were friendly either (a) before presentation of the stimuli or (b) before recalling the statements and estimating the numbers of each type. When the expectancy preceded the information, subjects remembered more behaviours consistent with the group label, and also estimated that they were more frequent than inconsistent behaviours (see also Hamilton and Rose, 1980; Slusher and Anderson, 1987).

There is, then, considerable evidence suggesting that retrieval of social information can be biased in the direction of confirming preformed stereotypical expectancies. Again though, apparently contradictory findings have emerged (see Stangor and Duan, 1991). In a paradigm very similar to that employed by Rothbart et al. (1979), Hastie and Kumar (1979, Experiment 1) presented subjects with twenty statements describing behaviours performed by target individuals who had previously been characterized by a series of adjectives. Twelve of these behaviours were congruent with the target's personality, four were neutral and four were incongruent. Subjects subsequently showed superior recall for statements *incongruent* with the target's personality, relative to other behaviours. In a second experiment it was shown that this effect became stronger as the ratio of congruent to incongruent behaviours was increased. These findings were later replicated by Hemsley and Marmurek (1982; see also Crocker, Hannah and Weber, 1983; Hastie, 1981; Srull, 1981; Wyer and Gordon, 1982).

Stern, Marrs, Millar and Cole (1984) offer a resolution of this apparent contradiction in the data. They suggest that preferential recall of inconsistent information holds under *individual* impression formation conditions (as in Hastie and Kumar, 1979), but not where a *group* image is in question (as in Rothbart et al., 1979). This is based on Stern et al.'s hypothesis that additional processing tends to be given to unexpected, potentially irreconcilable information, and that 'subjects do not expect members of some loosely knit group to behave consistently but do expect consistent behaviour from individuals' (p. 254). Their subjects were presented with a list of personality traits followed by twenty behaviours. In one condition these were attributed to a single fictional individual, whereas in the other subjects were told that the traits characterized a fictional group, 'as a whole', and the behaviours had each been performed by a different member. As predicted, it was found that in free recall the inconsistent behaviours were remembered better than consistent behaviours in the individual condition, but not in the group condition.

Findings from other studies support this suggestion that individual conditions produce superior recall of inconsistent information, whilst consistent information is favoured under group conditions. In an interesting study by Crocker et al. (1983) subjects were provided with either dispositional (e.g., 'He did this because he didn't care what others thought') or situational (e.g., 'He did this because he was paged for an emergency') attributions for consistent and inconsistent behaviours performed by a target. As predicted, it was found that superior memory for inconsistent behaviours held only where dispositional attributions had been presented, that is where the relevance of the behaviour to the target's individual identity was clearly established. With situational attributions, consistent and inconsistent behaviours were recalled equally well.

Studies conducted by Bodenhausen are also relevant here. Bodenhausen and Wyer (1985) presented subjects with vignettes containing biographical information about male targets who had committed transgressions. These transgressions were either stereotypic (e.g., Ashley Chamberlain from Cambridge, Massachusetts committed fraud; Carlos Ramirez from Alberquerque, New Mexico attacked a man in a bar) or non-stereotypic for each target. To simplify the rather complex findings, it appears that the target was treated in terms of a relevant group identity in the stereotype-consistent conditions, but more as an individual where the offence was stereotypically inconsistent. In the former case recall was better for stereotype-consistent details, while in the latter instance recall of inconsistent details was superior. Similarly, Bodenhausen and Lichtenstein (1987) constructed files of information about 'Robert Johnson' and 'Carlos Ramirez' and asked subjects either to make personality trait judgements about their target or to assess his guilt in relation to an assault described in the file. Hispanic category membership was expected, and found, to influence judgements of Carlos Ramirez more significantly in the guilt assessment than the trait judgement condition. Further, Bodenhausen and Lichtenstein report superior recall for stereotype-consistent information under these conditions (where the target was being treated as a group member), but equal recall of both consistent and inconsistent information in the trait judgement (individual) condition.

Forgas (1983) hypothesized that consistent information would be recalled better than inconsistent information where the target represented a 'culturally salient' social category, as compared with a less meaningful social grouping. Out of sixteen different 'person types' (or stereotypes), an initial experiment identified 'student radicals', 'surfies', 'Christians' and 'medical students' as highly salient categorizations in the subject population (Australian students), compared with 'engineers', 'sporty types', 'college students' and 'Asian students', which were less meaningful. In a second experiment subjects were presented with eight stimulus characters described by statements predominantly consistent or predominantly inconsistent with one of the stereotyped groups listed above. As predicted, stereotype-consistent information was subject to superior processing for the student radicals, surfies, Christians and medical students, but more inconsistent information was remembered about the engineers, sporty types, college students and Asian students.

Considered together, the findings of the above studies converge to suggest that where judgement or information conditions emphasize targets' social category memberships, stereotype-consistent information will be relatively important. On the other hand, where individual impression formation is emphasized, individuating (i.e., inconsistent) characteristics will be more salient. As we saw, Stern et al. (1984) base their distinction between group and individual conditions on the assumption that we expect consistency in individuals but not in groups. In our view, the evidence cited above suggests that we do expect quite specific stereotypical consistency in meaningful groups, and such consistency takes priority when group-based perception makes sense in the context (see Bodenhausen and Wyer, 1985). Overall, it appears that the early assumption of a more or less automatic tendency for stereotypic expectations to confirm themselves was rather simplistic. At the very least, we need to take into account motivational processes affecting impression formation, and distinguish conditions where group membership is the relevant and salient basis of perception from those where individual identity is of interest, or where the categorization is relatively unimportant or meaningless to the perceivers (e.g., Hymes, 1986; Forgas, 1983).

When Do We Stereotype?

One more or less implicit assumption underlying traditional stereotyping research was that if individuals hold stereotypes they use them. If I believe that Americans are aggressive and materialistic this will always influence my perception of Americans to some degree. However, from the perspective of the cognitive approach, the use of stereotypes, the engaging of the stereotyping process, becomes an empirical issue (e.g., see Hamilton, 1979, p. 59). As Taylor puts it:

> A categorization approach implies that the process of stereotyping has a contextual basis. It is clearly not the case that the social perceiver has a stereotype about a social group that he or she evenhandedly attributes to every member of that group with whom he or she interacts. Rather, there appear to be contextual dimensions that facilitate or inhibit the imputation of stereotypes to individuals. (S. Taylor, 1981a, p. 110)

Predicting the contextual basis of stereotyping formed an important aspect of Taylor's own early contribution. As part of a general account of spontaneous selective attention in social perception (see S. Taylor and Fiske, 1978), Taylor proposed a *distinctiveness or novelty principle*: relatively novel stimuli automatically attract attention (we referred to these ideas in the context of the illusory correlation effect). (McGuire and McGuire, 1981, McGuire, McGuire, Child and Fujioka, 1978, and McGuire, McGuire and Winton, 1979, have put forward similar ideas in relation to the salience of social categories in the self-concept.) The application of this principle to the issue of when we use stereotypes produces the hypothesis that where a cue to a category membership constitutes a novel stimulus it automatically attracts attention, making the relevant membership salient, and invoking the stereotype (McArthur and Post, 1977; S. Taylor et al., 1978). Thus, in general terms it is hypothesized that stereotyping is more likely where a category is in the minority, and increases in likelihood as the minority decreases in size, with 'solo' category members particularly likely to be perceived in stereotypical terms.

The third experiment reported by Taylor et al. (1978) includes a test of the prediction that a stimulus individual's sex category membership would increase in salience as it increased in relative novelty. The sex composition of the stimulus group was varied over seven conditions, from single-sex groups of six men or six women through the intermediate proportions to the 'solo' conditions (i.e., one man and five women, or one woman and five men). Subjects rated the stimulus group on several dependent measures including evaluations of each member on dimensions of sex stereotyping. The predicted positive relationship between relative novelty and sex stereotyping was not found on the stereotyping items, but the result on one other dependent measure was consistent with it. For each member of the group subjects were asked 'if this person had seemed to play any *special role* in the group and if so, what that role was (open-ended)' (S. Taylor et al., 1978, p. 786, emphasis added). Responses were blind-coded for sex stereotyping and a test for a linear trend in proportions revealed a non-significant tendency ($p < 0.09$) for more sex-typed roles to be attributed to male and female stimulus individuals the fewer the other members of their sex there were in the group.

There is, then, some support for the predicted link between stimulus novelty and stereotyping, though it is, as Taylor et al. concede, rather weak. Further, Oakes and Turner (1986a) have suggested that, because the relevant questionnaire item asked about *special* roles, it required subjects to focus on the stimulus individuals' distinguishing characteristics. This leaves the finding susceptible to at least one plausible alternative interpretation in that, for a solo male, for example, gender is a contextually distinguishing characteristic and stereotypically male behaviour would count as a special contribution to the group. Likewise, stereotypically female behaviour would appear relatively special in the solo female condition. In other words, task requirements (answering the 'special role' question) rather than a perceptual bias towards novelty may have mediated Taylor et al.'s linear trend.

Oakes and Turner (1986a) tested this alternative interpretation using an adaptation of Taylor et al.'s method, with the inclusion of a task variable; half the subjects ('individual' task orientation) were asked to focus on and describe one male target amongst the six stimulus individuals (the group varying in sex composition as in S. Taylor et al., 1978, with the exclusion of single sex groups), whilst the other half ('collective' task orientation) gave a description of each member of the stimulus group. Dependent variables included ratings on sex stereotype scales and, as predicted, the task variable had marked effects on the extent to which the male target was described sex-stereotypically. 'Collective' task subjects evidenced most sex stereotyping in the balanced, three male–three female stimulus group condition, whilst 'individual' task subjects described the target most sex stereotypically where his category membership was most novel (one male–five females) and where it was least novel (five males–one female). Although the pattern of stereotyping by 'individual' task subjects was not quite as predicted, Oakes and Turner (1986a) do confirm their hypothesis that stereotyping would be sensitive to contextually variable purposes, and provide no evidence supportive of any automatic tendency to focus on novel category memberships. Studies by Nesdale, Dharmalingam and Kerr (1987) and Abrams, Thomas and Hogg (1990) also fail to confirm the existence of an automatic distinctiveness bias. Nonetheless, the idea that novel category memberships are, in some sense, prepotent in social perception continues to influence discussions of the contextual basis of stereotyping (e.g., Brewer, 1988; Brewer and Kramer, 1985; Fiske and Neuberg, 1990; Hamilton and Trolier, 1986; Higgins and Bargh, 1987; Rothbart and John, 1985; Stephan, 1989).

The novelty-attention approach to category activation was very much a product of the emerging 'cognitive miser' emphasis in social cognition. If the need to conserve processing capacity is a major causal factor in stereotyping, perhaps stereotyping is more likely to occur where cognitive resources are strained. This hypothesis has been tested in a number of recent studies (e.g., Bodenhausen, 1990; Bodenhausen and Lichtenstein, 1987; Gilbert and Hixon, 1991; Kim and Baron, 1988; Macrae, Hewstone and Griffiths, 1993; Pratto and Bargh, 1991; Stangor and Duan, 1991). For example, Gilbert and Hixon (1991) tested the effects of 'cognitive busyness' on stereotyping. In two studies they found that subjects asked to rehearse an eight-digit number whilst watching a videotape of either a Caucasian or an Asian person stereotyped the Asian *less* than those not made 'cognitively busy'. However, in the second study subjects whose Asian stereotype had been explicitly activated before the video used that stereotype more under busy than non-busy conditions. Bodenhausen and Lichtenstein (1987) asked subjects to make judgements about either a Hispanic or Caucasian defendant in a mock jury trial. Both 'qualitative' (type of judgement required) and 'quantitative' (amount of information) demands on capacity were manipulated. Subjects making a more complex judgement (of guilt rather than of aggressiveness) were more likely to use stereotypes, but those expecting to receive a large amount of information about the defendant did not remember more stereotypical information than subjects expecting only a little information (see also Rothbart, Fulero, Jensen, Howard and Birrell, 1978). On the other hand, Stangor and Duan (1991) did find that subjects who had to form impressions of a number of groups, or who were distracted during impression formation relied more heavily on expected (stereotypic) information in their impressions. There is, then, mixed support for the idea that increasing demands on processing increases the likelihood of stereotyping (see chapter 5 for further discussion).

Also relevant to the question of when we use stereotypes is work on the relative *accessibility* of social categories. Bruner (1957) first introduced this idea to the categorization literature, suggesting that factors such as the contextual likelihood of particular objects or events, and the current goals and purposes of the perceiver would render certain categories highly accessible (i.e., likely to be activated; see chapter 5). More recent work has also studied frequency and recency of category activation (e.g., Higgins and King, 1981; Wyer and Srull, 1981), the salience of the category in memory (Nisbett and Ross, 1980), and the relation of a category to other accessible categories (Collins and Loftus, 1975) as determinants of current accessibility. Accessibility has also been conceptualized in terms of 'priming', i.e., 'activation of a category by unobtrusive exposure to exemplars of that category' (Herr, Sherman and Fazio, 1983, p. 323; see Higgins, Bargh and Lombardi, 1985). For example, James (1986) found that subjects were more likely to interpret an ambiguous adult–child interaction as a kidnapping incident when a poster requesting information about a genuinely missing child had been displayed at the entrances to the building where the study was conducted. It has been suggested that both short-term accessibility of this kind, and more chronic, long-lasting accessibility effects (e.g., see Bargh, Bond, Lombardi and Tota, 1986) can influence the use of social categorizations, and hence stereotyping, and that these effects tend to occur fairly automatically and without awareness (e.g., Brewer, 1988; Fiske and Neuberg, 1990).

A different approach to the contextual variability of stereotyping is that based on experiments by Locksley and her colleagues (Locksley, Borgida, Brekke and Hepburn, 1980; Locksley, Hepburn and Ortiz, 1982; see also Borgida, Locksley and Brekke, 1981). These authors relate stereotyping to the psychology of prediction, arguing that stereotypic beliefs function as 'base rates' which social perceivers tend to ignore in the presence of individuating, target-case information (see Kahneman and Tversky, 1973). Therefore, they argue, 'social stereotypes may not exert as pervasive or powerful an effect on social judgement as has been traditionally assumed', having 'minimal . . . impact' whenever information additional to social category membership is available (Borgida et al., 1981, p. 167).

Locksley et al. (1980) present evidence consistent with this analysis. For example, in their first experiment subjects read accounts of male and female students behaving in an assertive (male stereotypical) or passive (female stereotypical) manner in three social situations. The next day they were asked to predict how the target would behave in four new situations, and to describe their impression of the target on sex-stereotype dimensions. Results indicated that these inferences were based on the behavioural information subjects had been given about the targets and not on sex-stereotypical expectations. For example, targets who had acted assertively, whether male or female, were rated as more masculine and less feminine on the Bem Sex Role Inventory than were passive targets. In Experiment 2 assertive or non-assertive behaviour was described in a single vignette, and one condition was included in which subjects were provided only with the target's social category membership (as male or female). Again, in making inferences about the target's general behaviour and personality, subjects tended to use the information from the vignettes rather than stereotypic beliefs. However, where no behavioural information about targets was presented sex-stereotypic beliefs did determine judgement (see also Eagly and Wood, 1982; Hoffman and Hurst, 1990; Jussim, Coleman and Lerch, 1987; Nisbett, Zukier and Lemley, 1981).

As Krueger and Rothbart (1988, p. 188) comment, Locksley et al.'s research 'optimistically' suggests that stereotyping should be far less pervasive than it actually is. Clearly, we often do stereotype individuals about whom we know more than a category identification, a point evidenced by both everyday experiences (a close colleague with whom we disagree is a 'typical learning theorist'; our spouse who refuses to do the laundry/change a tyre on the car is a 'typical male/female') and empirical research (e.g., Bodenhausen, 1988; Bodenhausen and Lichtenstein, 1987; Grant and Holmes, 1981; Nelson, Biernat and Manis, 1990). The issue, then, is not whether information additional to category membership can override the stereotypical effect of the category, but when (under what specific conditions) this will tend to occur. The crucial factors appear to be the relationship between the category and the judgement to be made, and the nature of the additional, potentially individuating information provided.

First, category effects are more robust (i.e., stereotyping is more likely than individuated person perception) where there is a strong association between the category and the judgement to be made. Krueger and

Rothbart (1988) suggest that Locksley et al.'s results may have been partly a function of a relatively weak association between gender and assertiveness/passivity. Indeed, in Krueger and Rothbart's own pre-testing this dimension did not emerge as gender-stereotypic at all. Their experiments investigated judgements of aggressiveness, which they had found to be highly gender-stereotypic. In the first experiment, subjects judged members of gender categories (i.e., man/woman or construction worker/housewife) about whom information describing a single, recent behavioural act was also presented. This act was either neutral (e.g., 'recently bought the latest book of a bestselling author'), moderately diagnostic (e.g., 'yelled at his/her spouse') or highly diagnostic (e.g., 'beat his/her child') of aggressiveness. Ratings of the expected intensity and frequency of future aggressive behaviour were found to be determined by the targets' gender category, even in the presence of highly diagnostic behavioural information. So, for example, men and construction workers were always expected to be more aggressive than women and housewives. Krueger and Rothbart also manipulated the nature of the additional information, finding that relevant (diagnostic) behaviour apparently consistently engaged in (rather than a one-off example) and information in the form of a personality trait could effectively negate category effects.

Fiske and Neuberg (1989, 1990; Fiske, Neuberg, Beattie and Milberg, 1987) have attempted to systematize this and related research in their continuum model of impression formation. The model distinguishes between impressions based almost exclusively on social categories (i.e., social stereotyping), and those which are more 'attribute-oriented', formed by 'simply combining . . . the isolated characteristics of the individual other' (Fiske and Neuberg, 1989, p. 83). These 'extremes' form the poles of the proposed theoretical continuum (cf. Tajfel, 1978b; Turner, 1982; see chapter 4), along which the impression formation process moves, always beginning with category-based processes, which have priority, through to more individuating processes if certain conditions are met.

The perceiver first imposes an 'initial categorization' on stimulus input. This is 'an essentially perceptual process, preceding attention' (Fiske and Neuberg, 1990, p. 23), occurring 'regardless of the perceiver's intent' (Fiske, 1988, p. 66). It is based on categorizations cued by physical appearance, that are contextually novel, chronically or acutely accessible (e.g., through recency of activation), or congruent with the perceiver's current mood (see Fiske and Neuberg, 1990, pp. 9–12). The earlier emphasis on automatic selective attention to features such as novelty is thus incorporated in this model, and the emphasis on limitations in information processing capacity as the basis for this reliance on social categorization is retained (e.g., see Fiske and Neuberg, 1990, pp. 13–15).

Because categorization is 'adaptive . . . given the logic of human cognition' (pp. 14–15, i.e. given limited capacity), the tendency is to maintain this initial response and to perceive others stereotypically, unless information conditions make this inappropriate because others' characteristics do not 'fit' the initial categorization. The information conditions defining fit with a given category, although not specified exactly by the model (see Fiske and Neuberg, 1990, p. 6), relate to the degree of consistency between target information and the ascribed category. For example a description of a loan shark as opportunistic, shady and greedy is highly consistent (and likely to result in confirmation of the initial categorization), whereas a bored, obedient, uneducated doctor presents inconsistency which moves the perceiver along the continuum into recategorization attempts and towards relatively individuated, attribute-based impression formation processes and outcomes (see Fiske et al., 1987). Target information does not have to be glaringly inconsistent with the category for this to occur; a mixture of consistent and inconsistent (and sometimes category-irrelevant information) can negate a fairly weak category (e.g., Fiske et al., 1987, Experiment 1; Nisbett et al., 1981), whereas mixed information with a strong category label tends to be interpreted as consistent, producing confirmation and stereotyping (e.g., Bodenhausen, 1988; Bodenhausen and Lichtenstein, 1987).

Running throughout this analysis of the informational basis of impression formation is an emphasis on attention. Attribute-oriented attention is an essential prerequisite for progress along the continuum (Fiske et al., 1987, Experiment 2). Motivational processes also influence the probability and ease of movement along the continuum through effects on both the interpretation of stimulus information and the setting of information processing goals. For example, attribute-oriented impressions are more likely when the motivational structure of the situation requires accurate (i.e., in this model, individuated) impressions to be formed, whereas a perceiver may 'freeze' on a category-based impression that serves their current purposes (Erber and Fiske, 1984; Neuberg and Fiske, 1987).

We shall examine some of the underlying assumptions of this model in more detail in chapter 5. In relation to our current concern, the issue of when we stereotype, this model argues that impression formation always begins with stereotyping (as determined by novelty, accessibility, etc.), but whether or not this initial ('perceptual') response becomes significant depends on a far more controlled, attention-demanding process of weighing up its appropriateness in the face of the evidence available (i.e., the consistency of stimulus information with the category). Thus, in contrast with the implications of the earlier distinctiveness work (e.g., see Higgins and Bargh, 1987; Oakes and Turner, 1990), this model presents social perceivers as 'versatile, flexible human beings . . . remarkably skilled and often quite attuned in their use of situation-appropriate strategies' (Fiske and Neuberg, 1990, p. 62). Stereotyping is, nonetheless, seen as a non-preferred form of person perception. Only individuated impressions can attain the status of 'accuracy', and they are in general preferable to categorization because the latter 'by definition generalizes beyond the individual case and thus introduces error' (Fiske and Neuberg, 1990, p. 62; cf. Aronson, 1972).

A distinction between category-based, stereotypical impressions and more attribute-oriented, individuated impressions is also the central assumption of Brewer's (1988) dual process model of impression formation. Brewer also assumes, with Fiske and Neuberg, that category-based processes have priority, that the first step in impression formation is always an 'initial classification' which operates automatically, without conscious intent, and that cognitive limitations dictate a reluctance to move beyond categorization to more 'elaborate', individuated impression formation unless this is demanded by information conditions or perceiver goals and motives. Despite this initial agreement, however, the dual process and continuum models present divergent analyses of impression formation (see Fiske, 1988). The details of this divergence need not detain us here; rather, we shall summarize Brewer's account of the determinants of stereotyping versus 'personalization', i.e., individualized person perception. (Note that Brewer uses the term 'individuation' to refer to what Fiske and Neuberg call recategorization, i.e., a category-based perception, but involving some elaboration or recategorization of the initial impression. Brewer's term 'personalization' refers to what we, and Fiske and Neuberg, usually call individualized person perception.)

As the 'dual process' title suggests, Brewer's model posits two quite distinct impression formation paths, diverging immediately after the 'initial classification' stage towards social categorization and stereotyping (and potentially sub-typing, 'individuation') on one hand, 'personalization' on the other. A motivational variable, 'self-involvement', determines which path will be taken. If either the target person or the judgement task are ego-involving for the perceiver, impression formation will proceed towards personalization, whereas category-based impressions emerge in the absence of such attentional involvement. Thus, in general terms, Brewer predicts stereotyping will be more likely under conditions of minimal self-involvement.

Once embarked on the categorization path, the perceiver proceeds as dictated by stimulus characteristics, and by task demands influencing motivation and attention. In terms of stimulus characteristics, impression formation for Brewer involves a process of 'pattern-matching' in which pictoliteral representations of person-types are matched to incoming information. This continues, moving from the most 'general' level of categorization through to more specific subtypes, until an adequate fit is achieved. Relative category accessibility, contextual cues and the perceiver's processing goals affect category activation during this stage (see Brewer, 1988, p. 18). The 'individuation' or sub-typing process occurs where it is necessary to deal with information inconsistent with the category-based impression formed. The target is perceived as a 'special instance' of the category, thus the impression is still category-based (i.e., defined with reference to the category), though not stereotypical.

For Brewer, then, stereotyping occurs (a) with minimal self-involvement, and (b) depending on category accessibility, contextual cues and perceiver goals, in interaction with how well the stimulus information fits a particular category. One major weakness of Brewer's model is that, unlike Fiske and Neuberg, Brewer does not attempt to specify the conditions of good category/stimulus fit (see Zebrowitz-McArthur, 1988). She does, however, share Fiske and Neuberg's pessimism about the outcome of category-based impression formation, however well it might fit stimulus information, commenting:

> Because all category prototypes represent simplifications of the stimulus variability that actually exists among objects in the same general category, any typing of individuals is bound to lose much of the complexity and richness of detail that a more personalized representation of that individual would contain . . . category formation . . . is both efficient and functional, so long as the real world it is intended to represent is characterized by natural discontinuities in feature patterns. But the question remains as to how true this is of the world of social objects. (1988, pp. 28–29)

We shall return to these issues in chapter 5.

To summarize the extensive research reviewed in this section, social-cognitive analyses of the conditions under which stereotyping might occur have focused on both relatively automatic, uncontrolled processes like attention to novelty and accessibility effects, and on the more deliberate, controlled processes of fitting target characteristics to category specifications. The dependence of the latter on attention, and their vulnerability to motivational influences, have been emphasized. These more recent considerations of stereotyping as, at least in part, an outcome of current stimulus realities have not, however, led to a revision of the view that it is, fundamentally, a biased and erroneous way of representing that reality (Brewer, 1988, pp. 28–30; Fiske and Neuberg, 1990, pp. 13–15).

Stereotype Change

As we have seen, social-cognitive research produced evidence that many social beliefs were fairly resistant to change. This inertia was seen to be, in large part, an inevitable consequence of the normal operation of cognitive biases affecting, for example, selective memory (Rothbart et al., 1979) and the interpretation of ambiguous events (Duncan, 1976). Researchers appeared to face a rather 'depressing dilemma' (Hamilton, 1979, p. 80): processes which were necessary for adaptive human functioning (given limited capacity) served also to maintain and even bolster erroneous social beliefs. How could *necessary* processes be circumvented in order to facilitate stereotype change? This analysis breathed new life into the traditional view of stereotypes as rigid and unresponsive to reality.

On other hand, as we saw in chapter 2, traditional stereotyping research includes several demonstrations of significant revision of stereotypic beliefs in response to real changes in intergroup relations. Further, it has long been argued, under the heading of what has come to be known as the *contact hypothesis* (e.g., G. Allport, 1954; Amir, 1969; Cook, 1969; Pettigrew, 1969), that (prejudiced) beliefs about groups can be changed through specific types of positive interpersonal contact between in- and outgroup members. The task for social cognition was to translate these group-level analyses of stereotype change into an understanding of the individual cognitive processes involved (see Weber and Crocker, 1983).

In pursuit of this goal, the main strategy has been to analyse the conditions under which *disconfirming information* contributes to stereotype change (Hewstone, 1989b). The assumed power of disconfirming information was, of course, at the heart of the contact hypothesis. Interaction between group members was expected to reveal the relevant stereotypes as false, this disconfirmation then producing belief change and reducing prejudice. Whilst contact does often produce these effects for individual participants, research reveals that they seldom generalize to the group as a whole: beliefs about specific individuals change, but the stereotype does not (see Amir, 1976; R. J. Brown and Turner, 1981; Hewstone and R. J. Brown, 1986).

From the cognitive perspective, this can be seen as an issue of category–exemplar relations, and several researchers have argued that the exemplar (individual) must be seen as otherwise *representative* of the category if any disconfirming information it might convey is to have impact on the category (R. J. Brown and Turner, 1981; Hewstone and R. J. Brown, 1986; Rothbart and John, 1985). Consistent with this analysis, Wilder (1984) found that a pleasant interaction with a *typical* outgroup member produced a significant improvement in evaluations, although no comparable change in stereotypes. Weber and Crocker (1983) did demonstrate change in stereotypes about occupational groups where subjects were presented with counter-stereotypic information about otherwise representative group members. The importance of exemplar prototypicality for generalization to the category has also been demonstrated by Rothbart and Lewis (1988). Thus, contrary to the emphasis on interpersonal acquaintance evident in many discussions of contact, it appears that interactions which are unambiguously inter*group* may present the best opportunities for real change.

In terms of the more fine-grained, cognitive analysis of how disconfirming exemplar information revises stereotypes, three models have been presented and tested: *bookkeeping*, in which the stereotype adjusts to each new piece of relevant information (Rothbart, 1981), *conversion*, where radical change in the stereotype is brought about by a dramatic or highly salient event (Rothbart, 1981), and *subtyping* in which information inconsistent with the stereotype is represented in terms of a subordinate category structure (Weber and Crocker, 1983). As Johnston and Hewstone (1992) note, the latter is, in a sense, a model of stereotype maintenance rather than change, at least in its strong form in which disconfirming information is isolated in subtypes leaving the overall stereotype intact.

Weber and Crocker (1983) investigated these models by manipulating the *distribution* (concentrated in a few group members, or dispersed through the group) and *amount* (small vs. large sample) of disconfirming evidence. The bookkeeping model relies on the amount of information only (more change with more information, a fairly unremarkable prediction), but the distribution of that information is important for the other two models. Conversion predicts more change with disconfirmation concentrated in one dramatic example. Subtyping would predict the isolation of a dramatic disconfirmer as an exception, and more stereotype change where subtyping was more difficult, i.e., with disconfirming information dispersed across a number of individuals. Overall, results supported a moderate version of the subtyping model, with most change where disconfirming information was dispersed through a large sample (the sample size effect lending some support to the bookkeeping model). Despite the fact that extreme disconfirming members were isolated through subtyping in the concentrated condition, there was still more change here than in the control condition.

Further support for the subtyping model comes from a recent programme of research by Hewstone and his colleagues, which has also clarified the processes involved in stereotype change. In particular, and consistent with Hewstone's earlier work on the contact hypothesis, this research suggests that dispersed disconfirming information changes stereotypes because it is under these conditions that disconfirmation is evidenced by individuals who are otherwise representative of the category. Johnston and Hewstone (1992) found significantly more stereotype change under dispersed than concentrated conditions, and multiple regression results suggested strongly that it was the perceived typicality of disconfirming individuals (rather than the estimated proportion of inconsistent information or individuals) that mediated stereotype change. Hierarchical cluster analysis confirmed predictions for the concentrated condition, where disconfirmers were isolated through subtyping and their inconsistent attributes had little impact on the group stereotype. A second experiment confirmed the importance of dispersed disconfirmation for stereotype change. Hewstone, Hopkins and Routh (1992) present evidence of the limited impact of a police–schools liaison programme on stereotypes of the police as contradicting the conversion model. The police involved were subtyped as related to 'caring and welfare' professions, rather than seen as similar to police officers in general, or other authority figures.

Overall, then, the subtyping model receives strong support from Hewstone's research, although Johnston and Hewstone (1992) do note that it is rather vague and remains to be convincingly distinguished from the alternative hypothesis that perceivers simply discount atypical group members (although see Hewstone, Johnston, Frankish and Macrae, 1990, for evidence consistent with the subtyping analysis). Further, Johnston and Hewstone agree with S. Taylor (1981a) that the availability of subtyping as a response to disconfirming information bodes ill for prospects of significant stereotype change (cf. Pettigrew, 1981; Rothbart and John, 1985). In this context, we might note that the conversion model is not wholly bereft of support. Gurwitz and Dodge (1977) found that disconfirming information concentrated in one sorority member produced more stereotype change than the same information dispersed across all three members presented. Hewstone, Johnston and Aird (1992) report that concentrated disconfirmation had more impact than dispersed information on the stereotype of a homogeneous group (accountants). The latter authors urge integration of the work on stereotype change with that on perceived group variability.

A somewhat different approach to stereotype change has been taken by D. Mackie, Allison and Worth (1988; see also D. Mackie and Allison 1987) who identify a cognitive bias which, unlike others discussed in the stereotyping literature, may facilitate rather than obscure the perception of change. Specifically, they focus on *outcome biases* through which internal attributions (e.g., 'these people are conservative') are based on outcomes (election of a right-wing candidate) without regard to factors constraining those outcomes (the majority rule), and in the face of contradictory evidence (up to 49 per cent who did not vote for the elected candidate). Mackie et al. suggest that a sequence of judgements biased in this way, in which the outcomes changed over time (e.g., the right-wing candidate is overthrown by a left-winger) as a result of changes in factors such as electoral rules, could produce an *illusion* of change where none had occurred. That is, the group's attitudes could be seen as shifting to the left, when in fact the only reason the left-winger replaced the original victor was a change in the electoral rules, a change not taken into account because of the outcome bias.

D. Mackie et al. (1988) report two tests of the illusory change effect applied to stereotyping. In their second experiment, for example, subjects read about a group of either Black or Asian students who had taken a test of deductive reasoning in an attempt to qualify as representatives of their school in a competition with another college. On a first attempt at the test, the students apparently had to solve either 60 or 70 per cent (according to condition) of test items to qualify for the competition. Subjects in all conditions were told that the students had solved 65 per cent, representing success in the 60 per cent condition, but failure in the 70 per cent condition. After responding to a questionnaire, subjects read about a second qualifying attempt by the same students, but this time the pass mark had changed (to 60 per cent for those who had been told 70 per cent previously, and to 70 per cent for those told 60 per cent previously). Again, the group solved 65 per cent of the problems. Thus, some subjects read about failure followed by success, others about success followed by failure, although the group's actual performance remained invariant.

As predicted by the outcome bias, subjects told that the groups had succeeded then failed saw them (both Black and Asian) as less intelligent after the second attempt than after the first, and vice versa for those presented with failure followed by success. Thus, actually invariant performance was perceived as change as a result of the outcome bias. Mackie et al. also asked subjects to rate 'Asians', 'Blacks' and 'Whites' on twelve trait scales, including intelligence. The prediction was that if the biased inferences made about the student group generalized to perceptions of the relevant ethnic group as a whole, ratings of that group (but not the other two) should be higher in the failure–success than the success–failure conditions. This was confirmed in the Black target group condition, but only non-significantly for Asians.

The two approaches to stereotype change reviewed in this section, disconfirming information and illusory change, differ in two main ways. First, work such as that of Hewstone and colleagues is focusing on stereotype change in response to real change, i.e., under conditions where group members actually are different from the existing group image. In contrast, D. Mackie and her colleagues emphasize a disjunction between stereotypes and reality in their suggestion that stereotype change can involve altering the attributions made about behaviour that is actually invariant. Second, in the work on the effects of disconfirming information, the overall context (in terms of the pattern of disconfirming information presented) was seen to influence significantly the way that information was processed. In contrast, Mackie and colleagues argue that change can occur through a bias which takes one piece of information (the outcome) out of context (the decision rule).

In general, an approach to stereotype change which focuses on the effects of real change, in appropriate context, seems most consistent with both the traditional evidence of stereotype change discussed in chapter 2 and the intergroup perspective on contact (R. J. Brown and Turner, 1981; Hewstone and R. J. Brown, 1986) . The latter reminds us that group identifications are real and influential determinants of social interaction, and that stereotype change is as dependent upon *group* processes as it is upon individual attitudes and beliefs (Fishman, 1956).

Overview

This chapter has reviewed evidence of the contribution of normal, adaptive cognitive processes to the development and use of social stereotypes. Researchers have drawn upon knowledge in a wide range of areas (including the accentuation and evaluative effects of categorization, illusory correlations, the representation of social-structural relationships, basic issues of category representation and functioning in person perception, the influence of prior knowledge on the encoding and retrieval of new information, processes of selective attention, the psychology of prediction, and principles of belief change) in order to develop a better understanding of stereotyping as a normal process, engaged in by *all* perceivers.

Recent understanding of the complexity and context-dependence of social-cognitive processes can be contrasted with an early enthusiasm for identifying 'hard-wired' biases which would almost invariably produce certain outcomes. For example, contrast early ideas about the automatic activation of social categories through relative novelty, brightness, movement, etc. (S. Taylor and Fiske, 1978) with the far more complex analyses offered by Fiske and Neuberg (1990) and Brewer (1988), in which the appropriateness of the category as a representation of reality is taken into account. Similarly, the stereotype confirmation biases which attracted so much attention in the late 1970s are now recognized as context-dependent and subject to the motives of both perceivers and targets – stereotypes do *not* more or less automatically produce their own confirmation. Overall, one important message from this research is that whilst information processing factors are obviously critical in stereotyping, they do not cause it in the relatively 'mindless' (Langer, 1978), automatic sense implied by some of the early work (see Devine, 1989; Fiske, 1989). This shift in emphasis can be traced to both empirical disconfirmation of some early 'principles' and the influence of more social, group-oriented analyses in the area (e.g. Tajfel, 1981b; Turner et al., 1987; Turner and Giles, 1981a; see Fiske, 1993, for an example of the shift towards a more group-oriented appreciation of categorization).

The shift that we have observed is important to the issue at the heart of this book. The relationship between stereotyping and reality was understood to be negligible in the early cognitive miser period. Higgins and Bargh summarize the tone of that period with the following questions:

> To the extent that information processing is determined by variables such as accessibility, encoding specificity, salience, and so on, which in turn are associated with *potentially random contextual variables*, how do people master their cognitions? Just how good is the person – social environment fit? (1987, p. 415, emphasis added)

Stereotyping could, indeed, be a 'potentially random' matter, as determined simply by relative novelty or some other automatic process of selective attention. Recent models have moved away from the alluring simplicity of this 'meaning-free' type of analysis towards a recognition of the social perceiver as 'quite attuned in their use of situation-appropriate strategies' (Fiske and Neuberg, 1990, p. 62).

Cognitively speaking, then, the time seems ripe for a reappraisal of the relationship between stereotyping and reality. But we have also seen that stereotyping is still, even in the newer approaches, described as a bias, as non-preferred, as inaccurate, as overgeneralized – it may be the outcome of relatively sensitive cognitive processes, but it is still 'unfortunate'. In our view, the cognitive analysis of stereotyping cannot advance to a proper understanding of the validity of the process until its roots in the psychology of *the group* are revived and taken seriously. Stereotypes represent groups, and we need to think carefully about what groups are before we can fully understand what stereotypes are. This is our task in the next chapter.

Suggested Further Reading and References

Tajfel's 'Cognitive Aspects of Prejudice' is essential reading, not least for the eloquence with which he establishes the need for a cognitive analysis of stereotyping and prejudice. The first report of the minimal group experiments (Tajfel et al., 1971) is also well worth reading. Beyond that, the social-cognitive stereotyping literature is immense. Whilst landmark studies such as those of Hamilton and Gifford (1976), S. Taylor et al. (1978), Duncan (1976), and so on (cited in the text) are important for the reader wanting a detailed understanding of this tradition of work, useful overviews which reflect the general tone of the approach can be found in the Hamilton (1981a) book (now seen as something of a classic from this era) and the article by Hamilton and Trolier (1986).

Hamilton, D. L. (Ed.) (1981) *Cognitive processes in stereotyping and intergroup behaviour*. Hillsdale, NJ: Erlbaum. (a)
Hamilton, D. L. and Trolier, T. K. (1986) Stereotypes and stereotyping: An overview of the cognitive approach. In J. F. Dovidio and S. L. Gaertner (Eds), *Prejudice, Discrimination and Racism*. New York: Academic Press.
Tajfel, H., Flament, C., Billig, M. G. and Bundy, R. F. (1971) Social categorization and intergroup behaviour. *European Journal of Social Psychology, 1,* 149–177.
Tajfel, H. (1969) Cognitive aspects of prejudice. *Journal of Social Issues, 25,* 79–97.

4

Cognition and the Group: Social Identity and Self-Categorization

Even before the cognitive analysis of stereotyping had properly taken shape, Tajfel himself was applying his understanding of the categorization process and the insights gained from the minimal group experiments to a different, though closely related, research problem – intergroup relations. As we saw, the minimal group experiments were designed to investigate the determinants of intergroup discrimination, and the results suggested that social categorization *by itself*, an apparently purely cognitive division into groups, was sufficient under some conditions to produce discriminatory behaviour and attitudes in favour of the ingroup.

At the time the first minimal group experiments were reported, the most influential account of intergroup conflict was the functional theory of the Sherifs and their colleagues (see Sherif, 1967), which argued that it stemmed from real conflicts of interest. When minimal group members engaged in intergroup discrimination in the *absence* of any such conflict (or other assumed causes of ingroup bias), theoretical innovation was called for.

Initially, Tajfel et al. (1971) offered a 'normative' explanation, suggesting that the schoolboy subjects in their studies saw the experimental situation as one of 'team competition', in which it was appropriate for them to apply a general norm of ingroup favouritism which they had acquired from their culture and everyday life. However, as Tajfel (e.g., 1978a) and Turner (1975a) quickly pointed out, this explanation is trivial, largely redescribing the findings it is supposed to explain. No matter how the results had turned out, they could have been explained in terms of a social norm. Consistently fair matrix allocations, for example, could have been 'explained' as the product of a well-rewarded schoolboy or cultural norm of fairness. More importantly, Turner's early review of the intergroup literature (1975b) revealed no evidence for a real-world or experimental norm which consistently led people to favour ingroups over outgroups.

The search for an alternative to this explanatory dead-end culminated in a social psychological analysis of intergroup relations that has become known as *social identity theory* (Tajfel, 1972; Tajfel and Turner, 1986; Turner, 1975a). Later, Turner (1982, 1984) used the concept of social identity to provide insights into the social-psychological basis of group formation and developed a more general theory of group processes, *self-categorization theory* (Turner, 1985; Turner et al., 1987). This chapter summarizes these developments, focusing on the way in which ideas about the distinctive reality of group life (chapter 2) and the explanatory power of a cognitive analysis (chapter 3) come together in the concepts of social identity and self-categorization.

Social Identity

Social Groups and Meaning

Setting aside, for the moment, the fact that the behaviour of the minimal group members was specifically discriminatory, we might ask why subjects took any notice at all of the experimenters' categories. Tajfel (1972) addressed this issue, suggesting that the anonymity, lack of interaction, and absence of specific goals which the minimal group paradigm required left the subjects in a virtually 'meaningless' situation. This could be rectified through identification with, and action in terms of, the experimenters' categories:

> Meaning was found by [subjects] in the adoption of a strategy for action based on the establishment, through action, of a distinctiveness between their own 'group' and the other, between the two social categories in a truly minimal 'social system'. Distinction from the 'other' category provided *ipso facto* an identity for their own group, and thus some kind of meaning to an otherwise empty situation. (1972, pp. 39–40)

More generally, Tajfel (1978c) argued that individuals apply the categorization process in social interaction for the same purposes as in basic perceptual activity. Social categorization allows the perceiver to 'structure the causal understanding of the social environment' as a guide to action. Importantly, it also provides a system of orientation for *self-reference*, creating and defining the individual's place in society. Individuals' 'self-definition in a social context' (1978c, p. 61), the meaning and significance of their actions and attitudes in that context, depend upon social categorization. Where the relevant categorization divides individuals into social groups, action within that context will take on the distinct meaning and significance of intergroup relations.

This proposed link between the self and social categorization was formalized in the concept of *social identity*, initially defined by Tajfel as 'that part of an individual's self-concept which derives from his [sic] knowledge of his [sic] membership of a social group (or groups) together with the value and emotional significance attached to that membership' (1978c, p. 63). Bringing the *self* and the group together in this way helped to make sense of minimal intergroup discrimination and paved the way for Tajfel and Turner's (1986) more general analysis of intergroup relations. It also provoked new attempts to address the long-standing problem of the relationship between the group and the individual, between the social uniformities of group life and individual psychological processes (Tajfel, 1979; Turner 1987a,b; Turner and Oakes, 1986, 1989). The following sections discuss these two strands of theoretical development, together with a discussion of Tajfel's last published comments on social stereotyping (Tajfel, 1981a).

Explaining Intergroup Discrimination

Social identity theory assumes that people are motivated to evaluate themselves positively, and that insofar as a group membership becomes significant to their self-definition they will be motivated to evaluate that group positively. In other words, people seek a *positive social identity*. Since the value of any group membership depends upon comparison with other relevant groups, positive social identity is achieved through the establishment of *positive distinctiveness* of the ingroup from relevant outgroups.

Turner (1975a) argued that this was the basis of discrimination in the minimal group paradigm. Having identified with the minimal categories, subjects compared their ingroup and the outgroup in terms of the only available dimensions (the money or points represented in the matrices, or evaluative rating scales; see chapter 3) and sought positive distinctiveness for their own group by awarding it more money or points, or favouring it in other ways. Several lines of evidence converge to support this interpretation. For example, the distinctly *comparative* nature of the discrimination observed is clear from the strong influence of the maximum difference strategy in matrix choices. Turner (1978) has shown that *identification* with the minimal category is a necessary precondition for ingroup favouritism (cf. Sachdev and Bourhis, 1984, 1987, 1991) and there is some evidence that intergroup discrimination does raise group members' self-esteem (e.g., Chin and McClintock, 1993; Lemyre and Smith, 1985; Oakes and Turner, 1980; cf. Hogg and Abrams, 1990).

Early studies established that ingroup bias was by no means an automatic product of minimal social categorization (Turner, 1975a, 1981). Subsequent studies guided mainly by social identity theory showed that it was a function, *inter alia*, of (1) the degree to which subjects identified with the relevant ingroup and (2) the salience of the relevant social categorization in the setting, (3) the importance and relevance of the comparative dimension to ingroup identity, (4) the degree to which the groups were comparable on that dimension (similar, close, ambiguously different), including, in particular, (5) the ingroup's relative status and the character of the perceived status differences between the groups (Tajfel, 1978e; Turner, R. J. Brown and Tajfel, 1979; Sachdev and Bourhis, 1987). These studies also demonstrated that *outgroup* favouritism would eventuate where an outgroup was felt to be superior to the ingroup on the dimension of comparison. Along similar lines, experiments by Mummendey and her colleagues (e.g., Mummendey and Schreiber, 1983; Mummendey and Simon, 1989) have shown that outgroup favouritism can occur on dimensions that are irrelevant to an ingroup's preferred self-definition (for related discussions see van Knippenberg, 1984; van Knippenberg and Ellemers, 1990).

Beyond interpretation of minimal and other intergroup experiments, social identity theory sought to detail the different ways in which individuals can achieve positive ingroup distinctiveness and to specify the conditions under which various strategies (e.g., individual mobility, social creativity, social competition) might be pursued. The extent to which individuals perceived the current intergroup status relationships to be legitimate or illegitimate, and stable or unstable, were seen as important determinants of group members' actions (Tajfel, 1978e).

Overall, then, social identity research and theory emphasized the subtlety of the discrimination process and its sensitivity to the realities of social context and intergroup relations. Thus, social identity theorists and social-cognitive stereotyping researchers drew quite different conclusions from the minimal group findings. As we saw in the previous chapter, many stereotyping researchers concluded that Tajfel et al. had shown discrimination to be a direct, largely unavoidable product of the categorization process (e.g., Hamilton and Trolier, 1986; Messick and D. Mackie, 1989, p. 59; Wilder, 1981, p. 228). The social 'bias' of discrimination was seen to be as hard-wired and automatic as the cognitive biases (e.g., illusory correlation, the stereotyping of 'solo' group members) also identified as contributors to stereotyping (see Haslam, McGarty, Oakes and Turner, 1993a). In contrast, Tajfel and his colleagues argued that, in addition to categorization, a process of social identification, accompanied by motives for positive self-evaluation and intergroup distinctiveness, underlay intergroup discrimination and this psychological sequence itself interacted with conflicts of interest and the larger social context (Tajfel, 1979; Tajfel and Turner, 1979; Turner, 1975a). As Tajfel put it:

> The differentiation principle could be considered as part of the general syndrome of ethnocentrism . . . but this is an oversimplification. It is a dynamic process which can only be understood against the background of relations between social groups and the social comparisons they make in the context of these relations. (1981a, p. 162)

Whether or not intergroup relations were characterized by discrimination was seen as the complex product of a number of social and psychological factors. In rejecting the idea of any sort of 'generic' or automatic pattern of intergroup responses, Turner suggested the following:

> Social categories influence social interaction through their capacity to act as *social frames of reference* for interpretation of, and response to, individual behaviour . . . the real-life social category is like a condensed symbol of an existing intergroup relationship, but it is not the determinant of what is symbolized – to understand that we must examine how social categorization processes interact with other more dynamic factors at work in intergroup behaviour. (1978, p. 140; emphasis added)

Thus, whilst it may be the case empirically that social categorization *alone* appeared to cause discrimination in the minimal group experiments, subsequent theorizing and evidence of the variability of ingroup bias (e.g., Tajfel, 1978e; Abrams and Hogg, 1990; Turner, 1980) suggest that discrimination is not a simple, automatic effect of categorization. Rather, as Tajfel (1972) argued, the effect of social categorization is to imbue relationships with a certain group-based meaning, and what happens next depends upon what the relevant intergroup relationship means or implies.

Social Stereotypes and Social Groups

Subsequent to the development of social identity theory and after an absence of some years (since his paper on social categorization in 1972),

Tajfel returned directly to the issue of stereotyping in 1981. His paper was entitled 'Social Stereotypes and Social Groups'. Its clear message was that he felt that the cognitive analysis, including his own earlier work, was omitting a large part of the whole stereotyping story. Indeed, as we noted in chapter 3, he suggested that some recent cognitive analyses represented 'a theoretical retreat' (1981a, p. 151) from his original ideas because they neglected the role of values in social categorization and failed to specify the particular dimensions on which the accentuation effects of categorization would occur. The point of this paper was to bring the group, the realities of group life, back into stereotyping research.

Tajfel identified five basic functions of social stereotypes, two individual and three group-level functions. For the individual, stereotypes served the *cognitive* function of systematizing and simplifying the environment, and the *motivational* function of representing and preserving important social values. At the group level, stereotypes contributed to the creation and maintenance of group beliefs which were then used to *explain* large-scale social events and *justify* various forms of collective action. They were also involved in the creation and maintenance of *positive intergroup distinctiveness*, the tendency to differentiate the ingroup positively from selected outgroups – 'when such differentiation is perceived as becoming insecure and eroded; or when it is not positive, and social conditions exist which are perceived as providing a possibility for a change in the situation' (p. 161) – that was the subject of social identity theory. Tajfel pointed out that most stereotyping research through the 1970s had been content to deal only with the first of these functions, the individual cognitive function. He used both research (e.g., the New Look work in which he had been involved, see chapter 6) and historical examples (e.g., of witch-hunts, lay explanations of the plague) to illustrate the importance of the other four functions of stereotypes.

Building on these ideas, Tajfel emphasized two points as crucial to 'the potential development of a properly *social* psychological theory of stereotyping' (p. 162). First, he saw the group-level functions as laying the foundations for an analysis of stereotype *content* which would go beyond the cataloguing activities we reviewed in chapter 2. Second, he emphasized the need to link rather than set up false barriers between the group and the individual functions, suggesting that attempts to draw links should 'start with the group functions and then relate the individual functions to them' (p. 163). In other words, for Tajfel the group, and the 'cultural traditions, group interests, social upheavals and social differentiations' (p. 163) that go with it, was the *primary* causal factor in stereotyping, and other factors had to be understood in light of the fact that stereotypes reflect and make possible group life.

Tajfel saw two fruitful avenues in current research which could help effect the group–individual link in stereotyping. He saw work on social identity as relevant to framing the group explanation, justification and differentiation functions in terms of individual psychological processes such as self-definition, categorization and value-preservation. Second, research which was attempting to 'socialize' traditional attribution theory (e.g., Hewstone and Jaspars, 1984) seemed to hold out the promise of linking group explanation and justification with individual cognitive processes of attribution. These studies (e.g., D. Taylor and Jaggi, 1974; Duncan, 1976; see Hewstone, 1989a, for a recent review) had demonstrated that attribution, the explanation of social behaviour, was sometimes strongly influenced by the group memberships of the participants and the relationship between the groups involved. For example, Taylor and Jaggi showed that socially undesirable acts performed by ingroup members attracted *external* attributions, whereas identical acts performed by outgroup members were explained *internally*, as something to do with the character of the actor (and vice versa for desirable behaviour). Tajfel comments:

> These 'internal' . . . explanations are an instance of the functioning of social stereotypes. But the static, stable consensus implied by the older descriptive studies of stereotypes is replaced here by shifting perspectives closely related to the individuals' evaluation of the equally shifting social situations which are perceived *in terms of the nature of the relations between the groups involved.* (1981a, p. 166)

In other words, stereotyping is a context-dependent process which serves to represent the changing nature of intergroup relations.

Tajfel saw this paper as simply a 'hazy blueprint for future research' (p. 167). Sadly, he was not able to contribute to that research himself (he died in 1982), but he had taken important steps towards his aim of re-introducing the group to the social psychology of stereotyping, and the paper has been highly influential, not least in our own work (see also Condor, 1990; Huici, 1984; Leyens, Yzerbyt and Schadron, in press; Stroebe and Insko, 1989).

The Psychological Reality of the Social Group

Social identity theory has generated a number of disagreements, discussions, clarifications and critiques, some methodological (e.g., Bornstein, Crum, Wittenbraker, Harring, Insko and Thibaut, 1983a,b; Branthwaite, Doyle and Lightbown, 1979; St Claire and Turner, 1982; Turner, 1980; 1983a,b) and some theoretical and empirical (e.g., Abrams and Hogg, 1990; Doise, 1988; Rabbie, Schot and Visser, 1989; Turner, 1988). A book on stereotyping is not the place for a detailed review of these debates (many of the criticisms of the theory are best answered by close reading of the original sources). Nevertheless, they testify to the continuing force of its impact. Its analysis of intergroup conflict has proved fruitful and influential (e.g., Brewer and Kramer, 1985; R. Brown, 1986; Hogg and Abrams, 1988; Messick and D. Mackie, 1989; Turner and Giles, 1981a). Moreover, the theoretical work involved in trying to understand the minimal group studies, and in particular the elaboration of the concept of social identity, has taken the significance of this research beyond its original agenda. In this section we discuss the significance of the social identity concept for the issue of the relationship between individual and group, an issue which we see as lying at the heart of the social psychology of stereotyping.

Turner (1987a,b) reviews the significant skirmishes in one of social psychology's most fascinating and important battles. At stake is the psychological reality and distinctiveness of group phenomena. Turner expresses the issue thus:

> Does group behaviour imply social or psychological processes irreducible to or different from the properties of individuals, does the group possess a mental unity or reality *sui generis*? . . . Are groups real in the same vivid, tangible way that we tend to assume individual persons are real? (1987a, pp. 3–4)

Fundamentally, the issue is that of the interaction between social (e.g., the group, a social product) and psychological (individual group members' minds) processes, sometimes seen as 'the essential problem' of the science of social psychology (Asch, 1952, p. 256; see also F. Allport, 1962; Cartwright, 1979; Turner and Oakes, 1986).

Early pre-experimentalists such as LeBon (1895), McDougall (1921) and Freud (1921) took for granted some form of distinctive group psychology, emphasizing the role of instincts and emotions and tending to see group behaviour as a descent to more primitive, irrational forms of social interaction. On the other hand, the tenets of behaviourism led Floyd Allport (1924) to reject not only the rather metaphysical concept of a 'group mind' introduced by the pre-experimentalists, but also the very possibility of any distinctive group psychology. What may appear to be distinctive group *behaviour*, he suggested, was simply the individual reacting to a specific social stimulus situation. That person was still, in all senses, an individual, *psychologically* unaffected by the group context.

The development of *cognitive* social psychology provided an 'interactionist' alternative to these metatheoretical extremes. Interactionism (Turner and Oakes, 1986) indicates the idea that the psychological properties of individual minds are qualitatively changed by the interaction of individual and society. Turner summarizes the positions of Sherif, Asch and Lewin. In different ways, each argued that, through social interaction, group members created collective products such as norms, values, stereotypes, etc. which were *not* reducible to the activities of individuals. These were internalized by and thus *transformed* the psychology of individuals. In particular, Asch (1952) mounted a direct attack on both the group mind thesis and individualism. Individualism, he suggested, rests on two basic premises: (1) that psychological processes occur only in individuals and, therefore, (2) that individuals are the only psychological reality. It holds that, insofar as 'groups' have any meaning it is as 'shorthand expressions for the innumerable specific activities of individuals' (Asch, 1952, p. 241). The first premise, Asch argued, is an 'incontrovertible statement', but the second encounters several difficulties (see 1952, pp. 245–249), including the subjective reality of groups, the fact that they *seem* real to us. We talk of, for example, 'the Government', 'the Labour Party', 'Greenpeace', in reference not to 'the innumerable specific activities of individuals' but to the coherent, emergent activity of a distinct social unit: 'Greenpeace believes mining would threaten endangered species in the National Park', 'the Government predicts lower inflation figures next month', and so on. We perceive groups as endowed with psychological properties and the ability to act purposefully.

Asch went on to point out that if, as is patently clear, groups are real to us, and if we endorse individualism and its rejection of group reality, then:

> The logical conclusions would be that group facts are subjective constructions and that the facts of social life are the result of a *psychological error*. (1952, p. 246, emphasis added)

We saw in the preceding chapter that this conclusion has indeed been reached, roughly twenty-five years later, in the social cognitive analysis of stereotypes, and it is quite logical *given* an individualistic perspective. However, Asch himself rejected individualism (see 1952, chapter 9 for his eloquent analysis of this issue) and went on to detail his own early social cognitive answer to just how social, collective, 'group facts' could have individual, psychological reality (see Turner, 1987a).

Asch argued that it was the existence of a 'mutually shared psychological field' (1952, p. 142), through which the *relations between* interacting individuals were understood and internalized by all participants, that made group phenomena possible:

> Group actions . . . are possible only when each participant has a represen-tation that includes the actions of others and their relations. The respective actions converge relevantly, assist and supplement each other only when the joint situation is represented in each and when the representations are structurally similar. Only when these conditions are given can individuals subordinate themselves to the requirements of joint action. These represen-tations and the actions that they initiate bring group facts into exis-tence and produce the phenomenal solidity of group processes. (1952, pp. 251–2)

Further, he noted that the individual–group relationship was a 'part–whole relation unprecedented in nature' (p. 257) as it alone required the recapitulation of the whole, the group, within the part, the individual (i.e., the individual must be able to represent group relations as a whole within his or her mind in order to be able to act as an individual group member). He argued that the group and the individual, the social and the psychological, came together through cognitive representations of group relations and group facts. These transformed the individual into a *psychological* group member, a person whose actions and attitudes were regulated by an irreducibly collective product (see also Sherif, 1936).

Despite the power and breadth of these ideas a subtly transformed conception of the psychological basis of the social group took hold during the 1950s and 1960s. By the early 1970s an absolute decline in interest in group phenomena was apparent (Steiner, 1974). Rather than cognitive representation and the irreducible nature of group products, the emphasis shifted to the closely related concepts of interdependence and cohesiveness (Cartwright and Zander, 1968; Lott and Lott, 1965; Shaw, 1976; see Hogg, 1992; Turner, 1987b, for reviews). Further, whilst the concept of interdependence had been central to the work of Sherif, Asch and Lewin, in its modern guise it had lost the 'Gestalt' or 'field-theoretical' flavour they had given it, and there had been 'an almost universal return to a form of implicit individualism' (Turner, 1987b, p. 24; see also Hogg, 1992). Specifically, interdependence as a 'functional unity' which transformed separate individuals into *psychological group members* had become the interdependence of essentially separate indiuals for the mutual satisfaction of their individual needs and motives. Group relations were no longer seen as qualitatively different from interpersonal relations. Indeed Lott and Lott (1965), for example, argued that a group's cohesiveness, what held it together, could be completely equated with *interpersonal* attraction and that there was no such thing as *properties of the group as a whole* separate from the properties of individual members. A group was nothing more than a collection of mutually rewarding individuals in relatively stable relationships of interpersonal attraction, cooperation and influence. The idea that the relations between group members might be mediated psychologically by their membership in a joint social unit was lost. The psychological group became a superfluous concept, explanatorily redundant when it came to the analysis of determining psychological processes. These could be conceptualized at the interpersonal level in terms of variables such as interpersonal interdependence, attraction, similarity and influence.

This 'interpersonal interdependence' model of the group and the 'group dynamics' tradition from which it derived proved productive and influential (Hogg, 1992). It is clear that theoretical development in many areas of social psychology from the 1950s on has taken place on the basis of an implicitly individualistic perspective rather than an interactionist one (e.g., intergroup relations, Billig, 1976; group cohesiveness, Hogg, 1992; cooperation, Caporael, Dawes, Orbell and van der Kragt, 1989; crowd psychology, Reicher, 1987; social influence, Turner, 1991; for general discussions of this trend, see Cartwright, 1979, Sampson, 1977, Pepitone, 1981, Mansbridge, 1990, Turner and Oakes, 1986, Oakes and Turner, 1986b). However, in the 1970s both empirical evidence and theoretical argument emerged which questioned the adequacy of the interpersonal model.

Throughout the 1970s Tajfel had argued consistently against individualistic perspectives on intergroup behaviour. Agreeing with Sherif, he rejected the idea that problems of social conflict were explicable in terms of individual pathology, personality differences or interpersonal processes. Intergroup attitudes and stereotypes were large-scale social phenomena, formed and held in common by people as members of social groups, socially shared and socially diffused representations of their intergroup relationships, developed as normative group products within and as a function of the larger macro-social context. The task of social psychology, as he saw it, was not to perpetuate the myth of the asocial, as-if-isolated individual, but to understand how social realities influenced and interacted with psychological processes.

Social identity theory was developed self-consciously with this aim in mind. As Turner and Giles stated:

... the group is both a psychological process and a social product ... the psychological hypothesis is that group behaviour and relationships are mediated by a cognitive redefinition of the self in terms of shared social category memberships and associated stereotypes.

On the other hand, however, the group is a social reality. It refers to real interrelated people engaged in concrete social activities as a function of their social relationships and goals ... The cognitive processes instigate collective interaction and thus the emergence of social processes. The latter produce social structures, roles, norms, values, purposes, etc. which in turn become determinants of individual psychological functioning. The same also applies to the development of social identity itself ... This is apparent in that the theory takes for granted that real intergroup relations presuppose *shared* social categorizations and stereotypes, with a specific *sociocultural* content, related to members' *collective purposes* and the explanation, justification and evaluation of *concrete political and historical contexts* ... the group is a product of social influences as well as cognitive and motivational processes. (Turner and Giles, 1981b, p. 27)

Tajfel explained in great detail that the theory could not be reduced to an 'intrapersonal' need for self-esteem or solely to the psychological sequence of 'social categorization–social identity–social comparison' (1979, p. 184). This sequence was merely one leg of the theory's 'conceptual tripod': for the theory to contribute to explaining

certain selected uniformities of social behaviour ... we must know (i) something about the ways 'groups' are constructed in a particular social system, (ii) what are the psychological effects of these constructions; and (iii) how the constructions and their effects depend upon, and relate to, forms of social reality. (1979, p. 185)

Social reality can be described or analysed in terms of socio-economic, historical or political structures, but such descriptions or analyses are not within the competence of the social psychologist, he argued. What the social psychologist *can* do is to ascertain the 'shared interpretations of social reality' held by group members and such shared perceptions of intergroup relations in combination with the perceived location of groups within the particular social system can be used to formulate testable hypotheses.

As part of this general argument, Tajfel (1978b) revived theoretical discussion of the need to make a *qualitative* distinction between intergroup and interpersonal behaviour, opposing the reduction of the former to the latter. He suggested that the two kinds of behaviour might represent the extremes of a bipolar continuum upon which all instances of social behaviour could be placed (cf. Brewer, 1988; Fiske and

Neuberg, 1990). At the 'intergroup' extreme all of the behaviour of two or more individuals towards each other is determined by their membership of different social groups or categories (i.e., by group affiliations and loyalties to the exclusion of individual characteristics and interpersonal relationships). The 'interpersonal' extreme refers to any social encounter in which all the interaction that takes place is determined by the personal relationships between the individuals and their individual characteristics (i.e., idiosyncratic personal qualities are the overriding causal influences). The validity and usefulness of this distinction has been upheld in the interpretation of several research topics. For example, recent reformulations of the contact hypothesis of prejudice reduction recognize that to interact with an individual *as an individual* or *as a group member* are not the same thing, and do not have the same outcomes (Brewer and Miller, 1984; R. J. Brown and Turner, 1981; Hewstone and R. J. Brown, 1986).

Tajfel's continuum was largely descriptive, with the two extremes distinguished in terms of the presence or absence of social categorizations and the degree of uniformity or variability in intra- and intergroup behaviour. However, in the late 1970s Turner (1982) saw the opportunity for a more causal analysis. He noted that the findings of the minimal group studies were as inconsistent with the interpersonal model of group membership as they were with Sherif's realistic conflict analysis of discrimination. Minimal social categorization appeared capable of producing all the usual symptoms of psychological group formation (ingroup bias, mutual attraction, altruism, etc.) even though the paradigm was designed to exclude all its orthodox theoretical determinants (interpersonal interdependence, attraction, similarity etc.). The subjects did not even know which other persons were in their group. Group formation did not seem to reflect but to cause attraction between people: people liked others not as *individuals* but as members of the same *group*.

Subsequent research verified the ability of the categorization process, in the absence of attraction-related variables, to produce distinctively group-based responses (Hogg and Turner, 1985a,b; Turner, Sachdev and Hogg, 1983), and Turner (1982, 1985) demonstrated that findings in the area of social cooperation and influence were also incompatible with an individualized model of the group. On this basis, Turner (1982; 1984) proposed 'a tentative and provisional theory of group behaviour in terms of an *identity mechanism*' (1984, p. 526, emphasis added) in an attempt to explain movement along Tajfel's descriptive continuum.

Turner's 'self-stereotyping hypothesis' began the elaboration of the social identity concept into a 'cognitive' theory of the psychological group, 'in the tradition of Asch and Sherif' (R. J. Brown and Turner,

1981). Turner (1982) explicitly distinguished social identity ('self-defini-
tions in terms of social category memberships') from personal identity
('self-descriptions in terms of personal or idiosyncratic attributes', R. J.
Brown and Turner, 1981, p. 38), and recruited evidence of situational
variations in self-concept functioning to suggest that 'social identity is
sometimes able to function to the relative exclusion of personal identity'
(Turner, 1984, p. 527). Further, he asserted that:

> The adaptive function of social identity . . . is to produce group behaviour
> and attitudes . . . it is the cognitive mechanism which makes group behav-
> iour possible. (1984, p. 527)

The important causal process was *categorization*. Turner suggested
that the accentuation effects (i.e., accentuated intracategory similarity
and intercategory difference; see chapter 3) which accompany its operation influence *self*-perception in the same way as demonstrated in the
perception of others. In other words, the functioning of a social categorization in the self-concept produces *self-stereotyping*:

> Self-stereotyping produces the depersonalization of the self, i.e., the percep-
> tual interchangeability or perceptual identity of oneself and others in the
> same group on relevant dimensions. It is this cognitive redefinition of the
> self – from unique attributes and individual differences to shared social
> category memberships and associated stereotypes – that mediates group
> behaviour. (1984, p. 528)

Thus, social identity became the repository for the 'representation . . .
of group facts', as Asch (1952) had put it, and the application of our
knowledge about the functioning of categorization processes helped to
explain just how social identity transformed individuals into psychological group members. Turner comments:

> The identity perspective . . . reinstates the group as a psychological reality
> and not merely a convenient label for describing the outcome of interper-
> sonal processes and relations. (1984, p. 535)

An important theoretical shift had taken place, from Tajfel's conception
of social identity as *reflecting* group affiliations, to Turner's suggestion
that social identity comprised social categorizations of the self which
caused group phenomena. Whilst Tajfel had been tentative in his discussions of social identity, stressing its limited and domain-specific definition
(e.g., see 1978c, p. 63), the concept had now assumed centre stage and
demanded more rigorous theoretical specification and empirical explora-

tion. It was in this context that Turner developed self-categorization theory.

Self-Categorization Theory

Self-categorization theory is often introduced as a theory of processes underlying psychological group formation, and indeed its original mission was to explain the psychological basis of the social group. In effect, however, it attempts more than this, and is more accurately represented as a general analysis of the functioning of categorization processes in social perception and interaction which speaks to issues of individual identity as much as group phenomena. Turner and Oakes (1989, p. 270) comment:

> The theory should not be understood as an argument for the primacy of the group over the individual. It is called self-categorization theory (and not social identity theory) because it deals with the interrelation of personal and social, individual and group, and asserts the interdependence of individuality and shared, collective identity. The theory proposes that the group is a distinctive psychological process, but in so doing it reminds us that group functioning is a part of the psychology of the person – that individual and group must be reintegrated psychologically before there can be an adequate analysis of either.

In this sense, as well as dealing with group formation and related questions of social cohesion, cooperation and influence, the theory addresses the same general issues of social cognition, person perception and impression formation as some subsequent models (e.g., Brewer, 1988; Fiske and Neuberg, 1990; see chapter 3). Its direct relevance to stereotyping derives from the fact that it attempts to explain the nature of the relationship between cognitive processes (especially categorization) and group life (cf. Asch, 1952; G. Allport, 1954; Tajfel, 1969).

However, given its roots in the evidence and arguments outlined above, one distinctive aspect of self-categorization theory is its explicit aim to develop an interactionist, anti-individualistic analysis of these issues, that is, one which takes seriously the functional interaction of social and psychological processes, and the consequent validity and importance of collective as well as personal definitions of the self. It takes for granted that there is a reciprocal interdependence between social identity as cognitive representation and social product (see Turner and Giles, 1981b, p. 27).

Full details of the theory, its applications and much relevant evidence are readily available elsewhere (Hogg, 1992; Turner, 1985, 1991; Turner et al., 1987; Turner and Oakes, 1986, 1989; Turner et al., in press); we shall focus here on the basic propositions, in order to set the stage for the analysis of stereotyping to be presented in the next chapters.

Self-categorization theory develops the emphasis on categorization processes and their importance in self-conception which characterized social identity theory. It begins with the assumption that self-conception reflects self-*categorization*, the cognitive grouping of the self as identical to some class of stimuli in contrast to some other class of stimuli. As is the case with all systems of natural categories (Rosch, 1978), self-categorizations can exist at different *levels of abstraction* related by *class inclusion*. That is, a given self-category (e.g., 'scientist') is seen as more abstract than another (e.g., 'biologist') to the extent that it can contain the other, but the other cannot contain it: all biologists are scientists, but not all scientists are biologists. Going beyond the parameters of the previous analyses, self-categories both more and less abstract than personal and social identity are envisaged, but for purposes of theoretical exposition three levels of abstraction of self-categories are distinguished: the interpersonal (subordinate level of abstraction, personal identity, self as an individual person), intergroup (intermediate level of abstraction, social identity, self as a group member) and interspecies (superordinate level of abstraction, self as a human being). These are defined not by specific attributes but by the level at which people are being compared and categorized. For instance, 'altruism' could function as a cue to an individual identity, to a particular social category, or to being human, depending on the context.

Social categorical perception is more inclusive than individual person perception and in this sense more abstract (cf. Andersen and Klatzky, 1987; Andersen, et al., 1990), but it is assumed to be just as 'real', just as much a representation of the 'true' person. Human beings are *both* (and equally) individual persons and social group members.

It is perhaps in the detailed analysis of the functioning of the categorization process, in terms of both its antecedents and its outcomes, that self-categorization theory makes its most significant contribution. We shall discuss these ideas in some detail as this approach to categorization is an important aspect of our analysis of stereotyping. To begin with, the theory emphasizes the fact that categorization is a dynamic, context-dependent process, determined by *comparative relations within a given context*. Thus, to predict categorization, the entire range of stimuli under consideration, rather than isolated stimulus characteristics, must be considered (cf. Fiske and Neuberg, 1990). This point is formalized in the principle of *meta-contrast*, which is so called because it involves a contrast between contrasts, a judgement of difference between differences. The meta-contrast principle predicts that a given set of items is more likely to be categorized as a single entity *to the degree that differences within that set of items are less than the differences between that set and others within the comparative context* (cf. Campbell, 1958; Rosch, 1978; Tajfel, 1969; Tversky, 1977). This principle encapsulates but subtly transforms the classic idea that categories form on the basis of intraclass similarities and interclass differences. By proposing that categories form so as to ensure that the differences between them *are larger than* the differences within them, meta-contrast contextualizes categorization, tying it to an on-the-spot judgement of *relative differences*.

For example, consider the system of natural categories in figure 4.1. Meta-contrast predicts that we would categorize and perceive a given piece of vegetation as, say, a 'tree' (rather than as 'vegetation') to the extent that, in the current comparative context, the differences between trees (oaks, birches, etc.) are *less than* the differences between 'trees' and 'shrubs' – the distinction between trees and shrubs is more marked, and more relevant, than are the features that trees and shrubs share as 'vegetation'. Alternatively, the tree might be categorized and perceived simply as 'vegetation' to the extent that differences between types of vegetation (trees, shrubs, etc.) are *less than* differences between vegetation and, say, animals. The salient categorization will be 'oak' when the differences between individual oak trees are *less than* the differences between oaks and birches (or some other comparison species).

The meta-contrast principle applies similarly in person perception. Consider the hierarchy in figure 4.2. Here, we might categorize an individual as 'Australian' to the extent that, in the current comparative context, the differences between individual Australians (Isobel, Jane, etc.) are *less than* the differences between Australians and Americans. Alternatively, the salient category might be 'English-speaking' in a context where the difference between various English-speaking groups (such as Ameri-

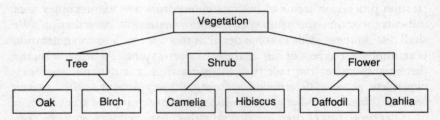

Figure 4.1 A categorical hierarchy of vegetation

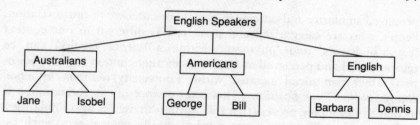

Figure 4.2 A categorical hierarchy of English speakers

cans and Australians) is *less than* the difference between English and non-English speakers.

These ideas can be expressed in terms of a *meta-contrast ratio*, that is the average perceived intercategory difference divided by the average perceived intracategory difference. For example, this might be:

$$\frac{\text{average perceived difference between Australians and Americans}}{\text{average perceived difference between individual Australians}}$$

The higher this ratio, the more likely it is that Australians will be perceived in terms of their shared national identity. Turner and Oakes (1989, p. 242) provide some more specific examples of how meta-contrast can be calculated, and the calculation and predictive power of meta-contrast are pursued in more detail in chapter 6.

Note, however, that the meta-contrast principle provides only a partial account of categorization. It describes the *comparative relations* between stimuli which lead them to be represented by a category, but it is also important to take into account the *social meaning* of differences between people in terms of the normative and behavioural content of their actions, and the relative accessibility of particular categorizations (Oakes, 1987; Oakes, Turner and Haslam, 1991). In general terms, the theory explains the salience of any given category as a representation of a set of stimuli as a function of an interaction between its relative accessibility (the 'readiness' of a perceiver to use a particular categorization) and the 'fit' between the category and reality. Meta-contrast is the theory's principle of 'comparative fit' (the match between category and the comparative properties of stimuli), but 'normative fit' (the match between category and the content properties of stimuli) is also always inseparably at work. These ideas about salience will be discussed in more detail in the next chapter.

This emphasis on categorization as highly variable and context-dependent produces a concomitant emphasis on the context-dependence of perceived similarity and difference, the major *outcome* of categorization. People who are categorized and perceived as different in one context (e.g., 'biologists' and 'physicists' within a science faculty) can be recategorized and perceived as similar in another context (e.g., as 'scientists' rather than 'social scientists' within a university) *without any actual change in their own positions*. This is the essence of categorization: it is a cognitive grouping process that transforms differences into similarities, and vice versa. We need some psychologically neutral term such as, perhaps, 'distances' to indicate the nature of precognized stimulus relations. There are 'distances' between people, but are they similarities or differences? Are physicists and biologists similar or different? Arising from the comparisons specified in the meta-contrast principle, categorization subjectively transforms 'distances' into similarities and differences, and from perceived similarities and differences flow, amongst other things, perceptions of attraction and dislike, agreement and disagreement, cooperation and conflict. In sum, categorization provides the fundamental basis of our social orientation towards others. Within the science faculty physicists might reject and deride the biologists, claiming they aren't 'real scientists', but in comparison with social scientists the two groups may present as inseparable allies.

As changes in the comparative context produce changes in ingroup–outgroup relationships, they also affect intracategory structure. The meta-contrast principle can be used to define the relative *prototypicality* of members within a group (see Turner and Oakes, 1989, pp. 259–265). In general terms, the more a group member differs from outgroup members and the less he or she differs from other ingroup members (i.e., the more this person exemplifies what ingroup members share and what they do not share with the outgroup), the more that individual will be perceived as prototypical of the ingroup. Clearly, if relative prototypicality depends on intergroup comparisons, then, for example, the prototypical physicist in a comparative context including biologists will be different from the prototypical physicist as compared with engineers. As we noted in chapter 3, this approach to categorization emphasizes context-dependent *judgements of prototypicality* rather than fixed prototypical images which represent groups as constants across changing contexts (cf. Brewer, 1988; Brewer et al., 1981).

The essential point of the meta-contrast principle, then, is that categorization depends on comparison, comparison of the difference within and the difference between potential categories. However, it is also apparent that comparison depends on categorization – what is available as a 'potential category' (i.e., what can be meaningfully compared with what) is constrained by the fact that stimuli must share category identity at some level in order to be compared with each other (Festinger, 1954; Goethals and Darley, 1977). Paradoxically, being able to say that two things differ always implies that they share a higher level identity in terms of which the comparison is meaningful. Thus, we have compared trees and shrubs as vegetation, Australians and Americans as English-speakers, physicists and biologists as scientists, but how do we compare biologists and babies, cabbages and kings? Only by seeking some common category, defined by dimensions in terms of which a meaningful comparison can be made – we might compare biologists and babies as 'types of humans', along dimensions defining that more abstract categorization (physical abilities, foodstuffs consumed, ability to hold their own in a conversation, etc.). In this way, less abstract categories (e.g., physicists) are based on comparisons within more abstract categories (e.g., scientists). A category forms from contrasts between stimuli in the implicit context of, and as constrained by, the definition of a higher-order identity, and the resulting category provides the dimensions for more finely grained comparisons which can lead to more finely grained categories, and so on.

This means, of course, that the different levels of identity discussed in self-categorization theory are seen as highly dependent upon each other. For example, personal identity depends on social identity – individual self-categorizations are based on and constrained by intragroup comparisons. The way in which Isobel and Jane (from the example above) perceive themselves as individuals will be affected by the nature of the intragroup comparison providing the context for the interindividual distinctions (Codol, 1975). Are they differentiating within the category Australian, or perhaps as women, or as physicists, and so on? At the same time, social identity can be said to depend on individual differences, as the latter play an essential role in determining the meta-contrasts from which social categorizations arise.

There is, nonetheless, a conflicting, competitive relationship between different levels of categorization as representations of the same stimulus situation. Following the meta-contrast principle, *social* categorization of the self and others becomes more likely as intergroup differences increase and intragroup, interpersonal differences decrease. On the other hand, categorization at the *personal*, individual level becomes more likely as intergroup differences decrease and intragroup differences increase. Further, the accentuation *effects* of categorization (chapter 3) work to enhance perceived differences between and similarities within categories associated with the salient level (e.g., the difference between Australians and Americans might be accentuated). At the same time they reduce perceived similarities and differences which are the basis of categorization at another level (e.g., differences between individual Australians may be minimized). In sum, there tends to be an inverse relationship between self-perception as a unique individual and as an ingroup category – the more Isobel perceives herself as similar to other Australians, the less she will be aware of her personal, idiosyncratic differences from them (and vice versa).

This idea of social and personal levels of self-categorization as in some sense in conflict, mutually antagonistic in their effects, brings us back to Tajfel's interpersonal–intergroup continuum, but in a more complex form. In its account of the psychological basis of group behaviour, self-categorization theory maintains the idea of such a continuum, hypothesizing that shift along it is a matter of the varying outcome of a continual conflict between personal and social identity as they vary in relative salience. Shifts towards social identity produce the *depersonalization* of self-perception and behaviour. As in Turner's earlier analysis, depersonalization is the direct effect of self-categorization at the social level. It is *self-stereotyping*, perception of increased identity between the self and ingroup members and increased difference from outgroup members (on relevant dimensions). Most importantly, self-categorization theory proposes that it is this process of depersonalization that makes group behaviour possible and produces its emergent, irreducible properties.

Thus, insofar as it is focusing on arguments for the psychological reality and distinctiveness of the group, self-categorization theory retains this emphasis on the two levels of social and personal identity. In a sense, the theory appears to be suggesting that there are, in Rosch's (1978) terms, two 'basic' levels in the cognitive representation of self and others, the social and the personal. In truth, however, one of the essential points of the self-categorization analysis is that *the appropriate level of categorization varies with the context*, and that to speak of any level as more 'basic' than another is misconceived. The idea of a given level is useful to indicate a theoretical extreme, but in reality there is a perceptual continuum that never fully embodies any one level but arises from a dynamic, fluid process through which tensions between different levels of abstraction are resolved. Human beings are both individual persons and social groups, but the extent to which they are one or the other varies. We see them as both, but represented in a single unique configuration at any given instant.

In sum, as an account of the group, the theory's key ideas are that (1) the level of inclusiveness at which and the degree to which one categorizes self and others as similar or different varies with the social context within which comparison takes place, (2) the salience of shared social identity leads to the depersonalization of self-perception, and (3) depersonalization produces group behaviour. Its relevance to stereotyping is that it outlines the conditions under which social categorizations of self and others become salient (i.e., under which people stereotype) and construes the stereotypic accentuation effects of ingroup–outgroup categorizations as the basic cognitive foundation of group behaviour. As we have seen, stereotyping is precisely what is meant by the depersonalizing of self-perception, which is seen not as a problem of intergroup relations and prejudice but as a basic adaptive process of social interaction. Importantly, too, in common with social identity theory, self-categorization theory takes for granted the social and psychological reality of groups. Its initial aim as a theory was to explain the psychological emergence of the group-level properties of social behaviour. It is these group-level properties that stereotypes describe.

In the following chapters we shall develop an analysis of stereotyping based on self-categorization theory. We shall emphasize and elaborate three aspects of the theory: (1) the dynamic, context-dependent nature of the categorization process, and of the judgements of similarity and difference which both determine and flow from categorization, (2) the definition of the self as an *outcome* of this categorization process, a definition which may focus, *inter alia*, on individual differences or on a shared group identification, and (3) the recognition of all levels of identity as equally 'true', real, psychologically valid definitions of the person. In chapter 5, we shall consider the 'salience' problem – when and why do we define ourselves and others in terms of social categories and stereotype? – in the context of a general discussion of the functions of categorization. In chapter 6 we shall explore the contextual basis of stereotypical accentuation and summarize evidence that such accentuation can be related to variation in self-categorization. Chapter 7 will illustrate the developing analysis by applying it to and re-interpreting the outgroup homogeneity and illusory correlation effects discussed in chapter 3. Finally, chapter 8 will summarize and draw together the major points of our analysis in a discussion of the issue of stereotype validity.

Overview

This chapter has traced the development of a social psychological theory of the group. The aim has been to make the problem of the individual–

group relationship explicit in the context of social stereotyping, and to outline the major recent efforts to confront this long-standing issue. We also hope to have shown that sophisticated hypotheses about specific processes now exist which address the role of 'social identity' in psychological group formation and social perception.

The focus of this book is the relationship between stereotypes and reality. It is important to keep reminding ourselves that stereotypes are representations of *groups*, representations which are often used to describe, interpret and predict the actions of *individuals*. Insofar as individuals are thought to be just that, only and always individuals, stereotyping inevitably distorts reality. We have seen in this chapter that social psychology has struggled with the individual–group relationship for many years, and that there is still no final agreement on the psychological status of the group. Are individuals only and always individuals, or are they also group members? On the one hand, the theories outlined in this chapter argue strongly that people can act as both individuals and group members and that intergroup behaviour is irreducible to interpersonal behaviour. In the following chapters we shall base ourselves squarely on this assumption. On the other, it seems that much of social psychology is still informed, explicitly or implicitly, by the individualistic conception of the group. That this is the case in current stereotyping research is apparent in a comment by Stephan and Rosenfield (1982), who suggest that the fundamental *problem* with stereotyping is 'that individuals are treated as group members . . . rather than as individuals to be judged on their own merits' (p. 116).

As one delves deeper into the cognitive analysis of stereotyping, it becomes apparent that two closely related assumptions contribute to the continued presentation of stereotyping as a biased, 'unfortunate' way of perceiving individuals. These are the (often implicit) rejection of the psychological reality of the group (along the lines of Stephan and Rosenfield's comment above), and the conceptualization of categorization processes that has come to dominate stereotyping research. As noted in chapter 3, Tajfel (1972) described categorization as a process which, amongst other things, *simplified* a complex social environment, and he understood the accentuation effects to be distortions of perception in the service of such simplification. In the age of the cognitive miser, these ideas became very influential. Categorization is widely described in the current stereotyping literature as designed to '*reduce* the total amount of information' (S. Taylor et al., 1978, p. 792, emphasis added), involving an inevitable loss of richness and distortion of reality. It is to the validity of these arguments and their contribution to our understanding of stereotyping that we turn in chapter 5.

Suggested Further Reading and References

For a general understanding of the individual–group relationship, and the ability of cognitive theory to address it, there is no more inspiring reference than Asch (1952) – this is something that should be read by all social psychologists. Turner and Oakes (1986) provide a more recent discussion of these issues. Hogg (1992) also gives a good overview of the individual–group problem as revealed through the study of group cohesiveness. Tajfel and Turner (1986) is the best statement of social identity theory, and Turner et al. (1987) spell out self-categorization theory and its application to several areas. Tajfel's final paper on stereotyping presents a strong critique of the cognitive 'push' and is essential reading (Tajfel, 1981a).

Asch, S. E. (1952) *Social Psychology*. New York: Prentice-Hall.

Hogg, M. A. (1992) *The Social Psychology of Group Cohesiveness*. Hemel Hempstead: Harvester Wheatsheaf.

Tajfel, H. (1981) Social stereotypes and social groups. In J. C. Turner & H. Giles (Eds), *Intergroup behaviour*. Oxford: Blackwell; Chicago: University of Chicago Press. pp. 144–167. (a)

Tajfel, H. and Turner, J. C. (1986) The social identity theory of intergroup behaviour. In S. Worschel and W. G. Austin (Eds) *Psychology of intergroup relations* (2nd ed.). Chicago: Nelson-Hall.

Turner, J. C., Hogg, M. A., Oakes, P. J., Reicher, S. D. and Wetherell, M. S. (1987) *Rediscovering the social group: A self-categorization theory*. Oxford: Blackwell.

Turner, J. C. and Oakes, P. J. (1986) The significance of the social identity concept for social psychology with reference to individualism, interactionism, and social influence. *British Journal of Social Psychology, 25*, 237–252.

5

Categorization, Selective Perception and Stereotyping: A Critical Re-examination

In this chapter and the next, we take a much closer look at the process of categorization – the treatment of a number of things as in some way equivalent, interchangeable. All the research we have discussed so far points to the central importance of categorization for stereotyping and for group processes in general. However, we have two quite distinct views of what categorization is for, its purpose, and what categorization produces, its outcome. Most stereotyping researchers (chapter 3) see categorization as, primarily, an information-*reduction* mechanism, designed to help the perceiver cope with limited information processing capacity. Its outcome is a distortion of perception, an overgeneralization and exaggeration of individuals' true characteristics. This is seen as regrettable, but nonetheless inevitable given the demands of cognitive economy.

On the other hand, categorization has also been identified as the basis of group formation and identification (chapter 4). In that context it was discussed as a process which gives us access to information about real similarites and differences between people occurring at varying levels of abstraction. For example, it allows us to be aware of given individuals as 'Tom', 'Mary', 'Jane' and 'Harry', but also as 'men' and 'women', or as 'the string quartet', under the appropriate circumstances. Thus, the purpose of categorization is assumed to be veridical selective representation of a complex and varying reality (i.e., one comprising people who can be both individuals and group members), and its outcome is not seen as, by definition, distorted or overgeneralized (see Oakes and Turner, 1990).

Questions about the purpose and outcome of categorization clearly lie at the heart of the issue we have set out to analyse in this book – the relationship between stereotyping and reality. In this chapter we address ourselves to purpose – what is categorization for, how does it achieve perceptual selectivity? This leads to a consideration of the antecedents of social categorization: when do social categories become salient in perception? We shall begin by summarizing the analysis of categorization processes offered in the social cognitive stereotyping literature.

Categorization and the Cognitive Miser

Hamilton and Trolier comment that 'we categorize people into groups as a means of reducing the amount of information we must contend with' (1986, p. 128). In general terms, most social cognitive researchers suggest that categorization is a process designed to reduce the amount of information flowing through the information processing system. However, the argument recruited to explain stereotyping is actually more specific than this. It is that social categorization reduces information *relative to* interpersonal perception. Stereotyping involves sacrificing the richness of interpersonal details for the overgeneralized images represented in social categorizations. For example, Fiske and Neuberg comment:

> We have neither the cognitive capacity nor the time to deal with all the *interpersonal* information we have available to us . . . Given our limited cognitive resources, it is both simpler (requires less effort) and more efficient (requires less time) for a perceiver to use stereotyped information to make inferences about individuals belonging to a group than it is to analyze *each person on an individual basis*. (1990, p. 14, emphasis added)

Similarly, as noted in chapter 3, Brewer (1988, p. 28) assumes that because categorization is designed to simplify perception, loss of 'the complexity and richness of detail that a more personalized representation of that individual would contain' inevitably accompanies stereotyping. Both models assert that this is efficient and functional 'given the logic of human cognition' (Fiske and Neuberg, 1990, p. 15), that is, given limited capacity. It is, nonetheless, seen as regrettable because, insofar as categorization deletes real complexity from our image of a person, it must be distorting that image to some degree, giving us a less accurate impression than we would otherwise have formed.

These related assumptions, that interpersonal perception is richer and more accurate than group perception, and that categorization (all categorization) necessarily distorts in its quest to simplify, underlie the fairly explicit notion within the stereotyping literature that whilst stereotyping involves categorization, individual perception does not. For example,

Fiske contrasts the two types of person perception in commenting that, 'stereotypers categorize because it requires too much mental effort to individuate' (1989, p. 253). Brewer's model contrasts top-down 'category-based processing' with bottom-up 'person-based processing' in which 'specific behaviours are first encoded at a relatively concrete level' (1988, p. 24). Similarly, Fiske and Neuberg (1990; see also Fiske et al., 1987) distinguish between top-down, category-based impressions and data-driven, attribute-oriented impressions, placing them at opposite ends of their continuum of impression formation. The latter involve 'an attribute-by-attribute consideration of isolated pieces of information' (Fiske et al., 1987, p. 401), with no attempt to establish relationships between these pieces of information, that is, no attempt to categorize. The final impression formed is then 'relatively uncontaminated by category-based generalizations' (Fiske and Neuberg, 1990, p. 8). In these models, then, interpersonal perception represents an accurate, almost unmediated appreciation of people's 'true' characteristics, in contrast with stereotyping which is category-based and hence unavoidably distorted.

Overall, then, the cognitive miser analysis presents social categorization as rather like one's least favourite close relative – unfortunate but unavoidable. If not for limited capacity we could, at all times, work at the level of piecemeal, data-driven impressions, treating each person as a unique individual with a unique configuration of attributes. This would greatly increase the richness, validity and accuracy of social interaction. However, we do have limited capacity, and as a consequence we have social categorization and stereotyping. Note that, from this perspective, social categorization and stereotyping are not ends in themselves, but unintended products of social cognition: '. . . social categorization is a necessary, if unfortunate, *byproduct* of our cognitive makeup' (Fiske and Neuberg, 1990, p. 14, emphasis added).* We can summarize the social cognitive explanation of stereotyping along the lines indicated in figure 5.1.

Is there any *direct* evidence that this is what is going on in stereotyping? As we saw in chapter 3, some studies have tried to test the idea that it is when information processing capacity is particularly strained that stereotyping is most likely. The results have been mixed. Further, we

---

* The point here is not that stereotyping occurs without the *stereotyper's* intent (see Fiske, 1989, for a discussion of this issue). It is, rather, that within the cognitive miser analysis stereotyping is seen as a side-effect of something else (capacity conservation), whereas we wish to argue that it is the fully intended outcome of categorization processes.

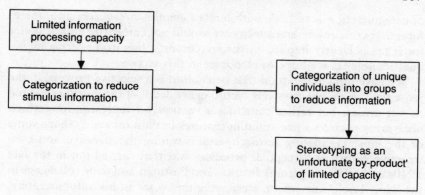

Figure 5.1 The cognitive miser model of stereotyping

should note the difficulty of manipulating something that can be unambiguously conceptualized as an increased demand for processing capacity. For example, Stangor and Duan (1991) increased the number of groups presented as a manipulation of cognitive strain, but this clearly also changes the comparative context in which judgements are made. Similarly, Macrae et al.'s (1993) manipulation of load involved providing subjects with a quite different task orientation. Bodenhausen and Lichtenstein (1987) expected a judgement of Carlos Ramirez's guilt to be more complex and therefore more capacity-expensive than a trait judgement. However, the finding of more stereotyping in the guilt judgement condition is likely to be an effect of the relevance of that judgement to the meaning of the category, rather than cognitive complexity. As Fiske and Neuberg (1990, p. 14) comment, aspects of the limited capacity argument 'still need to be tested more directly'. Isolation of demands on capacity from other contextual variables likely to affect categorization may prove difficult. In the next section we look at a different approach to the purpose of categorization.

Categorization and Perceptual Selectivity

There is a very simple, general sense in which categorization can be seen as promoting cognitive economy. Without it we would have to react and refer to every stimulus as a new and unique experience. As E. E. Smith comments, 'the mental lexicon required would be so enormous that communication as we know it might collapse' (1989, p. 501). However, even in this very simple form the argument that the *fundamental purpose*

of categorization is to cope with limited cognitive resources and, therefore, that with unlimited capacity we would not categorize and be better
for it (as is clearly implied in the stereotyping literature) seems highly
questionable, as we hope to elaborate in this section.

We have long understood that perception is a selective process, in the
sense that we do not passively record every detail of the world presented
to our senses, but rather construct a *meaningful* representation which
necessarily encodes some stimulus features but not others. Perhaps some
of the most fascinating research demonstrating the selective and constructive nature of perceptual processes was that carried out in the late
1940s and 1950s by Jerome Bruner, Leo Postman and their colleagues in
the 'New Look' movement. Reviewing this work in his autobiography,
Bruner comments:

> The mystery of perception, at least for me, is not that our senses tell us so
> much about the world, but that they tell us so little. Yet what they tell us
> is on the whole what we need to know ... Nature ... has given us so
> limited a span of attention that we can only sample lightly from the biased
> input that our senses permit us to apprehend ... But it is not random, this
> sampling of the world ... It is a filtering, a sorting out, and finally a
> construction, that world we perceive directly. The nature of the filter and
> of the construction processes that work with it – these constitute the *real*
> philosopher's stone. It does not turn base metal into gold, but turns
> physical 'stimuli' into knowledge, a much more valuable transformation.
> (1983, p. 66)

In his seminal paper 'On Perceptual Readiness' (1957), Bruner presents a
theory of selective perception in which categorization plays the pivotal
role. This paper is often cited as a source of the idea that categorization
contributes to perceptual selectivity by reducing the amount of information gained from stimulus input (e.g., Bargh et al., 1986), but in fact
Bruner portrays categorization in quite different terms.

Bruner argues that there is never perception without categorization:
'all perception is necessarily the end product of a categorization process'
(1957, p. 124; see also R. McCauley, 1987; cf. Neisser, 1987c). The
major reason for this is that it is the placing of percepts in general classes,
of which the defining properties are already known, which gives 'stimuli'
identity. Raw, uncategorized stimulus information may be abundant in
quantity but it is entirely lacking in human relevance, in meaning. Categorization gives a stimulus meaning through 'placement ... in a net-
work of hypothetical inference concerning its other observable
properties, its effects, and so on' (1957, p. 126). Far from reducing or
impoverishing perceptual experience, categorization enriches and ex-

pands it, allows the perceiver to, in Bruner's famous phrase, 'go beyond' (1957, p. 129) mere sensory stimulation to the identity of objects and events with '*more elaborated*, connotative meaning' (1957, p. 148, emphasis added). Similarly, in recent comments on the 'goals and purposes of social categorization', Medin (1988) is sceptical about the idea that categorization works to cope with information overload. He feels that 'categorization, including social categorization, is primarily to cope with the problem of too little rather than too much information' (1988, p. 122). He emphasizes the vital ability of categorization to generate expectations about a stimulus, and notes the importance of paying due regard to context in this process, noting that the same category can have different implications in different contexts.

Thus Bruner and others argue that the principal purpose of categorization is to turn 'stimuli' into objects and events with human relevance and elaborated meaning. If our experience of the world is so dependent upon the way we categorize it, understanding the origins and nature of our category systems obviously becomes a priority. This issue has received considerable attention in cognitive psychology in recent years (e.g., Murphy and Medin, 1985, and the chapters edited by Neisser, 1987a), and this is not the place to review those proceedings in detail. What is noteworthy, for our purposes, is the emphasis on both 'ecological' and 'intellectual' factors in the definition of what makes a category a category, what holds it together (Medin and Wattenmaker, 1987 refer to this as 'category cohesiveness') and thus why we categorize the world in certain ways rather than others.

On the ecological side, we can begin with what Neisser (1987a, p. vii) refers to as the 'Roschian revolution' in our understanding of categorization processes. As well as the ideas about prototypes and levels of inclusiveness outlined in chapter 3, Rosch (1978) made a further important contribution in arguing that the category systems we employ are not arbitrary, purely subjective constructions. Rather, they represent real and relevant invariances in the material world, 'natural discontinuities'. The commonly used example is the category 'bird' which reflects, among other things, the fact that wings and feathers really do co-occur far more frequently than do wings and fur. Neisser develops a similar argument in his own approach to categorization, where he discusses the importance of 'the ecological distribution and characteristics of the to-be-categorized domain itself' (1987b, p. 3) as a vital determinant of the category systems we develop and use. Indeed, Bruner also touches on this idea when he notes that perceivers develop 'a system of categories-in-relationship that fit the nature of the world in which [they] must live' (1957, p. 127), and it is more generally implicated in his concept of 'fit' between stimulus input and category specifications as one determinant of category activation. 'Fit' clearly implies that there is actual invariance in stimulus input which cognitive categories represent and make meaningful. In summary, several writers argue that categorization does not impose purely subjective structure on a formless environment, but rather selectively draws our attention to aspects of real, material structure. Reality, with its natural 'joints', is the source of conceptual order (see R. McCauley, 1987, for a review).

On the other hand, the 'intellectual' argument is that abstract, idealized 'theories' about the world and the way it works mediate between reality and the categories used to represent it. For example, Medin and Wattenmaker (1987; see also Medin, 1989; Murphy and Medin, 1985) chart the inadequacy of similarity-based models of category cohesiveness. One illustrative example of theirs is the relationship between a plum and a lawnmower. Clearly these are 'similar' on a number of dimensions (both weigh less than 1,000 kg, both cannot hear, both have a smell, both can be dropped, . . .) but these 'similarities' do not define any meaningful categorical identity shared by a plum and a lawnmower. What is lacking here is a way of defining *relevant attributes*, on the basis of which a meaningful categorization decision can be made. How do we decide that some similarities between objects are decisive for a given categorization decision, whereas others are irrelevant? Medin and Wattenmaker argue that it is consistency with people's 'background theories or naive knowledge of the world' that determines what qualifies as a good category and what does not. They briefly outline some fascinating empirical illustrations of the influence of background theories in the categorization process. The studies looked at rule induction. Subjects were presented with stimuli in two categories and asked to work out the rule determining placement in one category rather than the other. The stimuli for one experiment are shown in figure 5.2. This particular study differed from the basic rule induction procedure in that the cover stories and category labels were more elaborate than usual, and varied across subjects. Some were told that the two groups represented trains run by smugglers versus legal trains, others that they travelled in mountainous versus flat terrain, and so on. The different labels, which presumably activate different background theories, were found to influence rule induction in systematic ways. For example, some subjects given the smuggler label included mention of 'diamond-shaped load' in the categorization rule they developed.

In a further rule induction study subjects looked at children's drawings, again with varying category labels. Some heard that mentally healthy versus disturbed children had done the drawings, others that they

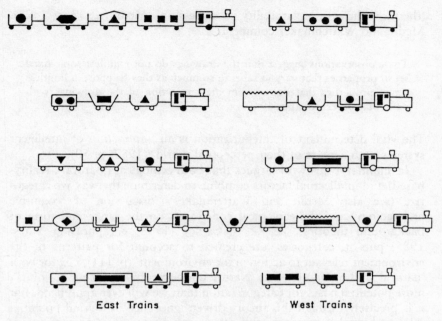

East Trains   West Trains

Figure 5.2   Example of stimuli used in a rule induction study discussed in Medin and Wattenmaker (1987)

The subject's task was to work out what separates the Eastbound trains from the Westbound trains. Some were told that they were smugglers' versus legal trains, others that they travelled on mountains versus flat terrain, etc.

were by farm versus city children, and so on. Again, these labels affected rule induction, and in a way that led Medin and Wattenmaker to argue that the effect is not simply to alter the relative salience of fixed attributes of the stimuli. For instance, subjects given the farm/city label might note the use of animal parts in some of the farm children's drawings, and develop an abstract rule along the lines of 'each drawing reflects some aspect of farm life' (1987, p. 49). No subject given an alternative label would mention anything of this kind. Furthermore, the *same* feature (e.g., expressions on the faces) could be used quite differently by subjects given alternative labels in order to validate different categorization rules. Subjects identifying one set of drawings as the work of mentally healthy (as compared to emotionally disturbed) children often noted that all the faces were smiling. In another condition exactly the same objective information was used as evidence that the drawings were done by noncreative (as compared to creative) children, with comments such as

'the faces show little variability in expression' (Medin, 1989, p. 1478).
Medin and Wattenmaker comment:

> These observations suggest that the drawings do not manifest some fixed
> set of properties that vary in salience so much as they 'support' a limitless
> set of properties that derive from the interaction of the drawings with
> particular observers. (pp. 49–50)

The vital determinant of categorization is an *'interaction* of intelligent
systems with aspects of their perceptual world' (1987, p. 50).

In summary, this work argues that both ecological ('natural', reality-
based) and intellectual factors combine to determine the way we categorize (see also Medin and Wattenmaker's discussion of 'cognitive
archaeology' and the ecological constraints on the range and form of
background theories). As C. McCauley (1988, paraphrasing Yates,
1985) puts it, categories 'are created to account for patterns of the
environment relevant to action in the environment' (p. 111), i.e., for both
'natural' and human reasons. Nature undoubtedly has far more 'joints',
more potential bases for categorization than we will ever apprehend. But
it is precisely through this theory-driven ignorance of myriad potential
relationships that categorization effects *selectivity* in human perception.
Bruner, Goodnow and Austin comment that 'psychological equivalence
is only limited by and not determined by stimulus similarity' (1956, p. 8,
and see Neisser, 1987a, p. vii). In other words, we cannot perceive
similarities and differences that do not exist, but of the practically infinite
potential bases for categorization available we actively select to attend to
a limited sample.

Thus, the critical mechanism for adaptive selectivity is not so much the
fact of categorizing but the process through which particular categorizations become activated to produce one subjective representation of a
stimulus context. For example, a given perceptual scene could be categorized and therefore experienced as 'traffic', or as 'cars and trucks', or as
'Hondas, Fords, BMWs etc.'. Whilst the objective stimulus information
on which these different instances of categorization operate may well
remain unchanged, what does vary is the subjective experience of similarity and difference. Objects perceived as similar in one instance (e.g., as all
'cars') are perceived as differing in another ('Hondas, Fords, etc.'). Recall
that in the cognitive analysis of stereotyping the idea was that the more
abstract categorization (in terms of a group stereotype) represented information reduction relative to the less abstract (interpersonal relations and
individual differences). Is it the case that a perceiver seeing 'cars' draws
less information from the context than one who differentiates between

Hondas, Fords and so on? One important issue here is the basis on which one categorization is used rather than another – when and why do we focus on 'cars' rather than Hondas, etc? We shall discuss this in detail presently, but for the moment imagine a perceiver who is trying to cross a busy road. Distinctions between Hondas and Fords are not informative, whereas these clearly would be for someone looking out for a friend driving a Honda, or eyeing a used car yard for a bargain. Defining 'information' in the abstract seems inappropriate here. Information is what the perceiver needs to know at any given moment in order to construct a meaningful representation of reality, and to achieve their goals. We would argue that categorization works to *maximize* information in this sense (Rosch, 1978, p. 28) by selectively drawing out aspects of structure, of similarity and difference in stimulus information, which are relevant to the perceiver's current requirements within the stimulus context as a whole (Turner and Oakes, 1989).

To recap, let us return to the question we posed at the beginning of this section – if the primary purpose of categorization is to reduce information as a rearguard action against limited capacity, then, if capacity was somehow boundless, would we choose to desist from categorizing, and achieve a more veridical, useful perspective on the world as a result? We believe the answer to this must be 'no'. Notwithstanding the obvious fact that categorization does afford us the economy of not having to react to each stimulus we encounter as a new event, the *purpose* of categorization does not appear to be information reduction. Categorization itself elaborates rather than reduces the information available in a stimulus. It is the crucial process which brings together our general understanding of and theories about the world on the one hand, and the material reality in which we live on the other. Without it perception would be meaningless, it would not be human.

In our view, the characterization of categorization and its purpose that we have outlined here is *incompatible* with the cognitive miser emphasis on information reduction. It seems contradictory to argue, as some recent accounts have argued, that categorization functions *both* to elaborate and give meaning to experience *and* to reduce the informativeness of stimuli (e.g., see Fiske and Neuberg, 1990, pp. 13–14). Categorization elaborates experience as construed *at one particular level of abstraction* (see chapter 4). This is, in principle, neither more nor less informative than any other way of construing the situation. However, as we have noted, insofar as categorization is determined (at least in part) by the perceiver's current goals, the categorization used is decidedly *more* informative than currently irrelevant alternatives. There is, then, in our view no important sense in which categorization functions as an information-reduction mechanism.

Perceptual selectivity through categorization is not a matter of imposing cognitive structures which simplify by reduction and thus deny the perceiver potentially valuable information. Rather, selection is achieved through active engagement with the environment such that the perceiver constructs it in the most appropriately informative manner. We agree with Neisser that 'selection is a positive process, not a negative one' (1976, p. 80), and that 'the very concept of "capacity" seems better suited to a passive vessel into which things are put than to an active and developing structure' (p. 98). With this perspective in mind, let us now return to issues raised in the cognitive miser analysis of social categorization and person perception.

Social Categorization and Person Perception

First, is it the case that stereotyping is inherently less rich and less accurate than interpersonal perception? We have outlined above our view that no one level of categorization is inherently less informative than another. However, the argument that group perception is impoverished relative to interpersonal perception is closely bound up with the suggestion that it is less *accurate*, that individual personality represents not only richness but also the *real* person, and any deviation from that must involve distortion and impoverishment.

We can recognize here the influence of the individualistic perspective that we discussed in chapter 4. We can recall that social identity and self-categorization theories provided an alternative perspective consistent with the (social and psychological) reality of the group. They argued that stereotypes were group products, determined by intergroup relationships, that intergroup behaviour could not be reduced psychologically to interpersonal behaviour, and that the concept of social identity provided an explanation of the psychological emergence of group-level phenomena. It is worth asking why it is so commonly assumed that the individual person is 'real', whereas the group, which is what stereotypes represent, is not. Asch (1952, chapter 9) examines the assumptions underlying the most explicit statement of the individualistic doctrine, by Floyd Allport (1933), and concludes that Allport makes a fatal error in attempting to distinguish between 'things' and 'relations'. 'Things', according to Allport, are concrete, tangible, we can bump into them or pick them up – stones, trees, individual people are things, and are accorded full reality. On the other hand we have 'relations', abstractions which we cannot see or touch, pick up or trip over – the principle of gravity, waves on the surface of water, human groups. These are relations, conceptions formed in our minds to describe the way things relate to each other. The individualist warns that we should not reify these mental artefacts. They are imaginary rather than real.

Asch argues that these ideas are 'untenable in terms of natural science' (p. 245). Clearly 'things' like diamonds, buildings, animals can be reconceptualized as 'relations' (e.g., a certain order of arrangement of carbon atoms, a given structure of bricks, glass, etc.). Further, in the preceding section we outlined the view that all perception is categorization, and categorization is fundamentally concerned with relations, with representation of the *variable relations of similarity and difference* in our environment. From this perspective, a stone could be just a single stone (and experienced as a separate 'thing'), or it might be part of a farm wall, it might be amongst a variety of missiles, it might crumble when used as pavement chalk – how far is it a fixed 'thing'? To some extent, we might turn Allport's injunction on its head, and argue for the (psychological) lack of importance of 'things' and the pre-eminence of 'relations' in our conception of the world.

This leads in to the second point we wish to raise here, the issue of whether, as the models discussed above suggest, stereotyping is categorization whereas interpersonal perception is not. Asch comments that an individual person is a 'thing' (as opposed to a relation) only insofar as we restrict our consideration of him or her to physical properties, size, weight and so on. The *psychological reality* of the person is a matter of judgements, abstractions, categories. It is widely argued that an impression of individual personality is as much an act of categorization as is social stereotyping (Cantor and Mischel, 1979; C. McCauley, 1988; Mischel, 1981; Turner et al., 1987, see chapter 4). In self-categorization theory, the difference between the two types of categorization is the level of inclusiveness at which they define similarity and difference. Whereas a stereotype defines similarities across a group (and differences from a comparison group), a personality categorization defines similarities within the individual across situations (and differences from other comparable individuals). The validity of this latter type of person categorization has attracted as much critical attention as the validity of stereotypes has. The 'consistency' debate (see Mischel, 1977) concerns precisely the extent to which personality categorizations overgeneralize personal characteristics.

All person perception (as all perception) involves categorization. Comparing personality (individual level) and stereotypical (ingroup-outgroup level) person perception, the level of identity is different but the processes are the same and, we have argued, one level is not by definition any less real, or any more of a distortion, than another; people are both individuals and social group members. Both types of person categorization are potentially vulnerable to, and have been accused of representing, overgeneralization. The crucial issue, as Mischel (1981, pp. 175, 520) has pointed out, is the way in which different types or levels of categorization are used in different situations. Do we perceive people in terms of the contextually appropriate categories?

The Selective Activation of Social Categories

In this section we present the self-categorization analysis of the selective activation ('salience', Oakes, 1987) of social categories, one which meshes social identity ideas with the general view of the purpose of categorization that we have outlined above. It is based on the hypothesis outlined by Bruner (1957), who begins with the assumption that category activation works to produce a representation of reality which is both as veridical and as appropriately selective as possible.

Bruner suggests that category activation is determined by an interactive process involving the relative *accessibility* of the category within the perceiver's repertoire (the 'readiness' of a perceiver to use a particular category) and the *fit* between input and stored category specifications. The relative accessibility of a category depends upon the perceiver's past experience, present expectations and current tasks, goals and purposes. It reflects the active selectivity of the perceiver in being ready to use categories which are relevant, useful and likely to be confirmed by the evidence of reality. It ensures that perception is appropriately selective, gearing categorization to changing circumstances and motives. Fit ties perception firmly to reality; however perceptually 'ready' we may be to see a given object or event in terms of category accessibility, we do not do so until something with at least some requisite characteristics enters the perceptual field.

We have applied this 'accessibility × fit' hypothesis to the salience of social categorizations (Oakes, 1987; Oakes et al., 1991; Turner, 1985; Turner and Oakes, 1986; 1989). The accessibility principle has been elaborated by social cognition researchers (Brewer, 1988; Higgins and King, 1981; Wyer and Srull, 1981; see chapter 3), and it is clear that there can be variation across both context and perceivers in the latent readiness of a given social categorization to become activated (e.g. Gurin and Markus, 1988). As well as the cognitive bases of varying accessibility identified in this research, it seems likely that social category accessibility will be affected by a wide range of social and contextual factors including the beliefs, norms and values of relevant reference groups (McGarty and Turner, 1992; Turner et al., in press). We see this as an important avenue for future research in this area, but our own work has concentrated on the specification of fit for social categories. What are the distinctive characteristics of stimulus input defining a fit to an ingroup–outgroup categorization rather than, say, personal identities within that context?

At the most general level, our answer is that social categorizations fit those aspects of reality characterized by the distinctive, emergent properties of group relationships and collective action. It is the *social invariances* (i.e., across different individuals) of human behaviour that social categorizations describe. The empirical specification of these conditions begins with the application of an important general principle from self-categorization theory: meta-contrast. In chapter 4 we discussed the role this principle plays in contextualizing the categorization process by making it dependent on a context-specific judgement of relative differences. In this context we can use it to define conditions under which individuals' similarities and differences are more appropriately perceived at the level of a particular group membership than at the level of personalities.

By the principle of meta-contrast, a given categorization is likely to form or become salient to the extent that differences *within* categories are less than differences *between* those categories in the comparative context. This has also been expressed as a meta-contrast *ratio*: a categorization with a contextually high ratio of inter- to intracategory differences is likely to become salient. Thus, for social categories salience is predicted in contexts where intergroup rather than intragroup differences predominate. For example, a perceiver observing a number of people, some of whom are Catholic and some Protestant, is more likely to categorize them in terms of religious identity to the extent that attitudes and behaviour are similar within but not between the religious groups (i.e., to the extent that they are correlated with the religious categorization; Tajfel, 1969). Extensive evidence from a tradition of research investigating the conditions of group membership salience points to the importance of relative intragroup similarity and intergroup difference (see Oakes, 1987 for a review). In the context of defining fit for social categories we have termed this aspect *comparative fit*. It describes the character of comparative relations between people which would lead them to be represented by a social category.

It is also important, however, to take into account the social meaning of these comparative similarities and differences. Would we categorize a group of individuals as Protestants and Catholics if those identifiable as

Protestant vehemently opposed birth control and abortion whilst the Catholics supported 'a woman's right to choose'? It seems unlikely. A categorization in terms of reactionary/progressive social attitudes, or some related political dimension might be more appropriate. The point is that, in representing the emergent properties of group action, social categorization must be able to make sense of the *content* of that action as well as its structure. We know what particular ingroups and outgroups are like or are supposed to be like and we employ social categorizations that are consistent with these 'background theories' and 'implicit knowledge'. Background knowledge and theories include cultural and religious beliefs, social representations, political and social ideologies and more formal, scientific and philosophical conceptions. We select social categorizations and defining stereotypical dimensions to match what is observed in terms of the *specific content dimensions* of comparison and the *direction of the observed differences* in the light of this broader interpretative matrix. The specific social categories that become salient and the stereotypical dimensions that define them must correlate with the shared similarities and differences between people in terms of the social meaning, the content, of what is observed (Boyanowsky and Allen, 1973; Festinger, 1947; Herman and Schild, 1960; Kelley, 1955). We use the term *normative fit* to refer to the match between category and reality in terms of content.

Oakes et al. (1991) report two studies directly testing this analysis of fit for social categories. In the second experiment the two aspects, comparative and normative, were manipulated orthogonally. The categorization involved was the undergraduate faculty membership (arts or science) of university students. The subjects were British undergraduate science students who watched video presentations of six-person stimulus groups ostensibly comprising three arts and three science students. These stimulus individuals discussed their attitudes to university life, an issue on which the student community expected arts and science students to disagree. Specifically, the stereotype of arts students included the idea that they viewed an active social life and extensive extracurricular activites as priorities for their years at university, whereas science students were expected to emphasize the importance of hard work, good grades and a consequently impressive career.

Normative fit was manipulated through the specific attitude expressed by one female arts student, designated the target individual. This was either consistent or inconsistent with the arts faculty stereotype ('consistent' versus 'inconsistent' conditions). The pattern of agreement within the stimulus group constituted the manipulation of comparative fit. There were three agreement conditions: 'consensus', all six individuals agreed on the issue; 'conflict', the three arts students expressed one attitude and the three science students took an opposing view; 'deviance', the target disagreed with the other five students. Normative and comparative fit were thus varied to form a 2 × 3 factorial design (consistent/inconsistent × consensus/conflict/deviance), as set out in table 5.1.

Subjects rated the target and the stimulus group as a whole on a variety of measures, including assessments of the degree to which the arts and science categories were differentiated from each other and attributions for the expressed attitude (was it to do with 'the objective facts of the case', the target's personality, or her arts faculty membership?). There were several specific predictions, but here we shall simply mention the two major hypotheses. First, we expected the arts/science categorization to become most salient where both comparative and normative fit were maximized, that is in the consistent/conflict condition (where the three science students emphasized hard work, and the three arts students prioritized their social life). Second, we hypothesized that the social categorization of students into arts and science groups in these circumstances would help to explain their attitudes, producing attributions to the category membership *as an aspect of the person* (i.e., internal rather than external in traditional attribution theory terms; see Oakes, 1987 for more detailed discussion of this aspect of the study).

These hypotheses received comprehensive support. The most relevant findings were that the target was categorized as more similar to the other arts students and different from the science students (i.e., stereotyped as

Table 5.1 Pattern of stimulus individuals' attitudes used to manipulate comparative and normative fit in Oakes et al. (1991, Experiment 2)

Conditions	Stimulus individuals					
	Science				Arts	
	1(M)	2(F)	3(F)	4(F)	5(M)	6(F)
Consistent/consensus	A	A	A	A	A	A
Consistent/conflict	S	S	S	A	A	A
Consistent/deviance	S	S	S	A	S	S
Inconsistent/consensus	S	S	S	S	S	S
Inconsistent/conflict	A	A	A	S	S	S
Inconsistent/deviance	A	A	A	S	A	A

A = arts stereotypic script (pro-'social life'); S = science stereotypic script (pro-'hard work')
M = Male; F = Female
Stimulus person 4, an arts faculty member, is the target individual in every condition. The consistency variable is defined in terms of the behaviour of this person.
(From Oakes et al., 1991, table 3)

an arts student), and expected to like the former more and the latter less in the consistent/ conflict condition, indicating increased intercategory differentiation between the arts and science categories under these conditions. Further, the target's attitude was explained more in terms of her arts faculty membership in the consistent/conflict condition, her personality in the inconsistent/deviance condition, and externally in the consensus conditions (all as predicted). Attribution to social category membership in consistent/conflict did seem to refer to an 'internal' (i.e., of the person) rather than external (e.g., social pressure) locus of causality as much as did personality attributions in inconsistent/deviance. In summary, it was where input fitted the comparative relations *and* the stereotypical content specified by the arts/science categorization that it properly explained and gave meaning to what subjects observed, and so became salient.

The first study also showed that a male target was stereotyped (selectively) more as a male under conflict conditions where three males disagreed with three females than under other conditions. Both these studies illustrate that social category salience depends upon intergroup differences being perceived as larger than intragroup differences.

A comparative fit principle also predicts that intergroup comparisons tend to make social identity salient whilst intragroup comparisons tend to make personal identity salient (Turner et al., 1987, pp. 48–49). A number of studies have reported supportive evidence (e.g., Abrams and Hogg, 1987; Dion, Earn and Yee, 1978; Gaertner et al., 1989; Haslam and Turner, 1992, 1993; Hensley and Duval, 1976; Hogg and Turner, 1987; Oakes, 1987; Oakes et al., 1991; Wilder, 1984; Wilder and Shapiro, 1984; Wilder and Thompson, 1988). We shall look at some of the relevant findings in more detail in chapter 6, where variations in the expected level of self-categorization are used to predict stereotypic assimilation and contrast. In chapter 7, we shall present other supportive data showing that the outgroup homogeneity effect can be re-interpreted in these terms (i.e., as a consequence of the comparative basis of self-categorization). There is also support for the general prediction in the classic intergroup literature on the role of a common enemy, intergroup relations or social conflict in creating a sense of 'we-ness' in the group (McDougall, 1921; Oakes, 1987; Sherif, 1967; Turner 1981, 1982).

The importance of the normative aspect of fit is also evident in recent work investigating the conditions and processes of stereotype change that we discussed in chapter 3. For example, Rothbart and John (1985) discuss the conditions under which contact between groups can influence stereotypes. They suggest that the association of experience with the social category rather than with individuals is important (see also R. J.

Brown and Turner, 1981; Hewstone and R. J. Brown, 1986), and predict that 'pairing an individual with a social category is determined by the degree to which the individual's attributes match those of the category' (pp. 89–90). Rothbart emphasizes that this matching occurs in terms of the social stereotype of a group rather than 'objective' defining attributes of the category (e.g., morphology, skin colour; see Rothbart and Lewis, 1988, p. 862). Thus, he argues, the more generally prototypical of a category a representative appears to be, the more their behaviour has potential to influence the group stereotype. To test these ideas Rothbart and Lewis (1988, Experiment 3) presented subjects with information of varying prototypicality about individual fraternity members. They found, as predicted, that subjects' tendency to generalize a target behaviour to the group as a whole increased as the prototypicality (i.e., degree of normative fit to the category) of the presented individual increased.

Fiske and her colleagues also discuss normative factors influencing whether or not input is perceived as fitting a social categorization. In Fiske and Neuberg's model, fit is determined by the extent to which a target's attributes are consistent with a category label. Fiske et al. (1987) report studies in which subjects were presented with stimulus individuals depicted by occupational category labels and a number of attributes under conditions designed to elicit either relatively attribute-oriented or relatively category-based processing. For example, in the consistent condition subjects might encounter a politician described as selfish, power-hungry, pragmatic, opinionated and smiley. An example of a stimulus person in the inconsistent condition might be a doctor described as bored, obedient, unenterprising, uneducated and efficient. As predicted, it was found that impression formation was particularly category-based in the consistent conditions, and more attribute-oriented in inconsistent conditions. There is, then, consistent evidence that a match between the meaning of a category and stimulus information is an important determinant of category salience and hence of stereotyping.

Note, however, that our results in the arts/science faculty study clearly indicated an *interactive* effect of the normative and comparative aspects of fit. The target's attitudes were equally consistent with the arts faculty stereotype across all three consistent conditions. The analyses of both Rothbart and Fiske would predict category salience here, but our findings were that, in general, the target's arts identity was no more salient in the consistent/consensus and consistent/deviance conditions (where there was low comparative fit) than it was in inconsistent conditions.

What needs to be emphasized is that in our view the relationship between attribute dimensions and categories is not fixed but highly dependent upon the comparative context (Haslam, Turner, Oakes, McGarty and Hayes, 1992). For example, taking a radical feminist position may be perceived as stereotypically 'female' under some conditions (e.g., at a trades union conference; in comparison with men) but roundly rejected as in any way definitive of 'women' under others (e.g., at a mothers' group; in comparison with lesbian separatists; David and Turner, 1992). Thus, we do not define normative fit for social categories as a matching of fixed individual attributes with a category (cf. Rothbart and John, 1985; Fiske et al., 1987) – a given individual attribute could, in principle, match any number of categories. For us, social categorization is about moving to a *different level of abstraction in the construal of social behaviour*, and this involves an understanding of comparative relations and normative factors in a complex interaction with each other.

The key point is that content-matching is not passive. There is no one-to-one correspondence between the long-term knowledge we have about what different kinds of groups are like and the actual social category which is constructed to represent them in a given setting. Directional differences between people are observed on specific content dimensions, and we selectively construct a meaningfully matching category. The meaning of the salient social categorization will vary to reflect the content of the diagnostic differences between groups in specific contexts (Ford and Stangor, 1992). The content of categories is selectively varied to match what is being represented in terms of our background theories and knowledge. It is therefore not a fixed category content being applied: the stereotype content is selectively constructed to describe, make sense of and rationalize the context-specific differences observed, to differentiate the groups meaningfully in terms of the interplay between background knowledge and immediate data (as in Oakes et al., 1991, Experiment 1).

Illustrations of this point are provided by two studies (see also chapters 6 and 7). Haslam et al. (1992) showed that the content of the stereotype of Americans (what Americans are like) varied significantly from the beginning to the end of the 1991 Gulf War and as a function of the groups which comprised the frame of reference. For example, during the war, when the frame of reference encouraged comparison with the Soviet Union Americans were seen as aggressive, but when it also encouraged comparison with Iraq Americans were seen as less aggressive. Inclusion of Iraq in the frame of reference also increased the perceived arrogance of Americans at the beginning of the war but reduced it at the end of the war. At one time, compared to one group, being American meant one thing; at another time or compared to another group, being American meant something else. In an outgroup homogeneity study

(Haslam, Oakes, Turner and McGarty, 1993b), Australians judged on their own (by Australians) are seen as happy-go-lucky, straightforward and sportsmanlike; judged in the context of Americans (where perceived ingroup homogeneity increased), they are seen as even more sportsmanlike but less happy-go-lucky, and a new trait also makes its appearance, pleasure-loving.

Another way to approach variable category content is through the idea of prototypicality. We can think of a social category as being defined by the individual member who best represents it, the member who is most prototypical (see chapter 4). Meta-contrast predicts that the internal structure of social categories will vary with the social context within which the group is defined. Social categories are not defined by a fixed prototype (nor a fixed set of exemplars), but vary in the relative prototypicality of their members as a function of context (cf. Barsalou, 1987). This derivation is easily demonstrated (Turner and Oakes, 1989; see chapter 4). It can be shown, for example, (in research on group polarization) that as a group becomes more extreme in an intergroup context, its more extreme members will gain in relative prototypicality over more moderate ones. There is a growing body of data supporting this analysis (see Turner, 1991).

The implications for stereotype content are simple and direct. Since the internal structure of a social category, the relative representativeness of members, naturally varies with the comparative context, these aspects of its stereotypical content will also vary likewise. As more extreme members become more representative, or as minimally prototypical members in one context become maximally representative in another, or as different dimensions of social comparison become relevant, redefining the basis of relative prototypicality, the judgement of the category as a whole will change. The same social categories can in fact have opposite meanings depending on context (Hogg, Turner and Davidson, 1990).

Comparative and normative fit are therefore interactive and inseparable. A fitting category must optimize meta-contrast on the right dimensions and the differences which optimize such contrast define category content. The content of a stereotype is not a fixed set of attributes applied in an all-or-none manner, but is shaped selectively by the context of its application.

It should be clear from these points that our analysis of fit as a determinant of categorization does not imply that particular categorical representations are demanded by particular stimuli, and thus that there is not necessarily a one-to-one relationship between a given context and a given categorical representation. For example, a given pattern of agreement and disagreement amongst six men arguing about the importance of football versus classical music in the course of world history might be perceived as fitting a class-based categorization for some perceivers, a 'jock'/intellectual grouping for others, or perhaps even a straight/gay distinction for some. We quoted Medin and Wattenmaker earlier in this chapter: categorization reflects an '*interaction* of intelligent systems with aspects of their perceptual world' (1987, p. 50). The 'intelligent system', the person, is always contributing as much to categorization as is the external world, and one implication of this is that categorization, like other social-cognitive products such as attitudes and prejudices, is very open to social influence. There is not one 'right' way to categorize in social interaction, and the way we choose will be strongly influenced by our own social identity and associated norms and values (McGarty and Turner, 1992; Turner et al., in press).

In summary, our analysis of social category activation emphasizes the *context-dependence* of all social perception and judgement. As determined by meta-contrast, categorization processes always reflect the stimulus context as a whole rather than any one stimulus in isolation. We know that meaning depends on context, and categorization is able to fulfil its meaning-giving function in perception by representing stimuli-in-context. It may be, in part, a failure to understand this context-dependence which has led us to the view that individual personality represents accuracy (Brewer, 1988; Fiske and Neuberg, 1990), a 'standard' in comparison to which the outcome of social categorization (stereotyping) is a distortion. Taking this perspective on the arts/science faculty study, the highly individualized perceptions of the target in the inconsistent/deviance condition are in some sense 'correct', whereas those in the consistent/conflict condition (where the arts/science categorization was most salient) are distorted, overgeneralized. In contrast, we would argue that both images of the target rely on context for their validity, and that the variation in impressions formed reflects the adaptiveness and sensitivity of the categorization process.

Overview

In this chapter we closed in on the process at the heart of social stereotyping: categorization. We asked what its purpose is, and whether or not its characterization as an information reduction mechanism, which is so central to the view of stereotypes as distortions of reality, was defensible. We have put our view that this is not the purpose of categorization.

Rather, its purpose is to bring together stored knowledge and current input in a form which both makes sense of the world and facilitates our goals within it. It is the goal- and context-dependence of this elaborative process, the fact that it operates on selective levels of abstraction and selective dimensions, that allows perceptual selectivity.

We have portrayed social categorization as a sensitive, dynamic process of imputing meaning to action. Through processes determined by relative accessibilitiy and fit, it selectively represents social interaction at the appropriate level of abstraction. Building on the ideas presented in chapter 4 about the psychological reality and distinctiveness of the social group, we have developed the argument that some social interaction is most appropriately represented by social categories, and we have defined the conditions under which this is the case.

Our argument thus far indicates no *necessary* basis on which stereotypes distort reality. Of course, stereotyping (as other forms of person perception) can be a route to overgeneralization and other distortions, but we have argued that it is not *by definition* distorted simply because it represents people as other than unique individuals. To reach this point we have had to examine important assumptions about (a) the psychological reality of the group and the apparently privileged position of personality in defining the 'true' person, and (b) the purpose of categorization processes in perception. Having done that, we argue that people are group members as much as they are individual personalities, and that social categorization and stereotyping are the means by which we are able to apprehend that fact. But we have not yet examined the outcome of that categorization process. Recall that the cognitive analysis of stereotyping began with Tajfel's demonstration that categorization produces the *accentuation* of intragroup similarities and intergroup differences. It leads us to perceive people as if they are more similar and different than they *really* are. In the next chapter we present ideas and data relevant to this aspect of the argument that stereotyping necessarily distorts reality.

Suggested Further Reading and References

The classic paper by Bruner (1957) should be read by anyone who has not yet had that pleasure. The chapters edited by Neisser (1987a) are a good source of current developments in the cognitive literature, as is the paper by Medin (1989). The approach to categorization outlined here was first published in Oakes and Turner (1990), and the study discussed in some detail towards the end of the chapter can be found in Oakes et al. (1991). It is also worth reading Fiske and Neuberg (1990) for a clear exposition of an alternative, cognitive miser type of analysis.

Bruner, J. S. (1957) On Perceptual Readiness. *Psychological Review*, 64, 123–152.

Fiske, S. T. and Neuberg, S. L. (1990) A continuum of impression formation, from category-based to individuating processes: Influences of information and motivation on attention and interpretation. In M. P. Zanna (Ed.) *Advances in Experimental Social Psychology* (vol. 23). New York: Random House.

Medin, D. L. (1989) Concepts and conceptual structure. *American Psychologist*, 44, 1469–1481.

Neisser, U. (1987) (ed.) *Concepts and Conceptual Development: Ecological and Intellectual Factors in Categorization.* Cambridge: Cambridge University Press. (a)

Oakes, P. J. and Turner, J. C. (1990) Is limited information processing capacity the cause of social stereotyping? In W. Stroebe and M. Hewstone (Eds) *European Review of Social Psychology* (vol. 1). Chichester, UK: Wiley.

Oakes, P. J., Turner, J. C. and Haslam, S. A. (1991) Perceiving people as group members: The role of fit in the salience of social categorizations. *British Journal of Social Psychology*, 30, 125–144.

6

The Social-Contextual Basis of Stereotypic Accentuation

In the preceding chapter we addressed the question of *why* people categorize. In terms of the analysis that we have developed, it is suggested that a group of individuals might be stereotyped in terms of a particular social categorization (as Irish, say) not because this is cognitively economical but because groups are real and in some contexts it is entirely appropriate to perceive and interact with people in terms of their group membership. As an illustration of this point, imagine that you are one of the people sitting in the foreground of the photograph below. This was taken during a demonstration held against the Thatcher government's Poll Tax in London in April 1990. In all probability, you would tend to think of one of the policemen in the picture *as a policeman* not because to consider him as an individual would be too demanding but because he has contextually important features which arise *solely* from the fact that he is a member of the police force. He might drag you away and lock you up not because he is Constable X *rather than* Constable Y, but because in this context he *shares* a number of attributes with Constable Y (the power to arrest you, possession of a truncheon, and a presumed antipathy to demonstrators). Here, then, you would engage in stereotypic perception not because it is more economical than individuated perception but because it is more valid.

However, even if the above analysis is accepted, there are other issues of validity associated with stereotypic perception. These concern the *outcome* of the stereotyping process in accentuated judgements. For Lippman, G. Allport and Tajfel alike, one of the defining features of stereotypes was that they *misrepresented* reality through the process of *exaggeration* – a view exemplified in G. Allport's definition of a stereotype as 'an exaggerated belief associated with a category' (1954, p. 191). From this perspective category-based accentuation involves distortion

Riot police charging Poll Tax demonstrators, Trafalgar Square, London, April 1990
Photo Tim Marshall

because 'within-category similarity is perceived to be greater than it actually is . . . and between-category differences are perceived to be greater than they actually are' (Stephan, 1985, p. 611; see also Eiser, 1990, p. 49; Tajfel, 1981a, pp. 150–151). Thus in Tajfel and Wilkes' (1963a) experiment when the shortest of the long lines had been categorized as 'long', it was judged to be longer *than it really was*. Similarly, your judgement of the policeman in the photograph may lead you to see him as more aggressive than an objective personality assessment would indicate.

The consequences of this view were elaborated by Stephan in an analysis of the two principal components of accentuation (assimilation and contrast):

The implications of assimilation and contrast for stereotyping are as important as they are obvious. Assimilation and contrast lead to distortions in the processing of information about social groups that facilitate the formation of stereotypes, promote negative attitudes between groups, facilitate the generation of inappropriate expectations, lead to the dehumanization of outgroup members and hinder attempts to change stereotypes. (p. 611)

Similarly, Krueger and Rothbart (1990) have commented:

One important consequence of categorizing people into groups is the exaggeration of perceived intergroup differences ... This tendency contributes to unrealistic intergroup attitudes, as it emphasises differences rather than similarities and may thus exacerbate social conflict. (p. 651)

In this chapter we will examine the foundations of this analysis in previous research and theory before providing a new perspective on the psychological basis and validity of accentuation.

Theories of Accentuation

Although accentuation effects are clearly central to stereotyping, their theoretical analysis has not been confined to literature dealing with this topic. Indeed, because they are central to a variety of psychological effects, accounts of accentuation-related phenomena have been provided by researchers interested in a range of topics including prejudice and both physical (or 'absolute') and social judgement. Broadly speaking though, four distinct types of explanation can be identified: those provided by personality, involvement, psychophysical and social cognitive theories (for reviews see Eiser and Stroebe, 1972; Eiser, 1990; Haslam, 1990). We will consider these separately before presenting an analysis from the perspective of self-categorization theory.

Personality Theories

As we noted in chapter 2, in *The Authoritarian Personality* Adorno and his colleagues suggested that the classic authoritarian could be identified by, amongst other things, 'the dichotomous handling of social relations as manifested especially in the formation of stereotypes and of ingroup–outgroup cleavages' (Adorno et al., 1950, p. 971). Following this work, a number of personality theorists argued that accentuation effects reflect the distinct psychological profiles of those who are inclined to hold and use stereotypes.

A large body of research appeared to support this analysis. This indicated that people who have extreme positions on an issue (i.e., extremists) are particularly prone to making extreme, polarized judgements which accentuate intercategory differences (for reviews see Hamilton, 1968; O'Donovan, 1965). In particular, these effects were observed in a famous series of social judgemental studies conducted by Sherif and Hovland (e.g., 1961) in which subjects had to sort statements into categories of differing extremity. Although Sherif and Hovland actually rejected personality theories, their data showed that compared to less involved (typically moderate) subjects, people who were highly involved in particular social issues (typically extremists; e.g., pro-Negroes in issues of race; Hovland and Sherif, 1952) tended (a) to assign more statements to extreme categories and (b) to place many more items into categories with which they disagreed (in the authors' terms these subjects thus tended to have a larger *latitude of rejection*).

Similar findings emerged from a study reported by Pettigrew et al. (1958) in which they asked South African subjects to judge the racial identity of people in photographs where in some instances this identity was unclear because targets of different race were presented to different eyes. Amongst other things, it was found that, compared to subjects in other racial groups, prejudiced white subjects were more likely to judge the people they saw in these combined images (referred to as manifest fusions) to be (a) members of black African or white European rather than other racial groups and (b) as members of black African rather than white European groups.

As a corollary to these effects, several studies also identified a distinct response pattern associated with moderation or neutrality. Manis (1960, 1961) found that college students with neutral attitudes towards fraternities tended to assimilate all attitude communications on this topic to their own position (see also Manis, 1964). Similarly, in reviewing data collected during the 1956 United States presidential election, Sherif and Hovland (1961) noted that subjects holding middle-ground positions generally perceived all political statements to be less extreme than did other subjects. In summary, relative to extremists, moderate or neutral subjects were typically observed (a) to *assimilate* more stimuli to their own position (leading to a larger *latitude of acceptance*) and (b) to *reduce* the differences between stimuli representative of different extremes. More recent confirmation of this pattern has been reported by Romer (1983) in a study of attitudes to abortion.

Interpreting such findings from the perspective of personality theory, Brim and Hoff (1957) argued that extremists had both a greater 'desire for certainty' and a more intense need to 'tidy up' the stimulus field than did moderates. Similarly, Pettigrew et al. (1958) suggested that the pattern of judgement exhibited by their white subjects could be interpreted as a manifestation of 'intolerance of ambiguity'.

Although a number of studies established a relationship between particular personality variables and patterns of accentuation, the findings all tended to be rather ambiguous. One reason for this was that where such relationships were observed they tended to be quite weak (e.g., Feldman and Hilterman, 1975; Malhotra, Jain and Pinson, 1983; Warr and Coffman, 1970) and to be observed on only a small subset of measures (e.g., White and Harvey, 1965; Larsen, 1971). Furthermore, the correlational nature of these observations precluded conclusive causal analysis. Indeed, the explanatory constructs that were used by researchers typically involved a high degree of circularity. White and Harvey (1965, p. 338), for example, partly defined the personality variable 'concreteness-abstractness' as 'a greater tendency toward extreme and highly evaluative judgements', and so it is hardly surprising that this variable was found to be related to judgemental extremity. An additional problem was that in studies where only some subjects made polarized judgements of stimulus items (e.g., Hovland and Sherif, 1952; Sellitz, Edrich and Cook, 1965; Zavalloni and Cook, 1965) those who did so were the individuals that personality theories would predict to be the *least* disposed to such behaviour (e.g., 'liberal' pro-Negroes rather than 'authoritarian' racists).

Aside from these points, a range of empirical findings have argued directly against the view that personality factors are the key determinants of inter-item accentuation. In a replication of Pettigrew et al.'s (1958) study conducted in Austin (Texas), Lent (1970) found that levels of accentuation were essentially the same across subject groups who had different levels of intolerance of ambiguity, ethnocentrism, and strength of attitude. In a more extensive study, Warr and Coffman (1970) conducted a series of four experiments in which subjects performed up to ten social judgemental tasks. Their aim was to develop a model which would clarify the relationship between a range of variables and patterns of judgemental extremity. The resulting model indicated that the role of interindividual variation in levels of authoritarianism, dogmatism, and integrative complexity was less important than inter-task variability in involvement – involvement here being defined as 'a compound of construct relevance and stimulus importance' (p. 108; cf. Tajfel, 1957).

Involvement Theories

As in the mainstream study of stereotyping, one significant failing of personality-based explanations of judgemental accentuation was that these phenomena appeared to be the outcome of processes *common to all perceivers* rather than a select few. Consistent with this conclusion as well as Warr and Coffman's (1970) findings, one very influential account suggested that accentuation was a product of subjects' *involvement* in a particular judgemental task.

Early support for this analysis was provided by proponents of the 'New Look' – the research movement which gathered force during the 1940s and 1950s and sought to challenge established psychophysical theory by demonstrating that psychological processes responded to motivational concerns. Particularly influential in the study of social perception was the research of Jerome Bruner and his colleagues which examined the manner in which perceptual processes were affected by the *values and needs* of perceivers. For example, in one widely cited study Bruner and Goodman (1947) asked ten-year-olds to make judgements of the size of coins and valueless grey cardboard discs by varying the amount of light projected on a glass screen in a box. It was found that although the coins and discs were actually of equal size, subjects typically judged the coins to be larger. Two further findings confirmed the relationship between this effect and the children's subjective needs: (a) the overestimation of size was generally greater the more valuable the coin, and (b) children from poorer families always overestimated coin size more than those from 'well-to-do' backgrounds.

On the basis of this and other similar studies which involved the judgement of a *series* of physical stimuli, Tajfel (1957) forwarded the general proposition that 'the relevance of a series of stimuli [to subjects] is related to an emphasis of the differences between them' (p. 194). Moreover, Tajfel argued that this principle could be extended to account for similar effects in the judgement of *social* stimuli. Anticipating his later work (e.g., Tajfel and Wilkes, 1963a), he remarked:

> When judgements concerning some quantifiable or ratable aspects of stimuli which fall into distinct categories are called for, differences in value or relevance cannot fail to influence the quantitative judgements in the direction of sharpening the objectively existing differences between the stimuli. (1957, p. 202)

Later, in a systematic elaboration of this argument, Tajfel (1959) suggested that the accentuation of interstimulus differences was potentially adaptive in improving the acuity of discrimination between valued and non-valued categories. This position was consistent with the results of a famous experiment conducted in Atlanta by Secord et al. (1956). They asked forty-seven high school students and eleven members of B'nai B'rith ('a Jewish organization which stresses tolerance and brotherhood") to rate photographs of five whites and ten blacks (who ranged along a continuum of skin colour) on measures of physiognomic and personality stereotyping (p. 78). It was found that compared to neutral judges, both pro- and anti-Negro subjects (for whom the judgement was more relevant) accentuated the stereotypically negroid features of Negro photographs (although the difference between neutral and pro-Negro judges was non-significant). However, with respect to personality stereotyping, relative to neutral subjects, pro-Negro judges de-emphasized the predominantly negative Negro stereotype, while anti-Negroes enhanced this unfavourable characterization. Both effects clearly reflected the particular values of the subjects.

A study conducted by Tajfel and Wilkes (1963b) provided more direct support for Tajfel's claim that the accentuation of differences between stimuli was related to their relevance for the judge. In this experiment subjects first rated photographs with respect to ten attributes of their choice. At a later date they rated new photographs using the first and last four attributes from the initial ratings. Tajfel and Wilkes anticipated that these two sets of items should differ in terms of their importance for subjects and thus that greater accentuation of inter-stimulus differences would be apparent in ratings made on the first four dimensions. Their findings confirmed this hypothesis and subsequent studies have shown that it is a robust effect (e.g., Ward, 1965; Judd and Harackiewicz, 1980; Judd and Krosnick, 1982).

In a slightly different manner to Tajfel (1957), Sherif and Hovland (1961) also looked to the role of subjects' involvement in a particular judgement in order to explain the effects observed in their own studies. Their 'assimilation-contrast model' (or *social judgement-involvement theory*) rested upon two interrelated assertions. First, it was argued that judges assimilate (i.e., displace towards their own position) stimuli with which they agree (i.e., those that fall within their latitude of acceptance) and contrast (displace away from their own position) stimuli with which they disagree (those that fall in their latitude of rejection). Second, the extent of judges' latitudes of acceptance and rejection was seen to be determined by their involvement in the issue with respect to which stimuli are judged: greater involvement leading to a smaller latitude of acceptance and a larger latitude of rejection. Sherif, Sherif and Nebergall (1965) thus proposed that:

> The crucial determinant of the relationship between extremeness of stand and the pattern of evaluations is not extremeness *as such*, but rather the high probability that the individual extreme in his position will be highly involved in it. (p. 233)

Several experiments conducted in light of this analysis appeared to confirm that it was subjects' involvement and not their extremity that led them to accentuate inter-stimulus differences. Prothro (1955, 1957) reported two studies in which Arab subjects rated statements concerning either (a) an identified group (Jews or Arabs) or (b) a non-specified group. He found that even though all subjects were extremely anti-Jewish and pro-Arab, they exhibited relative accentuation of the former statements only where there was strong personal involvement with the *particular* item sorted.

Psychophysical Theories

Whilst involvement-based theories were largely developed with the specific goal of addressing issues of *social judgement* (i.e., relating to judgements about people and things associated with them), a number of psychophysical theories of so-called 'absolute' judgement were also adapted for this purpose (see Eiser and Stroebe, 1972). And where theories of social judgement have typically been used to account for the effects of a perceiver's own position and values, psychophysical theories have typically been developed in order to explain effects associated with changes in a perceiver's *frame of reference*.

Particularly important in this regard was Helson's (1948) *adaptation level theory*. This proposed that judgements of stimuli are made in relation to a psychological point to which the perceiver has adapted (in general terms this being the mean value of other stimuli to which he or she has been exposed). Accordingly, objects of moderate weight (e.g., 500 grams) will appear heavier to a watchmaker accustomed to handling light objects than to a professional weightlifter used to heavy ones (Tresselt, 1948). In an attempt to generalize from this theory to the analysis of attitude judgement, Fehrer (1952) presented subjects with statements drawn from a common pool (Thurstone's 'Attitudes to War'). These statements were ordered in eleven categories ranging from 0 (pacifistic) to 10 (militaristic). In two experimental conditions subjects were presented either with militaristic items containing statements only in the range 3 to 10 or pacifistic statements ranging from 0 to 7. A control group was presented with the complete range. In support of predictions derived from adaptation level theory, Fehrer found that compared to this control group, the items common to all scales (i.e., 4 to 7) were judged to be more militaristic by subjects initially given the pacifistic range, and more pacifistic by those primed with the relatively militaristic statements.

Adaptation level theory also formed the basis of more recent work which has investigated the relationship between judges' frame of reference and their perception of the extent to which judged stimuli are (a) attractive and (b) similar to their own position (reviewed by Brewer, 1979). Mascaro and Graves (1973) found that the same target person was perceived as more or less similar to a judge and more or less favourably as a function of the character of a previously presented person. Thus a target of 'medium' similarity to the judge was perceived as more similar and also liked more where the judge had previously been exposed to an extremely dissimilar person. However, this same target was seen as less similar and liked less where the initially presented person had been highly similar to the judge.

In a study reported by Hensley and Duval (1976), male college students were asked to express their opinions on justice in a hypothetical court case. They then received a graphical presentation of the supposed opinions of the ten subjects present. Each subject was led to believe that he was person G, who always appeared in a cluster of eight subjects (Group S). Subjects D and E (Group O) were placed apart from the cluster within a range of two to ten inches, the precise distance varying over five conditions with increasing distance between the clusters indicating increasing opinion dissimilarity. As the distance between the two clusters increased, so did the perceived similarity within group S, subjects' liking for Group S, and subjects' perception of Group S's opinions

Table 6.1 Judges' perceptions of their similarity to, their liking for, and the correctness of, Group S and Group O as a function of the extremity of Group O

| | *Condition* | | | | |
	1	*2*	*3*	*4*	*5*
Similarity to S	30	33	37	46	54
Similarity to O	28	28	27	11	5
Liking for S	37	31	33	36	47
Liking for O	20	16	19	9	8
Correctness of S	33	39	38	50	53
Correctness of O	24	22	23	13	7

Higher numbered conditions indicate that Group O is more distant from the judge.

The results show that as Group O becomes more distant from the judge it is perceived to be less similar and correct and is liked less, whilst at the same time Group S comes to be perceived as more similar and correct and is liked more.

(Adapted from Hensley and Duval, 1976, tables 1, 2 and 3; note that conditions are numbered differently here. Copyright 1976 by the American Psychological Association. Adapted by permission.)

as correct. On the other hand, with this increase in distance, liking for and perceived correctness of Group O decreased. These results are summarized in table 6.1.

Wilder and Thompson (1988) note that the effects observed by Hensley and Duval did not vary in a regular fashion across conditions. It was only the comparison between the two smallest distance conditions on the one hand and the three largest on the other that produced significant differences in perceived liking, similarity and perceived correctness. In other words, subjects appeared either to assimilate Group O towards their own group *or* to contrast it away from their own group. This pattern was confirmed in Wilder and Thompson's own experiments. These used a mock jury paradigm in which subjects judged the decisions of other groups concerning damages awarded to plaintiffs. In Experiment 1, a group which proposed an award of damages moderately different from that proposed by the subjects was judged either on its own or in the context of a third group proposing an extremely different award. The measure of most interest related to the displacement of the moderately different target group – this being either towards the judges' own position (i.e., assimilation) or away from it (contrast). The principal finding was that where there was no extreme comparison group, the target group was contrasted away from the judges' own position. On the other hand, where the extreme group was included, the target group was assimilated. This finding was elaborated in two further studies.

While these findings were consistent with the view that a judge's frame of reference is an important determinant of judgement, they served to question the assertion of adaptation level theorists that there might be a simple one-to-one relationship between features of this comparative frame (e.g., its range) and stimulus displacement. That is, it appeared not to be the case that stimuli were assimilated and contrasted simply as a function of their absolute difference from a *single* position (typically, the subject's own). A similar conclusion was reached by Brewer (1979), who also noted that assimilation and contrast effects of the type observed by Hensley and Duval (1976) appeared to derive from the salience of the division between ingroup and outgroup categories.

A study conducted by Manis, Nelson and Shedler (1988) provided some further insights into the processes by which stimuli are displaced as a function of alterations to the frame of reference. These workers formulated a 'discrepancy hypothesis' which asserted that assimilation and contrast are in part a function of the discrepancy between presented information and the background provided by a judge's prior stereotypical beliefs. In their study distinct stereotypes of patients from two hospitals were induced by linking pathological and non-pathological word definitions to patients from each hospital. So, for example, a patient from Central Hospital defined 'cushion' as 'to sleep on a pillow of God's sheep', while a Metropolitan Hospital patient defined it as 'a padded device for comfort'. Across a number of conditions the degree of pathology associated with each hospital's patients (i.e., the extremity of hospital stereotypes) was manipulated by altering the mix of pathological and non-pathological definitions attributed to their patients. Subjects then had to evaluate which of a pair of mid-scale (i.e., medium pathology) definitions was the more pathological, one definition being attributed to a patient from each hospital.

Manis and his colleagues found that judgements of these mid-scale definitions varied as a function of the extremity of the initially induced hospital stereotypes: where a hospital's patients were initially understood to be extremely pathological mid-scale definitions were contrasted from the hospital stereotype, yet where a moderate stereotype was induced mid-scale definitions were assimilated to that moderate position. In this manner definitions of the same absolute degree of pathology were seen to be less pathological in the former context than the latter. In light of these findings Manis et al., like Wilder and Thompson (1988; see also Kahneman and Miller, 1986), concluded that assimilation and contrast effects are determined, at least in part, by the *discrepancy* between the primary stimuli being judged (e.g., group decisions, word definitions) and other salient social elements (e.g., information about other groups, stereotypical beliefs).

Along similar lines to adaptation-level theory, other psychophysical theories of judgement have implied that judgements are made relative to the midpoint (rather than the mean) of a judge's frame of reference. These ideas are central to Volkmann's (1951) rubber-band model and Upshaw's (1962) variable perspective model. Refinements to this approach have also been suggested by Parducci (e.g., 1963). His *range-frequency model* suggests that rather than judgement being determined by either the *range* of salient stimuli or the *relative frequency* of those stimuli (which affect the median and mean values respectively), it is a product of a compromise between these features. As summarized by van der Pligt, Eiser and Spears (1987) this model proposes that:

> Judges attempt to 'compromise' between the tendency to judge ... different response categories to refer to roughly equal proportions of the stimulus range and the tendency to use ... categories with roughly equal frequency. Thus judgements of individual stimuli are influenced by (a) implicit comparisons with other stimuli and (b) the tendency to distribute responses fairly evenly over the categories provided. (pp. 269–270)

This theory was consistent with findings from a series of experiments reported by van der Pligt et al. (1987). Questionnaire respondents rated the contribution which a range of technologies (e.g., nuclear power, coal, solar and 'other') should make to total energy production. It was found that judges' approval for any one energy source was determined in part by the number of response alternatives with which they were presented: the more alternatives, the lower was the approval for any single source. In Experiment 3, for example, when only nuclear power was rated, subjects suggested it should meet 28 per cent of energy demands, but this figure was only 16 per cent where respondents were presented with eight alternatives. Like the findings from earlier studies (e.g., Fehrer, 1952), these experiments can thus be taken to suggest that there is no such thing as an *absolute* representation of social stimulus reality, since all forms of judgement (from ratings of other stimuli to expressions of one's own beliefs) are made relative to, and critically shaped by, the context of salient alternatives (see Eiser and Stroebe, 1972; Tajfel, 1972; Sherif, 1935, p. 374; van der Pligt et al., 1987, p. 278).

Social Cognitive Theories

Although the social judgement-involvement model seemed to provide a better explanation of the relationship between extremism and accentuation than did personality theories, it too had certain shortcomings. First, as some personality theorists argued (e.g., White and Harvey, 1965, p. 334), because Sherif and Hovland's analysis was tested using between-subjects designs (where groups of involved and non-involved subjects were compared, but there was no direct manipulation of level of involvement within *the same* subjects), the influence of personality factors was not ruled out. Second, and more importantly, the theory could not explain why accentuation seemed in a number of cases to depend upon *which* extreme of a given judgemental dimension judges supported. To deal with this problem, Eiser (1971, 1973) proposed his accentuation theory based on the earlier work of Tajfel (1969, Tajfel and Wilkes, 1963a).

As noted in chapter 3, Tajfel proposed that differences between classes of stimuli would be accentuated where the focal dimension on which those stimuli were judged was perceived to be correlated with a peripheral dimension of classification. He noted that some of the features of stereotypes (primarily their tendency to cluster certain stimuli together and to exaggerate differences between others – as apparent, say, in the stereotypes that 'Jews don't drink' and 'the Irish are whisky-soaked';

G. Allport, 1954, p. 192), could be seen to arise from the stereotyper's belief that two dimensions of categorization (here ethnic group membership and drinking habits) were correlated.

Elaborating on this analysis, Eiser (e.g., 1971) argued that in judgemental tasks the judge's own *agreement* or *disagreement* with attitude statements could function as a correlated cue to differentiation. Extremists should display greater accentuation than moderates, he suggested, because for them the correlation between the position of attitude items and their agreement/disagreement with those items would tend to be higher. (Extremists might tend to agree with all items at one end of the scale and disagree with all items at the other, whereas moderates might tend to agree with statements on both sides of the issue). However, Eiser (e.g., Eiser and van der Pligt, 1984a) goes on to note that *response language* (generally the evaluative connotations of the labels used by the experimenters to identify scale extremes) will affect the extent to which judges will be willing to agree or disagree with items and therefore the extent to which they will categorize on this basis. It is the effect of response language on categorization which explains why typically only subjects identifying with one scale extreme display judgemental polarization. For example, a person who is in favour of drug use is more likely to agree with pro-drug statements and disagree with anti-drug statements and accentuate the differences between them when the pro-drug scale extreme is labelled 'broad-minded' and the anti-drug extreme 'narrow-minded' than when the respective labels are 'irresponsible' and 'responsible' (Eiser and van der Pligt, 1982). On the other hand, someone who was opposed to drug use would display the opposite patterns of agreement and accentuation in both cases. In the earlier findings of one-sided polarizations (e.g., by liberal pro-Negro judges rather than authoritarian racists), Eiser suggests that the scale response language was more positive at one end of the scale than the other, facilitating accentuation by only one group of extremists.

Over the past two decades a considerable amount of research has supported Eiser's theory and it has been widely accepted as an explanation of effects associated with judges' own positions (e.g., Eiser and Mower White, 1975; Eiser and van der Pligt, 1982; van der Pligt and van Dijk, 1979; for reviews see Eiser and van der Pligt 1984a, 1984b). McGarty and Penny (1988), however, have presented a re-interpretation of one-sided polarization effects in terms of *social identity theory*. Noting that attitude statements and rating scale labels are implicitly associated with underlying social categories (i.e., real social groups), the essence of McGarty and Penny's argument has been to suggest that judges will be more likely to seek to differentiate between those categories – and thus display judgemental polarization – where their own position is identified with a favourably-defined pole. It is suggested that by this means those judges who do polarize achieve positive intergroup distinctiveness.

They conducted a study in which judges rated a range of political statements. They established that left-wing terms were evaluated more positively by their subjects than right-wing terms. Consistent with social identity and accentuation theories, it was found that left-wing subjects displayed greater accentuation of the difference between political statements than did right-wing subjects. It was also found that intercategory accentuation was further enhanced by increasing the salience of distinct stimulus categories. This was achieved (a) by identifying the left- and right-wing statements with distinct authors and (b) by providing 'fitting' information (see chapter 5) about the political characteristics of those authors.

These findings were in part replicated by McGarty and Turner (1992). These researchers showed that explicit categorization (in terms of authors) increased accentuation (of interclass differences and intraclass similarities) and that social influence – where subjects were informed that a group of students from the previous year's class had made judgements that were discrepant from their own – reduced it. Interestingly, the effect of fitting information was only apparent where subjects received discrepant feedback. It was as if the meaning of that information became particularly important in encouraging subjects to use the authorship categorization only when they had been made uncertain by reference group influence.

A Self-Categorization Theory of Accentuation

Operationalization and Hypotheses

It can be seen from the foregoing discussion that the primary contribution of latterday judgemental research has been to emphasize both the *normality* and the *contextual basis* of accentuation effects. While stereotyping researchers have accepted for over two decades that accentuation is an outcome of normal, general processes, the context-dependency of these processes has tended to be overlooked. As we noted in chapter 3, until very recently, stereotyping in the cognitive tradition has tended to be conceptualized as the product of hard-wired information-processing biases.

On the other hand, as McGarty and Penny (1988, p. 151) note, judgemental research has tended to neglect the association of accentuation effects with group memberships. For example, the relevance of relations between blacks and whites is particularly striking in the studies reported by Pettigrew et al. (1958) and Secord et al. (1956) but the explanations developed by these researchers attribute very little (if any) direct causal role to these social realities. Notable exceptions to this trend were the Sherifs who argued strongly on the basis of Sherif and Hovland's (e.g., 1961) work that the displacement of stimuli on psychosocial scales 'is a psychological phenomenon ... that rests in the last analysis upon the social actualities of group life and intergroup relationships' (Sherif et al., 1965, p. 245). However the awareness underpinning this conclusion was never integrated in any predictive way with a detailed understanding of accentuation processes. As a consequence (and also reflecting the general tendency of judgement researchers to play down the significance of group processes), it has been little apparent in the body of research that has developed Sherif and Hovland's work.

In contrast, as noted in previous chapters, the starting point of self-categorization theory's analysis of accentuation is an acknowledgment of the social realities of group life and an awareness of their distinct impact upon the psychological processes of individuals. From this perspective we can move towards an understanding of accentuation effects which is consistent with the approach to stereotyping we developed in chapters 4 and 5. Rather than manifestations of distortion, we can begin to see accentuation effects as reflecting real outcomes of the altogether appropriate division of stereotyped stimuli into ingroup and outgroup categories.

In essence, we are suggesting that patterns of accentuation reflect the properties of stimuli that derive from their membership in, or association with, social groups that stand in relation to the stereotyper's own. *Accentuation is a social categorical response to people as members of groups in a social context.* To be more specific, self-categorization theory proposes that patterns of assimilation and contrast relative to the self serve to represent the degree to which a given stimulus is perceived to share (or not share) the same social category membership as the stereotyper.

As a starting point in the elaboration of this argument, let us summarize some of the implications of the ideas presented earlier for the understanding of accentuation. Three central points can be drawn from self-categorization theory and research. First, as an intergroup phenomenon, stereotyping arises from a depersonalizing shift in the level of abstraction of self-categorization such that both the self *and other people* are perceived as group members (Turner, 1982). Second, to the extent that individuals, including the self, are perceived to be members of the same group or social category they will be *psychologically interchange-able* (Turner, 1982). Third, the salience (or current psychological signi-ficance) of social categories is understood to be mediated by the interaction between the perceiver and features of his or her stimulus environment (Oakes, 1987).

Two further arguments, which are central to the analysis of accentua-tion, can be derived from the above points. First, tŏ the extent that a person sees others as members of his or her own social self-category (i.e., as ingroup members) those others will be perceived as similar to the self, and, conversely, to the extent that others are seen as members of a social nonself-category (as outgroup members) they will be perceived as differ-ent from the self. Second, the psychological definition of social categories (in relation to the self) is flexible rather than rigid, because it is deter-mined by social comparisons that are specific to a particular setting (Turner et al., in press; cf. G. Allport, 1954).

By elaborating these principles of social category formation and sali-ence, it is possible to provide a new explanatory, and predictive, model of stereotypic accentuation. The idea that the division of social stimuli into social categories is determined by the principles of comparative fit, through the operation of meta-contrast, is especially relevant. As noted in chapter 4, the principle of meta-contrast specifies degrees of categorical entitativity in a context-sensitive manner, suggesting that:

> Any collection of individuals in a given setting is more likely to categorize themselves as a group (become a psychological group) to the degree that the subjectively perceived differences between them are less than the differ-ences perceived between them and other people (psychologically) present in the setting (i.e., as the ratio of intergroup to intragroup differences increases). (Turner, 1985 p. 101)

The following hypothesis is a corollary of this principle:

> H1 That any stimulus will be perceived to share the same social category membership as a stereotyper to the extent that that stimulus is per-ceived to be less different from the stereotyper's own position than from all others that are psychologically salient for the stereotyper. (Haslam and Turner, 1992, p. 255)

In order to explore some implications of this hypothesis, we can look at calculations of meta-contrast in more detail. Consider a case where a stereotyper (the subject, S) who is moderately left-wing on some political issue is judging a person or statement (the target, T) that is representative of a moderately right-wing position. Imagine too, that as in a typical judgemental task this is done with respect to an seven-point rating scale – where, as Turner (1987c, pp. 81–82) has pointed out, this scale functions as a dimension of social comparison making salient a range of possible responses (the 'o's) each of which could be associated with the position of a particular social group:

$$\text{left-wing} \quad \underset{-3}{\text{o}} \quad \underset{-2}{\text{S}} \quad \underset{-1}{\text{o}} \quad \underset{0}{\text{o}} \quad \underset{+1}{\text{o}} \quad \underset{+2}{\text{T}} \quad \underset{+3}{\text{o}} \quad \text{right-wing}$$

In this situation it is possible, by means of the principle of meta-contrast, to compute the extent to which T should be perceived to share the same category membership as S: here the value of the meta-contrast ratio (MCR) – equal to the mean difference between T and the 'o's divided by the difference between T and S – is 0.6 {[(5 + 3 + 2 + 1 + 1)/5]/4}. In this example, then, the target person should be perceived as representative of a different social category to the stereotyper because the difference between target and stereotyper is greater than the mean difference between the target and all other scale positions (i.e., the value of the MCR is below unity).

Now the *manner* in which the stereotyping process is predicted to reflect the extent of shared identity (or the degree to which stimulus and self are *psychologically interchangeable*) can be stated formally in terms of the following hypothesis:

H2 That stimuli will be *assimilated* to a stereotyper's identity (i.e., displaced towards his or her own position and perceived as more similar to the self) to the extent that they share the same category membership as the stereotyper (i.e., are members of an ingroup). Conversely, it is hypothesized that stimuli will be *contrasted* from the stereotyper's identity (i.e., displaced away from his or her own position and perceived as different from the self) to the extent that they are representative of a nonself-category (i.e., an outgroup). (Haslam and Turner, 1992, p. 255)

In the above example, then, we would expect that having categorized the target (T) as an outgroup member (representative of a nonself-category), the stereotyper (S) would contrast that person from his or her own position. Accordingly, they might be represented as occupying a position of +3 on the judgemental scale. The general principles of both social identity and self-categorization theories might also lead us to expect that on dimensions relevant to that judgement (i.e., on political dimensions) the target would tend to be represented unfavourably (e.g., as reactionary).

Following on from this example, it can be shown that the extent to which any stereotyper and target share identity can be represented in terms of (at least) three variables, these being (a) the extent of the comparative frame of reference (i.e., the number of alternative positions), (b) the position of the stereotyper, and (c) the position of the stereotyped stimulus. This observation is of initial interest given the findings of established judgement research that these three variables are heavily implicated in accentuation phenomena. Furthermore, on the basis of these hypotheses it is possible to *simulate* patterns of accentuation associated with manipulation of these three elements.

Haslam and Turner (1993), discuss patterns of assimilation and contrast associated with simulated manipulations of the second of these elements – the stereotyper's *own position*. As a first stage in this process, figure 6.1 plots levels of shared stereotyper–target identity (i.e., the MCR of T for S) for stereotypers whose own position relative to a frame of reference corresponds (a) to the most extreme position (i.e., S = −5) and (b) to the most moderate position (S = 0).

As can be seen from this figure, two distinctive patterns emerge from such computations. First, to the extent that a stereotyper's own position

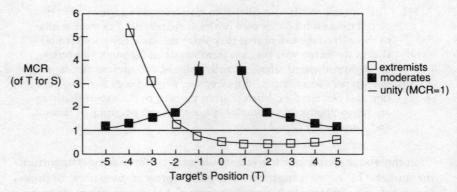

Figure 6.1 Shared stereotyper–target identity for extremists (S = −5) and moderates (S = 0), from Haslam and Turner (1993)

The graph shows that for extremists, compared to moderates, there is greater variation in the shared identity of other targets and that more targets do not share their identity.

is extreme there is greater variability in the degree to which other stimuli share his or her social identity (i.e., there is greater range in the values of the MCR). Second, to the extent that a stereotyper's own position is extreme there are fewer other stimuli that share his or her identity (having an MCR above unity) and more other stimuli that do not share that identity (having an MCR below unity).

In light of the hypothesized link between levels of shared social identity and patterns of assimilation and contrast (H2), these observations lead to the following predictions:

P1   That people whose own position is extreme (i.e., extremists) would tend to display greater assimilation of certain stimuli and greater contrast of others (relative to their own position) than people whose own position is moderate (moderates) – in other words, that extremists would make more polarized judgements.

P2   That extremists would tend to contrast more and assimilate fewer other stimuli (relative to their own position) than moderates.

These predictions are broadly consistent with the body of social judgemental findings associated with differences in own position reviewed earlier in this chapter. In particular, of course, they are supported by Sherif and Hovland's (1961; Hovland and Sherif, 1952; Hovland, Harvey and Sherif, 1957) observation that, relative to moderates, extremists display greater accentuation of the difference between classes of stimuli and also have larger latitudes of rejection and smaller latitudes of acceptance. The predictions are consistent too, with other research which has shown (a) that extremists tend to display both assimilation and contrast of other stimuli relative to the self – leading them to represent the social stimulus domain in a relatively bifurcated ('black and white') manner (Pettigrew et al., 1958, Secord et al., 1956), and (b) that moderates typically display a pattern of general assimilation – leading to a 'greyer' or more homogeneous representation of the stimulus array (Manis, 1960, 1961; Romer, 1983; Weiss, 1959; see also Sherif and Hovland, 1961).

Along similar lines, Haslam and Turner (1992) consider predicted patterns of accentuation associated with simulated manipulations of the stereotyper's *frame of reference*. Figure 6.2 plots values of shared stereotyper–target identity (i.e., the MCR of T for S) as a function of the range of the frame of reference (the number of scale points; N). As this illustrates, the following pattern emerges from calculations of metacontrast: that while the positions of both the stereotyper and target remain unchanged, the extent to which they share social identity increases as the frame of reference extends. Indeed, it can be shown that as

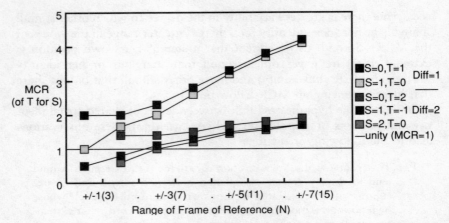

Figure 6.2   Shared stereotyper–target identity as a function of the range of the
frame of reference, from Haslam and Turner (1992, p. 256, reprinted by
permission of John Wiley and Sons, Ltd.)

Lines join points of equal absolute difference (Diff) between target (T) and stereotyper (S).
The graph shows that as the range of the frame of reference extends, a target that is the
same absolute distance from the stereotyper will be perceived to share more identity with
him or her.

N increases, the gradients of the lines on this graph tend towards a
constant (shared identity increases at a uniform rate as the frame of
reference extends) where the absolute difference between subject and
target remains the same.

On the basis of this observation, self-categorization theory leads to the
following prediction:

P3   That a target of constant absolute difference from a stereotyper will be
      perceived to share more identity with that stereotyper, and should
      therefore be assimilated more to his or her own position, as his or her
      frame of reference is extended.

This prediction is supported by findings from a range of studies which
have investigated the effects of changes to a judge's frame of reference
(e.g., Hensley and Duval, 1976; Mascaro and Graves, 1973). The theoretical analysis is also consistent with the empirical observation that
patterns of assimilation and contrast are partially determined by the
frame of reference relevant to a particular comparative judgement
(Biernat, Manis and Nelson, 1991) and by the discrepancy between
primary and other 'background' stimuli – this being the inter-class component, or numerator, of the meta-contrast ratio (Manis et al., 1988;

Wilder and Thompson, 1988). Our analysis is consistent as well with Brewer's (1979) claim that such frame of reference effects are attributable to changes in the definition of stimuli as members of ingroup or outgroup categories.

Empirical Investigation

Manipulations of Frame of Reference

One of the areas in which self-categorization theory's analysis of accentuation has received a large amount of direct support relates to manipulations of subjects' frame of reference. The experiments reported by Wilder and Thompson (1988) explicitly tested and supported the prediction that extension of subjects' frame of reference would serve to heighten the perceived similarity of stimuli that were a constant absolute difference from the perceiver's own position (cf. P3 above). Just as self-categorization theory predicts, they found that a group who are categorized as an outgroup at one level of self-categorization can be recategorized as an ingroup in contrast to an even more different outgroup (see chapters 4 and 5). Abrams and Hogg (1987) provide a demonstration of similar effects occurring in the evaluation of speech dialects. In their study Scottish subjects from Dundee evaluated the dialects of people from Glasgow (another Scottish city) more positively in contexts where middle-class English dialects (i.e., the dialects of a more different outgroup) were also presented. Further support for this analysis was provided by Hogg and Turner (1987) in a study where individuals were organized into four-person mixed-sex groups or same-sex dyads. Here it was found that individuals were more likely to define themselves in terms of gender and to accentuate their similarity to other same-sex individuals where men and women were present rather than just men or just women (i.e., in intergroup rather than intragroup contexts).

Similar patterns also emerged in the studies conducted by Oakes et al. (1991) that were discussed in the previous chapter. In contexts that were meaningfully defined in intergroup terms (i.e., collective or consistent conflict conditions) subjects were more likely to perceive the target individual in stereotypic terms and (in Experiment 2) to accentuate her similarity to other members of the same group. An experiment reported by Gaertner and his colleagues (1989) also supported self-categorization theory's predictions concerning the effects of frame of reference and level of self-categorization upon perceived attraction to others. In this study all subjects were initially defined as members of one of two groups each comprised of three members. At a later stage two-thirds of the subjects were induced to recategorize that array as either one superordinate group of six people or as six individuals. As predicted, it was found that intergroup discrimination was reduced by both these recategorization strategies and that patterns of liking for other group members reflected the categorical boundaries established by the experimental manipulation. Relative to the two-groups condition, liking for outgroup members increased in the superordinate-group condition and liking for ingroup members decreased in the six-individuals condition. On the basis of their findings the authors argued that changes in stereotypic bias arise from, and reflect, changes in the salience of ingroup–outgroup categorization.

This point was confirmed in an experiment of our own which investigated changes to stereotypes as a function of both (a) alterations to subjects' frame of reference and (b) changes over time (Haslam et al., 1992). In this study Australian students characterized Americans using the Katz–Braly checklist (after Katz and Braly, 1933; see chapter 2) both before and during the 1991 Gulf War and did so in situations where a list of other countries which they might have been asked to characterize included (a) Australia and Britain, (b) Australia, Britain and the Soviet Union, or (c) Australia, Britain, the Soviet Union and Iraq. It was found that stereotype content varied as an interactive product of study phase and comparative context: overall stereotypes were quite negative, but they were significantly more negative (a) at the end of the war than at the beginning when only Australia and Britain were comparison groups, and (b) in the first phase of the conflict when the frame of reference was extended to include Iraq. On specific traits, for example, Americans came to be seen over time as more arrogant and less straightforward, and in comparison to Iraq they were seen as less ambitious and more tradition-loving. The general pattern appeared to reflect the fact that Americans were an outgroup for this subject sample and that both the prosecution of the Gulf War and the inclusion of Iraq as a comparison group in its early phase served to reinforce the basic ingroup (anti-war Australians) versus outgroup (pro-war Americans) division.

In an attempt to provide a more controlled test of self-categorization theory's frame of reference predictions (i.e., P3) a series of three empirical studies were conducted by Haslam and Turner (1992). These involved the systematic manipulation of the stereotyper's frame of reference and, on the basis of calculations of meta-contrast, sought to predict both the direction and the degree of stimulus displacement.

The experiments all employed a common experimental paradigm which involved assigning individuals group identities on the basis of a bogus personality inventory. These identities indicated different levels of idealism/pragmatism and were identified in relation to a number of other possible identities. Having been assigned to groups, subjects then had to judge a target person whose 'objective' position on the dimension of idealism/pragmatism had previously been established using control subjects. Judgements were made on a number of measures including placement of the target and the self on a rating scale and characterization of the targets' group using a version of the Katz–Braly checklist.

In all three studies the identity of both the subjects and the target to be judged remained constant across conditions while information about the nature of other possible identities was varied. In Experiment 1 these other identities extended one pole of the frame of reference, in Experiment 2 they extended both poles, and in Experiment 3 the positions of subject and target were extremitized relative to the frame of reference (the social context was displaced to one side but without changing either the absolute positions of self and other or the extent of the frame of reference). In all cases extension or extremitization led to increases in the extent to which, on the basis of calculations of meta-contrast, the target was expected to share identity with the subject (following H1). And as predicted (on the basis of H2), in all three experiments this increase in shared identity led to enhanced assimilation of the target to the subjects' own position and to some change in the content of stereotypes of the target's group.

In Experiment 1, for example, where all subjects were told that they were 'slightly pragmatic' and judged a predominantly pragmatic target (a male), subjects indicated that the difference between their position and that of the target was 3.69 (on a nine-point scale) where the frame of reference was restricted and included only three possible identities (and the MCR of the target for subjects was 0.50). However, this difference was 1.88 where the frame of reference was extended and included seven identities (and the MCR of T for S was 1.90). In addition, checklist responses indicated that the target's group was characterized more favourably when the target was categorized as an ingroup rather than an outgroup member (i.e. where his MCR for subjects was greater than 1.00 and he was assimilated rather than contrasted). So, for example, in the Restricted Range condition of Experiment 1 the target's group was characterized as 'materialistic' by 67 per cent of subjects and as 'practical' by 33 per cent, but in the Extended Range condition the corresponding figures were both 47 per cent.

Manipulations of own position

In an attempt to test self-categorization theory's predictions concerning the role of subjects' own position in determining accentuation, Haslam and Turner (1993) conducted further studies involving variations to their bogus identity paradigm. In the first of these, subjects were randomly assigned either to a control group or to one of five experimental conditions, each associated with a *different* level of pragmatism/idealism. These five group identities occupied positions 1, 3, 5, 7 or 9 on an eleven-point scale ranging from totally pragmatic (0) to totally idealistic (10). Subjects then judged the extent of a predominantly pragmatic male target's pragmatism and characterized the group of which he was said to be a member using an adjective checklist.

On the basis of the meta-contrast principle (H1) it was possible to calculate the degree to which the target should share identity with subjects in each experimental condition. Considering these values in light of the hypothesized relationship between shared identity and accentuation (H2), the primary prediction was that subjects assigned more pragmatic identities (at scale positions 1, 3 and 5) for whom the target should be representative of an ingroup (i.e., MCR > 1.00) would assimilate him towards the position associated with their identity, whilst those subjects assigned idealistic identities (at positions 7 and 9) for whom the target should be categorized as an outgroup member (i.e., MCR < 1.00) would exhibit relative contrast by displacing him away from their own position.

Results provided strong support for these hypotheses. They also supported a secondary hypothesis that stereotypes of the target's group would be more favourable to the extent that he was representative of subjects' own identity. Sixty-three per cent of pragmatists (at positions 1 and 3) described this group as 'practical' and only 33 per cent described it as 'materialistic', while for idealists (at positions 7 and 9) this pattern was reversed, corresponding levels of assignment of these traits being 55 per cent and 76 per cent.

Haslam and Turner (1993, Experiment 1) provided further support for self-categorization theory's predictions in a study where subjects were assigned to one of three identities as either extremely pragmatic (scale position 1), moderately pragmatic (3) or borderline pragmatic/non-pragmatic (5) and then had to judge *two* targets, one predominantly pragmatic (2) and one moderately non-pragmatic (7). Subjects' identities were again defined in the context of eleven identities ranging from totally pragmatic to totally non-pragmatic. On the basis of calculations of meta-contrast it was anticipated that extremely and moderately pragmatic subjects would assimilate the pragmatic target to their own position (because the MCR of this target for these subjects was greater than 1) but that they would contrast the non-pragmatic target (whose MCR for subjects was less than 1). Borderline subjects, however, were expected to assimilate both targets (because in both cases their MCR for subjects was greater than 1).

In raw form, this study was thus expected to reproduce a classic finding because the more extreme subjects were predicted to display greater accentuation of the difference between the two targets (following P1 above; cf. Hovland and Sherif, 1952). As can be seen from table 6.2, the results of the study provided strong support for this prediction. Analysis of the subjects' stereotypes of both targets' groups also showed that subjects assigned extreme identities tended to display greater accentuation of differences in the relative favourableness of the two groups.

These two studies thus both provide support for self-categorization theory's explanation of the previously observed relationship between the accentuation of interstimulus differences and the extremity of subjects' own position. However, the results are also inconsistent with a number of other accounts of this relationship. Most significantly, the random assignment of subjects to conditions ruled out personality and involvement-based explanations (e.g., Adorno et al., 1950; Sherif and Hovland, 1961; White and Harvey, 1965) as this procedure cut across potentially relevant individual differences between extremists and moderates. Furthermore, the findings were inconsistent with any explanation of accentuation effects couched in terms of inherent differences between extremists and moderates (e.g., in self-confidence or intellectual sophistication; Sidanius, 1988).

Table 6.2 Mean self-ratings of pragmatism, target ratings and differences in ratings of targets

Condition (Subject's position)	Self	Pragmatic target (Tp)	Non-pragmatic target (Tn)	Difference in target ratings
extremely pragmatic (Se)	1.27	1.20	7.75	6.55
moderately pragmatic (Sm)	2.80	1.90	7.65	5.75
borderline pragmatic (Sb)	4.81	2.14	6.62	4.48
control		1.76	7.00	5.24

Ratings of self and targets made with respect to an eleven-point scale (0 = totally pragmatic, 10 = totally non-pragmatic)

(From Haslam and Turner, 1993)

Manipulations of multiple comparative features: Reconceptualizing the roles of extremism and moderation

In supporting predictions derived from self-categorization theory, the results of the above two studies support the assertion that extremists represent the stimulus world as more 'black and white' than moderates because in self-categorical terms it *is* more black and white. This point follows from our discussion in chapter 4 of the manner in which comparative context can convert the same raw 'distances' into either similarities or differences. People who are close to an extremist's position are more similar than is the case for moderates because these people are generally more *distant from others*. Conversely, distant people are more different for extremists because they are generally *closer to others*. Importantly though, this point pertains only to the standard judgemental setting. It applies only where there is (or subjects assume there to be, cf. Poulton, 1968; van der Pligt et al., 1987) a uniform distribution of stimuli across the range of possible positions.

In order to test this analysis directly and to rule out the possibility that it was 'something about' extremism that led the subjects who were assigned extreme identities to accentuate the differences between targets (e.g., beliefs about the way extremists ought to behave), Haslam and Turner (1993, Experiment 2) conducted an additonal study. This manipulated both subjects' own positions *and* the configuration of comparative others that comprised their frame of reference. The experiment was designed to test the hypothesis that moderates would display more accentuation of interstimulus differences than extremists (i.e., a reversal of the standard finding) in conditions where most other people were seen to be closer to the extremists' own position than to that of moderates (i.e., where the distribution of comparison stimuli was skewed towards the extremists).

Subjects were assigned identities corresponding to scale positions of 2 or 5 on an eleven-point scale ranging from totally idealistic (0) to totally non-idealistic (10) and then judged two targets who were at these same positions. These judgements were made in contexts where a reference group (most of the students in the previous year's class) was said to be at scale positions 1 or 9, or was not mentioned (a control condition). Consistent with predictions derived from calculations of meta-contrast, it was found that in control conditions extremists displayed more accentuation of inter-target differences in idealism than moderates (reproducing the standard finding) but that this pattern was reversed where the reference group's position was skewed towards the pole occupied by the extremists. Some unexpected anomalies in the data (clarified in Experiment 3) reinforced the conclusion that the relative degree of polarization displayed by moderates and extremists is a function of the context of self-categorization.

Thus where extremism was comparatively 'normal' moderates displayed the pattern of accentuated responding typically associated with extremists. This finding confirms the point that *stereotypic accentuation is determined by stimulus reality and the perceiver's social categorical relationship to it*, rather than by own position *per se*. In this it questions both the popular view that extremism is psychologically inferior to moderation (a view first elaborated by Aristotle over 2,000 years ago and formalized by personality theorists; e.g., Adorno et al., 1950) and the less common view that it is actually superior (e.g., Sidanius, 1988). Instead, the findings make way for a novel conceptualization of extremism and moderation by supporting the theoretical claim that the cognitive processes of extremists and moderates *are the same* in being sensitive to context and generally serving to represent social categorical reality in an appropriate manner.

Accentuation and stereotype content

Although the discussion in the foregoing sections has focused on the manner in which changes in comparative context lead to predictable patterns of stimulus displacement, it is important to note that in all cases this displacement was also bound up with changes in stereotype content. Self-categorization theory presents a model of *stereotype change* in which the content of stereotypes is predicted and has been shown to vary in such a way as to reflect the categorical properties of groups and individual group members that accrue to them within a *specific* social context. It follows, for example, that psychologists' perceptions of sociologists should change in situations where they are compared with used car dealers rather than with physicists (see chapter 5). Furthermore, psychologists' *self-stereotype* is also likely to change across these different settings.

Both these points were demonstrated in a study conducted by Haslam, Brooks and Oakes (1993). In this, student nurses and non-nurses (business and sports science students) assigned traits to nurses using the Katz–Braly checklist and in two different comparative conditions also made judgements of doctors and mothers. As well as identifying a number of between-group differences in stereotypes of nurses, content analysis also indicated (a) that both groups of subjects were more likely to see nurses as courteous in contexts where they were compared with doctors, and (b) that nurses were more likely to see themselves as helpful when they compared themselves with either doctors or mothers, although non-nurses perceived nurses to be less helpf.." when they compared them with these other groups.

In an additional bogus identity study Haslam and Turner (1993, Experiment 3) also showed that the content of subjects' self-stereotypes changed as a function of the position and nature of a reference group. When extreme idealists believed that a group of Mormons was also extremely idealistic rather than slightly non-idealistic, they described themselves in less idealistic terms (e.g., as more practical and less sensitive and imaginative), but this pattern was reversed when the reference group was said to be comprised of members of the previous year's class.

Having made the point that stereotyping and the processes of social categorization which underpin it are products of comparative context, it is important to re-emphasize that both stereotyping and social categorization also have an interactive basis in *normative fit*. As we argued in chapter 5, the principle of normative fit implies that stimuli will only be represented in categorical terms where their assignment to categories is consistent with our background theories and knowledge. Categories will be selectively matched to stimulus differences in terms of the specific dimensions of comparison and the direction of observed differences, but, at the same time, category content will vary as a function of the intracategory structure and diagnostic intercategory differences in the context. We would expect, for example, that the fit of stimuli into ingroup and outgroup categories would be higher – and hence judgemental polarization stronger – to the extent that the stimuli included in the ingroup category are associated with positive connotations and those in the outgroup category with negative connotations. This prediction is consistent with Eiser's body of research (e.g., 1973).

In more complex situations than those that obtaining in the bogus identity studies conducted by Haslam and Turner (1992, 1993, where the identity of subject, target and comparison groups was deliberately minimal), we would thus expect contextual alterations to affect factors other than just meta-contrast. In particular, such changes would often be expected to affect the dimensions on which stimuli are compared and thus affect the *meaning* of particular judgements (see Spears and Manstead, 1989). For example, during the build-up to the 1991 Gulf War, extension of Australian students' comparative frame to include Iraq served to make the pro-war/anti-war dimension salient and led to less favourable stereotypes of pro-war Americans (Haslam et al., 1992). The content of stereotypic judgement can also be affected by *social change* over time: thus later in the Gulf War (perhaps as a result of the influence of anti-Iraq propaganda) subjects' stereotypes of Americans were slightly more favourable in the comparative context that included Iraq, a pattern which seemed to reflect the perception of this nation as a 'common enemy'.

Theoretical Implications

The research considered above builds upon two points which emerge from some of the previous work in this area (particularly as discussed by Eiser and Stroebe, 1972; Sherif and Hovland, 1961). First, we acknowledge that the processes of accentuation, like those of stereotyping, are common to all perceivers rather than just some. Second, we focus on the way in which accentuation effects are shaped by context.

Importantly though, our theoretical analysis differs from others in three important respects. First, it appears to provide a more parsimonious account of accentuation effects than other theories (Haslam, 1990). Thus where a range of psychophysical models have typically been used to explain different frame of reference effects, self-categorization theory is the only theory consistent with the array of findings reported by Haslam and Turner (1992). Similarly, this theory also explains effects associated with the subjects' own position where, as we noted earlier in this chapter, these have previously been accounted for by a totally different class of theory (i.e., non-psychophysical; see Eiser, 1990; Eiser and Stroebe, 1972).

Second, the explanatory construct central to our analysis is clearly very different from those employed by other theorists. Where most social (and other) judgemental theories of accentuation ascribe no special role to group memberships and intergroup relations, the utility of the principle of meta-contrast derives from the very fact that it relates to, and seeks to quantify, these very features of stimulus context. In regard to this point it is thus important to note that self-categorization theory does not propose a mathematical or reductionist solution to problems in the analysis of accentuation. We are certainly not suggesting, for example, that meta-contrast is simply an algorithm used by individuals to integrate a mass of complex information. On the contrary, meta-contrast (always in interplay with accessibility and content) is considered the principle underlying the social categorical definition of stimuli within a particular comparative context. In this sense it serves not to aggregate information mechanically but to abstract and epitomize the 'actualities of group life'.

The third difference between our approach and that of other theorists is that it leads to a very different way of thinking about accentuation. Self-categorization theory does not assume that accentuation perverts the truth that exists at the level of stimuli considered individually and in isolation (see e.g., Dawes, Singer and Lemons, 1972; Judd and Harackiewicz, 1980; Krueger, 1992; Krueger and Rothbart, 1990; Stephan, 1985). Instead we argue that accentuated judgements reflect the social reality that derives from the meaningful association of the people and things we judge with dynamically-constructed social groups. In support, the above studies show that judgements of individuals (and stereotypes of the group to which they belong) vary in order to reflect a categorical reality that changes in the face of alterations to social context and intergroup relations.

From our perspective, then, the very term 'accentuation' is actually misleading as it implicitly suggests that the appropriate representation for a particular stimulus would reflect properties apparent when it was considered in isolation and independent of any group to which it might belong. As we have argued in previous chapters, we do not believe that lower-level representation can be considered, in the abstract, to be any more basic, real or accurate than higher-order social categorical representation. On the contrary, we consider the appropriateness and accuracy of perception at a given level of abstraction to be fully relative to the social context. So, to return to the example that we considered at the start of this chapter, when protesters at a demonstration see a policeman not as an individual but as a person who shares group membership with other policemen and not with themselves, the emphasis of his difference from them on relevant dimensions of comparison is a veridical reflection of contextually significant social realities. For this reason, their perception is not distorted. Indeed, we would suggest that distortion would only arise if interaction in this context *was* dictated by a representation of the policeman as an individual.

The validity of this analysis may appear to rest on the idea that individuals' own behaviour is transformed by membership of a group (as evidenced, for example, by research into group polarization; see Turner, 1991). One could argue that the policeman actually would behave differently (typically in a more stereotype-consistent manner) when he was with a group of other policemen rather than on his own. Although this is undoubtedly true and is part of a clear dynamic within which stereotyping processes operate (see Vinacke, 1956), we do not think that the validity of our analysis rests on this point. Instead, we believe that even where the stimulus is incapable of effecting change itself (as in most judgemental studies), veridical perception will still involve accentuation (at some level of categorization).

This point applies to the results of Tajfel and Wilkes' (1963a) experiment where, as we noted in the introduction to this chapter, subjects are typically understood to have distorted reality by, amongst other things, representing the difference between the longest of the four short lines and the shortest of the four long lines as 1.9 cms. when the 'actual' difference was 0.9 cms. (as in table 3.1; see, for example, Eiser, 1990; Tajfel, 1981a). We would argue that judgements of lines made in isolation using a metric ruler are not inherently more valid, accurate and useful than judgements which reflect the category memberships of those lines. This is because the ruler itself must be understood simply as a classification device which is consensually employed to make judgements at a particular level of abstraction. As it is, subjects' responses served to reflect the fact that there were *important and meaningful* differences between the two categories of lines (A and B), a significant higher-level structural property of the stimulus situation that *cannot be conveyed* by use of a ruler.

We can summarize this broad debate by referring to a short verbal exchange that took place during the trial of the Black South African leader Steve Biko in 1976, sixteen months before his death in police detention.

JUDGE BOSHOFF: But now why do you refer to you people as blacks? Why not brown people? I mean you people are more brown than black.

BIKO: In the same way as I think white people are more pink and yellow and pale than white.

JUDGE BOSHOFF: Quite . . . but now why do you not use the word brown then?

BIKO: No, I think really, historically, we have been defined as black people, and when we reject the term non-white and take upon ourselves the right to call ourselves what we think we are, we have got available in front of us a whole number of alternatives . . . and we choose this one precisely because we feel it is most accommodating. (Biko, 1988, p. 121)

This extract provides a vivid example of the role of social context in determining accentuation. The judge's argument arises from a particular ideological position and reflects a conceptualization of the nature of social reality that is remote from the reality of intergroup relations and everday life. In rejecting the judge's position, Biko argued – as do we – that the accentuated representation of his own group as 'black' (chosen from a range of alternatives and standing in opposition to the ruling 'whites'), was the most valid, meaningful and appropriate representation, *even though* in an individualistic, decontextualized sense it might appear wrong.

Overview

In this chapter we have looked at how and why individuals make judgements of stimuli that typically exaggerate the properties remarked by 'objective' judges. Previously these effects have been explained either in terms of differences between perceivers (e.g., in personality or involvement) or in terms of psychophysical principles associated with mathematical properties of the stimulus context (e.g., as judgements made relative to the mean, median or mid-point of a scale).

In contrast to these positions, self-categorization theory suggests that stereotypic accentuation reflects the extent to which others share the perceiver's social identity in a given context. It relates assimilation and contrast to the salient level and kind of self-categorization in a given context. Consistent with this analysis, we have discussed findings from experiments which show that as features of the judgemental context change, patterns of accentuation – apparent both in the judgement of individuals and in stereotypes of the groups to which they belong – change too. Importantly though, this change was shown to reflect the categorical relationship of stimuli to self within the judgemental context (as operationalized in terms of comparative and normative fit). In this manner accentuation effects are seen to arise from a process which adjusts to, and allows realization of, the realities of ongoing intergroup relations.

This conclusion, and the evidence that supports it, serve to challenge two commonly advanced beliefs: first, that individuals who do accentuate (typically extremists) are psychologically inferior to individuals who don't (typically moderates) and, second, that accentuation (and stereotypes) distort reality through a simplifying process of exaggeration. Our analysis has allowed novel reinterpretations of experimental phenomena central to the stereotyping literature. In the following chapter we will attempt to demonstrate how self-categorization theory provides a basis for a similar reconceptualization of some other important stereotyping effects.

Suggested Further Reading and References

As reviews of social judgemental research, the books by Sherif and Hovland (1961) and Eiser and Stroebe (1972) are both landmark texts. Each conveys the vitality of the empirical and theoretical advances made by the researchers, and potentially turgid judgemental theory is rendered accessible and interesting. The self-categorization theory of accentuation and its relationship to the analysis of stereotyping is dealt with in more detail by Haslam et al. (1992) and Haslam and Turner (1992).

Eiser, J. R. and Stroebe, W. (1972) *Categorization and social judgement.* European Monographs in Social Psychology, no. 3; London: Academic Press.

Haslam, S. A. and Turner, J. C. (1992) Context-dependent variation in social stereotyping 2: The relationship between frame of reference, self-categorization and accentuation. *European Journal of Social Psychology,* 22, 251–278.

Haslam, S. A., Turner, J. C., Oakes, P. J., McGarty, C. and Hayes, B. K. (1992) Context-dependent variation in social stereotyping 1: The effects of intergroup relations as mediated by social change and frame of reference. *European Journal of Social Psychology,* 22, 3–20.

Sherif, M. and Hovland, C. I. (1961) *Social judgement: Assimilation and contrast effects in communication and attitude change.* New Haven, CT and London: Yale University Press.

7

Outgroup Homogeneity and Illusory Correlation Revisited

As this book has progressed we have moved away from the received view that stereotypes and stereotyping misrepresent social reality by simplifying, exaggerating and ossifying the richness of human interaction. Instead we have developed the argument that stereotypes serve to reflect the realities of group life as perceived from a particular vantage point and within a particular context.

In the preceding two chapters we have developed this reconceptualization in the context of basic questions concerning categorization. We have argued that both the purpose and the outcome of the categorization process can be recast in such a way that the assumptions of distortion and error currently inherent in their treatment are exchanged for an emphasis on the dynamic, context-dependent, veridical representation of reality. It is now time to confront data and arguments relating to two important topics in the cognitive stereotyping literature, outgroup homogeneity and illusory correlation.

These topics are of interest not only because they are currently the focus of a large amount of research attention, but because they can be seen as problematic for our analysis. The outgroup homogeneity effect has been explicitly identified as inconsistent with self-categorization theory and the theory does indeed make predictions about the effects of categorization which could be seen as contradicted by outgroup homogeneity. We shall outline why we do not see existing evidence as inconsistent with our analysis and discuss our own research into the comparative and normative basis of perceived group homogeneity. The discussion of illusory correlation is more speculative. Although self-categorization theory assumes that stereotype formation should follow principles related to meta-contrast and normative fit (rather than proceed in the absence of any relationship between categories and reality), it does not directly generate any specific explanation of illusory correlation. None-theless, it is interesting to demonstrate that it may be possible to reinter-pret the illusory correlation effect in a way that is consistent with our analysis.

Outgroup Homogeneity

We [Americans] know . . . that not all Americans are dollar-worshippers, breezy or vulgar. Nor are they all friendly and hospitable. On the other hand, Europeans, who know us less well, often view us as one big mono-lithic unit having all these qualities. (G. Allport, 1954, p. 172)

In this statement, Gordon Allport provides both an early illustration of the outgroup homogeneity effect and the essence of one contemporary explanation of its occurrence. As we discussed in chapter 3, the outgroup homogeneity effect refers to the tendency for people to see members of outgroups as less variable and more similar to each other than members of ingroups. Many empirical studies have revealed patterns of homogene-ity judgements consistent with Allport's anecdote (see Park et al., 1991), and a great deal of effort has been expended in an attempt to identify the *cognitive basis* of the outgroup homogeneity effect. The robustness and generality of the effect are rarely questioned (cf. Simon, 1992). It is accepted as 'almost a truism' (Linville et al., 1986, p. 165), and the colloquial phrase 'they all look alike' (with its inbuilt implication that 'we' don't) is often referred to as an illustration of widespread belief in outgroup homogeneity. Indeed, symptomatic of the way in which the effect is more or less taken as read in the stereotyping literature is Park and Rothbart's (1982, p. 1051, emphasis added) reference to it as 'the *principle* of outgroup homogeneity' which, together with the 'principle' of ingroup favouritism, they see as a central cause of negative outgroup stereotypes and intergroup conflict.

Consistent with the assumption that outgroups are, as a general principle, perceived as more homogeneous than ingroups, cognitive ex-planations of the effect have concentrated on identifying fundamental differences in the way in which ingroup and outgroup categories are represented. As we saw in chapter 3, Linville and her colleagues present an exemplar-based model (i.e., one which assumes that category infor-mation is represented in terms of specific, individual examples of cat-egory members), and argue that, largely as a result of greater familiarity with the ingroup (as alluded to in Allport's comment), perceivers encounter and store information about more ingroup than outgroup exemplars. In contrast, Park, Judd and their colleagues claim that a dual storage model of category representation, in which both exemplar and abstract, prototype-based, information about groups is stored, is better able to account for the outgroup homogeneity effect. They suggest that basic differences between ingroup and outgroup representations are established during both information encoding (where more variable abstractions are formed for ingroups) and information retrieval (where abstract variability information is supplemented by exemplar information for ingroups but not outgroups). These differences are traced to several factors, such as an assumed lack of elaborated contact with the outgroup (see chapter 3).

Thus, although they draw on quite different models of category representation, the two major explanations for the outgroup homogeneity effect agree that ingroup categories inherently contain more variability information than do outgroup categories and hence that *as a general rule* judgements of an outgroup will be more homogeneous than judgements of an ingroup.

This prediction, and the apparent accumulation of findings supporting it, have been seen by a number of researchers as problematic for self-categorization theory. For example, following their meta-analysis of relevant studies (which indicated that the effect was 'significant but small'), Mullen and Hu (1989) suggest that the data is 'inconsistent with the social identity theory assumption that the ingroup and outgroup will be perceived in terms of equivalent, low intragroup variability' (pp. 247–248). Indeed, self-categorization theory would predict symmetry in judgements of ingroup and outgroup homogeneity *under certain conditions*, and it is because we are able to specify the conditions of such symmetry that we do not regard existing evidence of asymmetry (in the form of outgroup homogeneity) as inconsistent with our analysis of categorization effects in social perception. Neither do we view outgroup homogeneity as a 'principle' of social perception. We see it as one of a number of different ways in which relations between and within groups can be represented, each of which is a product of the comparative and normative context in which judgements are made.

When, according to self-categorization theory, will a collection of individuals be perceived as relatively homogeneous, or as relatively variable? The theory predicts that *perceived similarity follows the categorization process*. Thus individuals will be perceived (and will perceive themselves) as homogeneous, as similar to each other, to the extent that they are categorized as members of one group *within* which similarity is accentuated. Alternatively, they will be perceived as variable to the extent that they are categorized at a lower level of abstraction, in terms of individual, personal categories *between* which differences are accentuated. Further, the categorization process is highly context-dependent. The salient level of categorization depends on the comparative context, as specified in the principle of meta-contrast, and on the normative fit of input with the categorization (in interaction with perceiver readiness). Shared social identity tends to become salient in the context of stereotype-consistent *inter*group comparison, whereas personal identity is based on *intra*group comparisons (Hogg and Turner, 1987). Indeed, in discussing the interdependence of comparison and categorization in chapter 4, we argued that personal identity can *only* become salient as a result of intragroup comparisons. In order to compare with other individuals and establish difference from them, there must first be an implicit recognition of shared ingroup membership, in terms of which intra-individual comparisons can be made. These principles are illustrated in figure 7.1.

Two conclusions relevant to outgroup homogeneity can be drawn from the above statements. First, we predict symmetry in ingroup–

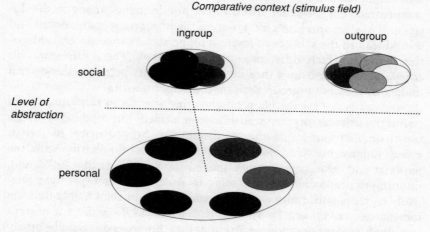

Figure 7.1   Categorization as a function of comparative context and level of abstraction, from Haslam et al. (1993b)

Solid lines indicate salient category boundaries. When the outgroup is present the intergroup context makes social categories salient. Similarities within these are apparent because individuals are categorically interchangeable. When the ingroup alone is present the inter-individual context makes lower-level (personal) categories salient. Differences between these are more apparent because individuals are not interchangeable.

outgroup judgements to the extent that they are both made in an explicitly intergroup context in which the ingroup–outgroup relationship is salient (i.e., there is high comparative and normative fit). Second, we expect that, insofar as individuals are perceived as variable, in terms of their personal differences from each other, this will always be an *intra*group judgement. Thus an overall asymmetry in experimental data in favour of outgroup rather than ingroup homogeneity (or ingroup rather than outgroup variability) is predicted by self-categorization theory, to the extent that ingroup judgements can be shown to have occurred in intra- rather than intergroup contexts.

In fact, it appears that a number of studies providing evidence of an outgroup homogeneity effect have inadvertently assessed outgroup homogeneity in an intergroup context, but ingroup homogeneity in an intragroup context. This is because subjects are often asked to make ratings *either* of the ingroup *or* of the outgroup (e.g., Brewer and Lui, 1984; E. Jones et al., 1981; Linville, 1982, Linville and E. Jones, 1980; Park and Rothbart, 1982, Experiments 1 and 2; Quattrone and Jones, 1980; Wilder, 1984). Rating of an outgroup always takes place in an at least implicitly intergroup context; the subject represents one group, the target category another. Comparison between the two groups should lead to the salience of social categories within which similarities are accentuated. On the other hand, ingroup judgements, made in the absence of any comparison group, encourage intragroup comparisons and should lead to the salience of lower-level personal (or subgroup) categories between which differences are accentuated. These differences in comparative context may thus be one factor contributing to the general finding of greater outgroup than ingroup homogeneity.

Some evidence for the plausibility of this analysis in fact comes from one of the first stereotyping studies ever published. Katz and Braly (1933, see chapter 2) found that the uniformity (i.e., homogeneity) of stereotyped judgements was *not* related to subjects' familiarity with the national and ethnic groups they judged (cf. Linville et al., 1986) and, importantly, uniformity of the ingroup American stereotype was relatively high (its uniformity was in the middle of a range of highly uniform judgements, see table 2.1). The fact that Katz and Braly did not observe ingroup heterogeneity (and relative outgroup homogeneity) can be attributed to the fact that American stereotypes were elicited in a judgemental context that was clearly intergroup in nature (recall that subjects made consecutive judgements of ten groups, with the ingroup being rated seventh).

In order to test our argument that existing findings reflect, at least in part, differences in the comparative context in which ingroup and outgroup judgements are made, we conducted two studies (Haslam et al., 1993b) in which subjects in one set of conditions judged both an ingroup *and* an outgroup (both judgements thus being made in an explicitly intergroup context) while subjects in other conditions followed the common procedure of judging *either* an ingroup or an outgroup. Our general hypothesis was that group homogeneity judgements would vary with the categorization process, as determined by comparative context, rather than with ingroup–outgroup status. More specifically, it was predicted that on stereotypic dimensions the ingroup and outgroup would be perceived as equally homogeneous in the intergroup comparative context (where both groups were salient for subjects). On the other hand, an outgroup homogeneity effect was expected where groups were judged alone, as this would represent an intergroup context for the outgroup judgement, but an intragroup context for the ingroup judgement.

This first experiment manipulated stereotyped group (Australia, an ingroup vs. America, an outgroup) and comparative context (no comparison vs. intergroup comparison) in a four-condition between-subjects design. Based on the methodology devised by Katz and Braly (1933), subjects were asked to assign five checklist traits either to Australians or to Americans, and they did this in the context of either that group alone or both groups. Having made these assignments, each subject then estimated the *percentage* (see Park and Judd, 1990) of people from the stereotyped country (and, where relevant, the comparison country) who could be characterized by each of the five traits the subject had themselves identified as stereotypical. Importantly, therefore, subjects *chose for themselves* the content dimensions on which the homogeneity of the stereotyped group (i.e. the ingroup or outgroup, depending on condition) was judged. For this reason we can be sure that the normative fit of that content was equally high for both groups. In contrast, it seems likely that in studies where subjects judge groups on dimensions chosen by the experimenter (on whatever basis) there might be some variation in the extent to which subjects are willing to accept particular attributes as ingroup- or outgroup-defining. Moreover, from our perspective, any such asymmetry would clearly have an impact upon judgements of homogeneity (any factor reducing the fit of a category should reduce homogeneity judgements). By controlling normative fit, an additional objective of this experiment was to assess the nature of this impact.

The main findings are presented in table 7.1. As can be seen from the results for stereotypical traits in the table, our predictions were strongly

Table 7.1 Mean percentage of group members to whom traits apply as a function of comparative context and stereotypicality of traits

| Judged group | Comparative context and stereotypicality of traits | | |
| | no comparison | intergroup comparison | |
	(stereotypic)	(stereotypic)	(counter-stereotypic)
Australians	57	74	48
Americans	75	74	68

(From Haslam et al., 1993b, tables 1 and 2)

supported. In the no comparison conditions, assigned traits were applied to significantly more outgroup members than ingroup members (75 per cent of Americans, 57 per cent of Australians) – the typical outgroup homogeneity effect. However, where both judgements were made in an intergroup context, levels of ingroup and outgroup homogeneity were equal (traits were assigned to 74 per cent of Americans and 74 per cent of Australians).

This analysis deals only with the ratings of both groups on stereotypical dimensions. Subjects in the intergroup comparison conditions also made some counter-stereotypical ratings, as they assigned percentages for the comparison group on the dimensions used to describe the stereotyped group (e.g., subjects who had assigned traits to Australians in the intergroup condition indicated the percentage of Australians *and* of Americans to whom these traits were applicable). These percentages are also included in table 7.1. Note that Judd and his colleagues (e.g., Judd and Park, 1988; Judd et al., 1991) explicitly define homogeneity in terms of both stereotypical and counter-stereotypical dimensions, with percentage ratings on the latter being subtracted from those on the former. In other words, these researchers define a homogeneous group as one to which stereotypical traits are applicable and counter-stereotypical traits are *not* applicable. In these terms, our results indicate a strong *ingroup* homogeneity effect in the intergroup conditions, as counter-stereotypic traits were assigned to 68 per cent of Americans but only 48 per cent of Australians.

This pattern differs from that reported by Judd et al. (1991) who asked subjects to provide percentage estimates of the homogeneity of both business and engineering majors on four trait and four attitude dimensions. Subtracting percentage estimates on counter-stereotypical dimensions from those on stereotypical dimensions, they found an outgroup homogeneity effect: ingroup majors were perceived as both less stereotypical and more counter-stereotypical than outgroup majors. Judd and his colleagues do not specify the source of the eight dimensions used in their study, but as we noted previously, our experiment incorporated an important procedural difference in that subjects defined for themselves the stereotypic dimensions on which groups were judged. In this experiment, then, we can be sure not only that particular traits were stereotypical of the groups involved, but also that they were explicitly recognized as such by the subjects (i.e., that the normative fit of stereotypic traits was high for both ingroup and outgroup). This does not hold for the study reported by Judd et al. (1991), even though the choice of traits may (or may not) have been justified on the basis of independent ratings.

Following on from this point, a further difference between these studies which may go some way towards explaining the different results obtained in each lies in the *favourableness* of the traits with respect to which ingroup and outgroup homogeneity were judged. In Judd et al.'s (1991) experiment it is apparent that the favourableness of the traits and attitude statements used did not differ systematically between groups. Indeed, each group seems to have been represented by one positive and one negative trait, and one positive and one negative attitude statement ('extraverted' and 'impulsive' were the traits stereotypic of business majors, 'analytical' and 'reserved' were the traits stereotypical of engineering majors). Although this balance may have been seen as desirable for reasons of experimental control, it is apparent from the content analysis performed on our own data that where subjects choose traits themselves they typically use favourable traits to characterize the ingroup and unfavourable traits to characterize the outgroup (the ingroup stereotypes generated by our subjects were significantly more favourable than their outgroup stereotypes; cf. Katz and Braly, 1933).

On the basis of this observation, it is possible to explain the ingroup homogeneity effect observed in our study in terms of both the motivational principles articulated within social identity theory (chapter 4) and the principles of category fit we have discussed above. It seems that although subjects were quite willing to see positive (ingroup) traits (e.g., 'sportsmanlike' and 'happy-go-lucky') as applicable to the outgroup they were much more reluctant to see relatively negative (outgroup) traits (e.g., 'extremely nationalistic' and 'ostentatious') as applicable to the ingroup. This divergence may reflect the fact that the former tendency was much less threatening to subjects' social identity than the latter. Although such motivations would be expected to vary with context (e.g., in the face of intergroup competition), it seems reasonable to suggest that it is generally more threatening for group members to acknowledge that 'we're very unpleasant' than that 'they're very pleasant'.

A second experiment (Haslam et al., 1993b, Experiment 2) was conducted in order both to replicate the effect for comparative context obtained in the first study, and to examine the motivational account of the link between perceived variability and trait favourableness more rigorously. The design of the study was very similar to the initial experiment, although the *favourableness of traits included in the checklist* was here introduced as an additional factor. That is, subjects characterized the ingroup or outgroup in either a single or two-group context but did so with respect to a checklist that included either only positive traits, only negative traits or both positive and negative traits. Predictions for the comparative context effect were the same as those for the first experiment, and two related effects were expected to arise from subjects' reluctance to apply negative traits to the ingroup, as discussed above. First, it was predicted that the ingroup would be represented as more homogeneous when the checklist included only positive rather than only negative traits. Second, we expected the outgroup to be represented as more homogeneous than the ingroup when the checklist included only negative traits.

The main results of this study are presented in table 7.2. A significant interaction between stereotyped group and comparative context on the stereotypical ratings replicated the effect found in the first experiment: there was outgroup homogeneity in the no comparison conditions (averaging across levels of trait favourableness, traits were applied to 74 per cent of Americans but only 66 per cent of Australians) but no difference in perceived homogeneity in the context of explicit intergroup comparison (traits were applied to 75 per cent of Americans and 74 per cent of

Table 7.2 Mean percentage of group members to whom traits apply as a function of comparative context, stereotypicality and favourableness of traits

Judged group	Trait favourableness	Comparative context and stereotypicality of traits		
		no comparison (stereotypic)	intergroup comparison (stereotypic)	(counter-stereotypic)
Australians	positive	68	78	59
	both	67	75	58
	negative	62	69	56
Americans	positive	71	72	67
	both	76	80	63
	negative	75	77	66

(From Haslam et al., 1993b, tables 4 and 5)

Australians). Further, detailed examination of a significant two-way interaction between trait type and stereotyped group revealed support for both predictions relating to trait favourableness. The ingroup was seen as more homogeneous when it had to be described using all positive rather than all negative traits (traits were applied to 73 per cent and 65 per cent of Australians, respectively), and the outgroup was seen as more homogeneous than the ingroup when subjects could assign only negative traits (here traits were applied to 73 per cent of Americans but only 65 per cent of Australians).

The effect for counter-stereotypical traits obtained in Experiment 1 was also replicated here: counterstereotypical traits were applied to fewer Australians (58 per cent) than Americans (66 per cent), producing an ingroup homogeneity effect in intergroup conditions, as defined by Judd et al. (1991). There was also a clear interaction between trait favourableness and trait stereotypicality. This provided some support for our valence-related analysis of the ingroup homogeneity observed in the first experiment, as subjects appeared to attribute counter-stereotypic traits to the ingroup more strongly where the checklist contained only positive items, and to reject the applicability of stereotypic traits when the checklist was limited to negative items (see Haslam et al., 1993b).

Overall, then, these two experiments provided strong support for our argument that homogeneity judgements follow the categorization *process* rather than fixed differences in category representation. Our analysis shares with Park et al.'s (1991) work an emphasis on the importance of the relative salience of individual category exemplars and abstracted category-level representations. However, where Park et al. (e.g., 1991, p. 220) see these two types of information as represented together in stable category structures, with varying proportions and salience of each across ingroup and outgroup categories, self-categorization theory conceptualizes them as distinct outcomes of categorization at different levels of inclusiveness. In our view, future research should explore further the functioning and consequences of this fluid categorization process rather than seek to establish whether an exemplar or prototype model is the 'true' model of category representation – an issue which Park et al. themselves see as 'extremely difficult' to resolve (1991, p. 222) and which, from our perspective, is necessarily unresolvable.

Our findings also emphasize the importance of the perceived group-relevance of dimensions available for homogeneity judgements (i.e., the normative fit of content to categories). It seems likely (and our findings involving trait favourableness tend to confirm this point) that ingroup homogeneity judgements would be more sensitive to this factor than would judgements of outgroups, because in associating characteristics with an ingroup subjects are essentially defining the social aspects of self. Any mismatch between the dimensions provided for judgement and subjects' own definition of the groups involved is thus more likely to reduce ingroup than outgroup homogeneity, and this may be another factor contributing to the prevalence of outgroup homogeneity findings in the research literature. More generally, it is clear that groups are not seen as homogeneous (or otherwise) in a general, content-free manner (Simon, 1992; Tajfel, 1981a; Tajfel et al., 1964). On the contrary, we would argue, and our results suggest, that homogeneity judgements can actually be a means by which people *communicate* the perceived links between content and group membership in a given context. When subjects made judgements in our studies they were essentially making a statement about how far a given trait was seen to be *group-defining* rather than judging inter-individual variation *per se* (Park and Judd, 1990).

As statements about 'groupness', we thus expect homogeneity judgements to be sensitive to any factors which affect the extent to which a collection of individuals is perceived (by both themselves and others) as a meaningful group. Whilst the studies outlined above tested the basic idea that comparative context and normative fit would influence homogeneity, we have also begun to investigate other factors. For example, we hypothesized that homogeneity judgements would be sensitive to the social influence process (McGarty and Turner, 1992; Turner, 1991), insofar as this worked either to validate or invalidate dimension-specific judgements of ingroups and outgroups.

In an initial study (Oakes and Haslam, 1993) subjects indicated the percentage of both Australians (ingroup) and Americans (outgroup) who could be characterized by group stereotypical traits. Prior to making these homogeneity judgements subjects were given information about how these groups were seen by others. For half the subjects these others were 'open-minded people' (who had been established as an ingroup for the subjects), whilst for the other half they were 'closed-minded people' (an outgroup). Further, the information provided by these others either confirmed ('good fit') or disconfirmed ('bad fit') subjects' pre-existing stereotypic beliefs about Australians and Americans. In the good fit condition it was suggested that Australians were happy-go-lucky, pleasure-loving and sportsmanlike, and Americans were extremely nationalistic, materialistic and ostentatious (all highly stereotypic attributions). Under bad fit this pattern was reversed so that Australians were attributed American-stereotypic traits, and vice versa.

As expected, we found that where good fitting information was thought to come from an ingroup rather than an outgroup (i.e., the subjects' beliefs about the groups were validated by like-minded others), perceived homogeneity of both ingroup and outgroup on stereotypical dimensions was enhanced. It was also enhanced where bad fitting information was provided by either an ingroup or an outgroup: when told that open- or closed-minded people thought Australians were extremely nationalistic and Americans were pleasure-loving, subjects rejected this view and emphasized that *they* thought Australians were pleasure-loving and Americans extremely nationalistic. We suspect that the basis of the rejection of the bad fitting information may have been different in the ingroup and outgroup cases. The information was easily rejected as invalid when its source was an outgroup since there was no reason for subjects to accept it. When it was provided by an ingroup, however, subjects may have been motivated to engage implicitly in minority influence (to argue with the ingroup to get it to change its 'open' mind, Turner, 1991) or to recategorized (subtype) the ingroup source as a deviant subgroup different from self.

What was striking was that the *least* perceived stereotypical homogeneity was found where good fitting information came from an outgroup. This is the condition where subjects found that they *agreed with an outgroup member* (cf. Boyanowsky and Allen, 1973). Turner (1991) has discussed the aversiveness of this situation, and suggests that the options available to the individual are to either re-categorize the other as ingroup (agreement with ingroup members is expected, aversiveness removed), or to change their opinion so that the situation can be recast as disagreement with an outgroup member (again, expected and less aversive). It appears that our subjects reduced stereotypical homogeneity judgements (e.g., they said that fewer Australians were pleasure-loving, and that fewer Americans were ostentatious) in order to communicate disagreement with the outgroup. Beliefs validated by an outgroup were revised (see David and Turner, 1992). In sum, these findings are consistent with our analysis of homogeneity judgements as expressions of beliefs about the characteristics of human groups, made by people who are also identified as group members. As such, homogeneity judgements are likely to be as dynamic and as context-dependent as are those group characteristics themselves.

Finally, it is interesting to consider our analysis of group homogeneity in the context of Simon's (1993) 'egocentric categorization' model, which both claims the outgroup homogeneity effect as supportive evidence, and aims for a more parsimonious explanation of the effect than previous models. A fundamental point in Simon's model is that idiosyncratic self-definition is preferred or 'basic' in Rosch's (1978) sense (at least in Western culture). From this, Simon suggests that many situations hitherto construed as intergroup may in fact be what he terms 'quasi-intergroup', being situations in which '(inter)group relations with outgroup members co-exist with *interpersonal* relations with ingroup members' (1993, p. 140). Because individual self-categorization is basic and preferred, it operates as 'a powerful counter-force' to processes determining the salience of ingroup–outgroup categorizations, and phenomena such as outgroup homogeneity (which seems to reflect group-level perception of the outgroup but individualized perception of the ingroup), 'emerge as "default" phenomena'.

Whilst there are some important points of agreement between Simon's model and self-categorization theory (in particular the idea that interpersonal differentiation is associated with ingroups), there are also points of sharp divergence (Simon, 1993). For one thing, we have already discussed our rejection of the idea of any 'basic' level in social categorization (chapter 4). Also, the hypothesized *co-existence* of group and individual level categorization is inconsistent with predictions from self-categorization theory (see Simon, 1993). It will be recalled from chapter 4 that self-categorization theory assumes a 'functional antagonism' between different levels of categorization, such that processes associated with categorization at the ingroup–outgroup level (processes necessary for others to be perceived as 'outgroup') work against awareness of interpersonal differences represented at a lower level of abstraction. We would argue that recognition of interpersonal differences must always follow a shift to that lower level of abstraction. This shift could be instantaneous, but would be predictably related to a change in comparative and/or normative context brought about by a change in factors such as the task facing perceivers, the judgemental conditions, expectation of interaction, and so on.

The main evidence that Simon cites in support of quasi-intergroup situations is the outgroup homogeneity effect. We have already discussed our interpretation of this effect as a reflection of, *inter alia*, in- and outgroup judgements being made in *different* contexts. In other words, we have suggested that judgement conditions were not characterized by *simultaneous* ingroup–outgroup and individual-level categorizations. In order to be convinced of the existence of quasi-intergroup situations we would need to have evidence of outgroup homogeneity and relative ingroup variability *within the same comparative and normative context and under the same judgemental conditions*. We have already indicated why the existing outgroup homogeneity literature does not appear to satisfy these conditions. In our own studies which operationalized these conditions we provided evidence of symmetry in homogeneity judgements.

In conclusion, self-categorization theory fully predicts asymmetry in experimental data in favour of interpersonal differentiation within groups defined as ingroups as compared to groups defined as outgroups. Whilst outgroups are always judged from an intergroup perspective, in the context of a salient ingroup–outgroup division producing stereotypic homogeneity, ingroups (and only ingroups) can be judged from either that same intergroup perspective or from the very different vantage point of an intragroup perspective (outgroup members can of course be judged from an intragroup perspective where they have been recategorized as ingroup at a superordinate level). Indeed, ingroup judgements will naturally tend to be intragroup, and thus highly differentiated and variable, unless particular conditions prevail which emphasize the salience of the ingroup–outgroup categorization. Our own findings indicate that when ingroup judgements are made under these conditions, they do reflect categorization at the ingroup–outgroup level, and are as stereotypical and homogeneous on ingroup-defining dimensions as are outgroup judgements on outgroup-defining dimensions.

We feel that it is important to acknowledge and emphasize this potential (and often actual) symmetry between ingroup and outgroup judgements. In contrast to the implicit assumption of a qualitative distinction between ingroup and outgroup perceptions which underlies the almost unquestioning acceptance of outgroup homogeneity as a 'principle' of person perception, our view is that *all* stereotypical homogeneity simply reflects perception operating at a distinct, collective level, and that this is appropriate for representing ingroup as well as outgroup members. Indeed, it is difficult to see how ingroups could actually exist as meaningful bases for social identification if their members did not appreciate that they *shared* beliefs, attitudes, expectations and traits – in other words, unless they were aware that the ingroup was homogeneous on relevant dimensions, in appropriate contexts. Enthusiasm for outgroup homogeneity may stem, in part, from an assumption that this 'groupness' is a distortion of perception visited largely upon outgroup targets. In contrast, and underlying our analysis of this literature, we would argue that it is also and equally something experienced as part of individuals' own self-definition.

Illusory Correlation

In chapter 3 we discussed the research of Hamilton and his colleagues (after Hamilton and Gifford, 1976) in which subjects are reliably found to over-emphasize numerically distinct (i.e., rare) behaviours performed by a numerically distinct group. Hamilton and Gifford (1976, Experiment 1) found that, as a result of this tendency, their subjects represented the smaller of two groups more negatively than the larger group even though the ratio of positive to negative behaviours was the same for both (9:4) in the stimulus information with which they were presented (see table 3.3 above). Not surprisingly, this study has been regarded as the paradigm case of distortion arising from basic and inherent strategies of human information processing.

Furthermore, as reasoned by Hamilton (1979, 1981b), this bias can be seen as fulfilling a critical role in stereotype formation as it can produce, independently of other motivational concerns, negative stereotypes of minority groups. If, as Hamilton argues, negative behaviour is non-normative and hence rare, processes of illusory correlation could lead quite straightforwardly to negative stereotypes of relatively small groups even though the behaviour of members of those groups is actually no worse (and could conceivably be slightly better) than that of members of larger groups. As Mullen and Johnson (1990) note on the basis of a meta-analytic integration of results from a large number of studies, this analysis is particularly disturbing in view of evidence that the strength of illusory correlation increases when subjects are exposed to more stimulus information, because in our everyday encounters with groups we are exposed to many more than the forty or so behavioural exemplars presented in typical illusory correlation experiments.

In spite of convincing evidence that the illusory correlation effect is robust under certain conditions (see Mullen and Johnson, 1990), there are two basic reasons why we are sceptical about Hamilton's analysis. The first, already noted in chapter 3, is that previous research indicates that the basic cognitive processes underpinning illusory correlation do appear to be sensitive to, *and to be shaped by*, group-based motivational concerns of the perceiver (McArthur and Friedman, 1980; Schaller and Maass, 1989; Spears et al., 1985, 1986).

This conclusion was confirmed in an experiment conducted in our own laboratory (Haslam et al., 1993a). Here, in six independent conditions Australian subjects formed judgements of two groups of stimulus persons about whom standard illusory correlation information was presented (i.e., there were eighteen positive and eight negative statements about Group A members and nine positive and four negative statements about Group B members). The two groups were subsequently said to come from *different* cities: either from Canberra (the subjects' own city) or Perth (another Australian city) or Detroit (an American city) in all possible pairings. Consistent with findings previously reported by McArthur and Friedman (1980) and Schaller and Maass (1989) there was evidence of strong illusory correlation where the subjects' ingroup (Canberrans) constituted the majority (Group A). However, a strong effect also emerged where Group A was said to come from Detriot and Group B from Perth. These patterns were also significantly attenuated when the pairings were reversed (i.e., in the two conditions where Canberrans were a minority and in the condition where Detroit was a minority and Perth a majority).

The effects for the Perth–Detroit pairing were predicted on the basis of work by Marques and his colleagues into the 'black-sheep effect' (Marques, 1990; Marques and Yzerbyt, 1988; Marques, Yzerbyt and Leyens, 1988). Working within the framework of social identity theory, they have shown that under certain conditions – specifically, where intra-group and intergroup comparisons are made simultaneously (Marques, 1990, p. 149) – poor exemplars of an ingroup will be under-evaluated and psychologically alienated in order to preserve overall relative ingroup positivity. In the case of the Perth–Detroit pairing, this motivational effect was attributable to two factors. First, the experimental context was one where subjects were making both intergroup and intra-ingroup comparisons (the former – between Australia and the United States – being explicit; the latter – between Canberra and Perth – being implicit). Second, in the specific historical context in which the study was conducted, Perth (the capital of Western Australia) was generally perceived very negatively within Australia. At the time of the study (9–14, May 1991) a number of its senior politicians and their associates had been implicated in corruption arising from the collapse of various financial institutions and state-run projects. In reaction to this, a high-level independent inquiry (a Royal Commission) was in the process of being conducted and this was unearthing fresh cases of improper conduct on a daily basis.

In contrast to suggestions made by some previous researchers (e.g., Wilder, 1981, p. 231), the findings of this study were significant in showing that neither illusory correlation nor ingroup favouritism are inevitable: in some conditions illusory correlation was attenuated when it would have resulted in negative characterization of the Canberra ingroup, but at the same time the effect was very strong when it led to the negative characterization of an unpopular exemplar of the Australian ingroup (Perth). The results thus confirmed the point that the processes underpinning both phenomena respond dynamically both (a) to motivational concerns associated with group membership (e.g., concerns to maintain a positive social identity) and (b) to features of the social environment within which they operate (e.g., historical and economic relations between groups).

A second basis of disagreement with Hamilton's model of stereotype formation relates to the theoretical explanation which he proposes to account for the illusory correlation effect. As we noted in chapter 3 this is founded on the belief that numerically infrequent stimuli are inherently distinctive and hence likely to be over-attended to (for related ideas see McGuire et al., 1978; S. Taylor et al., 1978). Hamilton suggests that this tendency is especially marked in the case of co-distinctiveness – that is, in instances where a distinctive group is linked to a distinctive behaviour. This belief is summarized by Hamilton et al. (1985, pp. 5–6; see also Acorn et al., 1988, p. 346; Hamilton, 1979, p. 62; Hamilton and Gifford, 1976, p. 393; Hamilton and Sherman, 1989, p. 61; Sanbonmatsu et al., 1987, p. 2):

> Given two classes of stimulus events, each of which contains both frequent and infrequent (distinctive) subcategories, the co-occurrence of the respective infrequent events will be highly distinctive to the perceiver, and hence will draw attention and be effectively encoded during information acquisition. As a result, these stimulus co-occurrences will be particularly available in memory for later retrieval when various kinds of judgments are called for. . . . A consequence of this information-processing bias is that one will perceive the two classes of events as being associated when in fact they are not.

There are a number of reasons why this distinctiveness account appears to us to be implausible as an explanation of stereotype formation. Most straightforwardly, it does not explain why *only some* instances of shared distinctiveness develop into fully-fledged stereotypes. Why, for example, did the Princeton students studied by Katz and Braly (1933) believe that Turks were cruel rather than aggressive, nationalistic, passionate or persistent (or for that matter, kind, loyal and tradition-loving) in view of the fact that all of these attributes are reasonably distinctive?

In earlier work (Oakes, 1987; see chapter 3), we have taken issue with the proposition that attention is automatically focused and concentrated on novel stimuli – the 'distinctiveness hypothesis' proposed by S. Taylor et al. (1978). As Oakes and Turner (1986a, p. 329) note, one of the major problems with this hypothesis is that the psychological mechanism it proposes is highly maladaptive. This is because novelty is seen to attract attention wherever and whenever it is found – novelty is novelty, whether it be observed in skin colour, eye colour or tie colour. If such a randomly-activated mechanism did underpin attention processes, perceivers would be led to expend processing energies on distinctions which had in general, no social-psychological significance and, in particular, no relevance for current behaviour. Such an implication flies in the face of the conclusions drawn by categorization theorists who have long recognized (a) that social influence works to draw our attention to certain bases for categorization (such as skin colour) but not, under most circumstances others (e.g., eye colour) (Bruner, 1958, p. 93; Tajfel, 1980, pp. 84–85) and (b) that a functional relationship holds between given categorizations and their use in given contexts (Bruner, 1958; Tajfel, 1972; Rosch, 1978). As these researchers have argued, categorization appears to draw attention only to regularities and irregularities that are relevant for the purposes at hand.

Consistent with this point, as already discussed in chapter 3, findings from their study which modified the design of Taylor et al.'s (1978) experiment led Oakes and Turner (1986a) to conclude that 'the evidence . . . weighs heavily in favour of the conclusion that there is no automatic bias directing perceivers' attention towards, and thus increasing the salience of novel category memberships' (p. 341). Similarly, results reported by Oakes et al. (1991, Experiment 1) showed that the extent to which a target person was perceived in terms of his gender was a function of the extent to which his arguments on a gender-relevant topic differed from those of females and were *similar* to those of males (i.e. the comparative fit of gender categories) rather than of his status as a distinctive solo person *per se*.

In order to assess directly the role of distinctive stimulus pairings within the illusory correlation paradigm, McGarty, Haslam, Turner and Oakes 1993 conducted an experiment modelled on that reported by Hamilton and Gifford (1976, Experiment 1).* Here though, the study incorporated a not-so-subtle twist: the subjects were not actually presented with any stimulus sentences describing group behaviours. At the start of the experiment subjects were all given the basic instructions used by Hamilton and Gifford (1976, p. 395) informing them that Group B was smaller than Group A. In four conditions they were then either (1) given no further information, (2) told that there were twice as many statements about Group A members, (3) told that about half of the statements described positive behaviours performed by members of Group A, or (4) given both the latter pieces of information. Subjects then went straight on to complete response material by (a) linking statements to groups (e.g., filling in the blank in the statement 'A member of Group – regularly forgets the names of people who work for him'), (b) evaluat-

---

* The following analysis of illusory correlation was developed in collaboration with Craig McGarty, who also wrote parts of this section (as in McGarty et al., 1993).

ing Group A and B on trait dimensions (of goodness, friendliness, pleas-
antness and honesty) and (c) estimating the number of undesirable behaviours performed by members of each group.

Here it was found, *inter alia*, that merely telling subjects that there
were twice as many statements about Group A members was sufficient to
lead them to evaluate Group A more favourably than Group B and to say
that members of Group B performed more undesirable behaviours than
members of Group A (in a ratio of about 2:1). In other words, the study
produced strong evidence of illusory correlation effects even though
subjects had not actually attended to any stimulus information. For this
reason, the results were clearly inconsistent with Hamilton's explanation
of the phenomenon which relies upon subjects selectively encoding specific behavioural instances – in this case negative behaviours performed
by members of the minority.

The question that arises, however, is how these and other standard
illusory correlation effects might be explained in terms of self-categorization theory. In addressing this issue, we can start our analysis with the
assumption that, in the standard illusory correlation paradigm, subjects
use their categorization of the two groups (A and B) to make sense of the
potentially confusing situation which confronts them. Following the
discussion of self-categorization theory in previous chapters we can argue
that they use the categories to perceive regularities in the stimuli. People
then accentuate similarities and differences between the stimuli in the
process of forming coherent, separable and useful categories. Categories
are formed on the basis of meta-contrast in a manner that maximizes
both between-category difference and within-category similarity. Categories are more likely to be salient, to be used as an appropriate basis for
representing reality, to the extent that they maximize the meta-contrast
ratio (MCR) of inter-class to intra-class difference.

To consider how this process might explain the pattern of responses
obtained in McGarty et al.'s first experiment, one can think of a situation
in which a person is placing nine marbles into two categories when he or
she also knows (a) that there are twice as many marbles in one category
as the other, and (b) twice as many red marbles as blue. This is analogous
to the experimental condition in which subjects were told that there were
twice as many statements about Group A as Group B and discover (on
reading through the statements to which they have to assign group
membership) that the ratio of desirable to undesirable behaviours is
approximately 2:1. Here there are four possible ways of sorting the
marbles into categories, and it is possible to compute a meta-contrast
ratio for each (assigning a value of 0 to a blue marble and 1 to a red

marble). These four resolutions and corresponding meta-contrast ratios are presented below:

Category A	Category B	MCR
1 1 1 1 1 1	0 0 0	++ (infinity)
1 1 1 1 1 0	1 0 0	2.00
1 1 1 1 0 0	1 1 0	0.00
1 1 1 0 0 0	1 1 1	1.67

From these calculations, it is apparent that the resolution associated with the highest meta-contrast ratio (i.e. the one which is most meaningful in categorical terms), involves placing the six red marbles in Category A and the three blue marbles in Category B. Following a similar line of argument, it can be shown that the most meaningful categorical representation of standard illusory correlation stimuli involves assigning all the undesirable statements to members of Group B (the minority). In these terms, the illusory correlation effect may have been reproduced in this study because it was the most appropriate way of making sense of the stimulus field.

Interesting as it is on its own, the obvious question raised by this explanation of effects observed in a study where no stimuli were presented is whether it bears any relation to the effects observed in standard demonstrations of illusory correlation. In seeking to answer this question, it is necessary to make a number of assumptions. The first is that in the standard experiment (as in the above study) subjects are confronted with a potentially confusing situation to which they bring the quite reasonable expectation that it can be resolved in categorical terms. The normal way stimuli are resolved in categorical terms is to find categories which the stimuli fit and seek relevant content dimensions which allow those categories to acquire *differentiated meaning* (McGarty and Turner, 1992).

This concept of differentiated meaning requires some explanation. It is the idea that on the basis of the perception of similarities and differences perceivers identify regularities which help them to explain the perceptual world in a particular setting. These differentiated meanings are associated with beliefs of the form 'Members of Class X are more likely to have Feature A than members of Class Y'. This form of statement must be distinguished from the non-comparative statements 'Members of Class X are likely to have Feature A. Members of Class Y are likely to have Feature B'. The second type of belief is not explicitly comparative: it does not include the assumption of comparison between categories unless the preface 'The difference between Class X and Class Y is that...' is included. Differentiated meaning, then, is meaning which makes concepts separate and clear.

In the case of the illusory correlation paradigm the categories have already been defined, and the stimuli have been selected to suggest comparison in terms of one primary content dimension: evaluation. Indeed, we would argue that subjects in the illusory correlation paradigm probably see their task to be a matter of working out which group is good and which group is bad. We think it is reasonable to suggest that subjects expect there to be a difference between Group A and Group B (even though they may have no prior expectation as to the direction of the difference).

Under these circumstances self-categorization theory suggests that to the extent that perceivers are able to detect regularities which enable them to apply a categorization they will accentuate the similarities and differences associated with the categorized stimuli. Therefore to the extent that they have seen one of the groups as good and the other as bad, they will see the former group as better and the latter as worse than they would have if they had not applied the categorization (Tajfel and Wilkes, 1963a; Turner, 1985).

While this analysis is plausible as an explanation of McGarty et al.'s initial results, the critical question is whether or not it can be claimed that subjects in the illusory correlation paradigm are accentuating psychologically *real* differences between the groups (noting that in Tajfel and Wilkes's, 1963a, experiments in order for subjects to accentuate the differences in the lengths of two sets of lines it was necessary for one set *actually to be* longer than the other). The very point of the frequencies used in the standard illusory correlation paradigm is that they are supposed to suggest that the groups are evaluatively equal (this is why the effect is described as 'illusory'). However, it can be argued that this equality is itself a consequence of the conceptualization of the stimuli in particular terms, namely in terms of the ratio of positive to negative statements. Indeed, we contend that there are several real contrasts in the standard illusory correlation stimuli which suggest the positivity of Group A over Group B (see McGarty et al., 1993).

To illustrate one of these real differences we must retain the assumption that the subjects bring to the stimulus situation (or at least rapidly develop) the expectation that one of the stimulus groups is generally more positive than the other, and that they see the point of the exercise of watching the stimuli as being to determine the direction of this difference. Under these circumstances subjects may entertain two competing hypotheses. When perceivers test between these hypotheses, they are in effect imbuing the two groups with differentiated meaning:

H₁ Group A members are good and Group B members are bad.
H₂ Group B members are good and Group A members are bad.

Under this decision scheme, positive statements about Group A ($n = 18$) and negative statements about Group B ($n = 4$) are evidence in favour of H₁ and positive statements about Group B ($n = 9$) and negative statements about Group A ($n = 8$) are evidence for H₂. From the stimuli to which subjects are exposed there are thus twenty-two pieces of evidence in favour of H₁ and seventeen pieces of evidence in favour of H₂. Under the binomial distribution this difference (given the prior probabilities that p (H₁) $= .5$ and p (H₂) $= .5$) translates to a probability of .26.

While an experimenter might not be swayed by an event that is likely to occur by chance about once in every four occasions, this level of probability is potentially far more convincing when applied to naturalistic conditions. The situation is roughly analogous (leaving aside the possibility of the revision of prior probabilities during the course of the experiment) to imagining, for example, that the experimenter had taken a coin which the subjects believed to be biased, tossed it twice, obtained two heads, and asked the subjects which direction the coin was biased towards (which if we set the prior probabilities at .5 yields a probability of .25). Given the prior information that the coin is biased, then the rational response given the events is to conclude that the coin is biased towards heads. Of course, one might also conclude that there is not enough information to decide the direction of bias, but it would be irrational to decide that the coin is biased towards tails. This pattern is, in fact, what standard illusory correlation data shows: subjects generally conclude that Group A is better than Group B or that there is no difference, they very rarely conclude that Group B is better than Group A (evidence from our own standard studies suggests that the latter conclusion is reached by only about 10 per cent of subjects).

In order to lend further weight to this theoretical analysis, McGarty et al. (1993) conducted a second study which closely followed the procedure of their first experiment. Here though, subjects were presented with the thirty-nine statements to which they would have to assign group membership *before* they performed this task. These statements were presented one at a time on a large screen, each for ten seconds in the form 'A member of Group _ regularly forgets the names of people who work for him'. This modification was incorporated for two reasons. First, the unlabelled stimulus information was expected to allow subjects to establish the relative preponderance of desirable behaviours in the stimuli as a whole prior to their completion of the response sheet – this information being necessary in order to maximize the comparative fit of group members into desirable and undesirable groups (as in the marble example above). Second, it was expected that this procedure would tend to increase subjects' motivation to perceive the stimuli in categorical terms because they would need to identify some purpose for, and impose some meaning on, the display of stimulus sentences.

Consistent with predictions, this second study led to much stronger illusory correlation on every measure than was observed in the initial experiment. Furthermore, very strong illusory correlation was apparent on every measure even in the condition where subjects were given no more than the basic instructions used by Hamilton and Gifford (1976; i.e., informing them that Group A was larger than Group B). Illustrative of this point, in this condition the mean ratings of Group A and Group B on the four evaluative dimensions (ranging from 0 = bad to 10 = good) were 7.59 and 4.13, respectively.

Taken together, these studies thus suggest that the pattern of illusory correlation previously reported in a large number of studies (Mullen and Johnson, 1990) can arise from processes other than those envisaged by Hamilton and his colleagues (for similar conclusions, see Fiedler, 1991; E. R. Smith, 1991). More significantly, it is apparent that these processes need not involve any bias of the type which is central to Hamilton's shared distinctiveness analysis. Indeed, the analysis derived from self-categorization theory and supported by the findings of McGarty et al. (1993), suggests that illusory correlation arises from fully rational processes which serve to reflect significant and meaningful categorical realities – namely, the fact that in the standard illusory correlation paradigm there are actual differences between the stimulus groups that serve to confirm subjects' expectations of intergroup difference. Put more strongly, we believe that there are grounds for arguing that the correlation effect reported by Hamilton and Gifford (1976) is not strictly 'illusory' at all.

Overview

In this chapter we have reconsidered two of the most important of the topics that we discussed in chapter 3 – outgroup homogeneity and illusory correlation. Investigation of illusory correlation has dominated research into stereotype formation since the mid-1970s, which means that stereotype formation has been seen almost exclusively as the outcome of biased information processing which distorts perceptions of groups. Similarly, belief that outgroup homogeneity is 'almost a truism' has meant that stereotyping research has been dominated by the implicit view of stereotyping as a distortion visited mainly upon outgroups.

We have tried, in this chapter, to show that both of these effects can be recast as the outcome of fully adaptive categorization processes which work to represent reality. It is important to note that, unlike other social cognitive researchers (see Hamilton, 1981c), we are not saying that these effects are the outcome of processes which are adaptive at one level because they conserve processing capacity, but maladaptive at another because they simplify and distort. In our view, both illusory correlation (as an outcome of the assumption that there are differences between different groups) and outgroup homogeneity (as evidence of the fact that judgement is affected by comparative and normative context) can be seen to arise from categorization processes which allow us to perceive the realities of both the individual and the group.

Judgements of group homogeneity are crucial to understanding stereotyping and central to self-categorization theory. We feel that work in this area needs to focus on the understanding of *process*, as affected by comparative context and other factors, and to move away from the view that homogeneity is a relatively stable property of category representations (see also Simon, 1992). The analysis of illusory correlation that we have presented may or may not be confirmed in future research and does not derive so directly from self-categorization theory as does our reinterpretation of outgroup homogeneity. Nevertheless, it does show that it is possible to find explanations of the effect which are consistent with the theory and inconsistent with notions of irrational bias. There is clearly enormous scope for the study of stereotype formation to move beyond illusory correlations and investigate the way in which the realities of group life, as they change across time and contexts, are represented in stereotypes (e.g., Ford and Stangor, 1992; Haslam et al., 1992; Haslam et al., 1993b). However, in talking of the need to study 'real intergroup differences' we are not advocating a return to the kernel of truth hypothesis, assuming that fixed group truths are partly distorted by the influence of comparative context (cf. Ford and Stangor, 1992, p. 365). We see variable intergroup comparison as a fundamental condition of stereotype formation. The question of how comparative and normative context affect the formation and expression of stereotypes is likely to attract considerable research attention in the near future.

Having examined the ability of our analysis of stereotyping to deal with two specific topics in the field, we now need to step back and reconsider some of the broader implications of our approach. We now move to address questions that were raised in the infancy and adolescence of stereotyping research (i.e., from Lippman, 1922, to the mid-1960s) but which have been side-stepped as it has matured (i.e., since Tajfel, 1969). Is stereotyping simply the cognitive component of prejudice? How can we assess the validity of stereotypes? Is stereotyping just unwarranted over-generalization? Do stereotypes have a kernel of truth?

We believe that the failure of latterday research to make substantial progress in relation to these questions arises from a failure to confront the issue at the heart of this book – the relationship between stereotyping and social reality. This, then, is this focus of our final chapter.

Suggested Further Reading and References

The papers by Park and Rothbart (1982) and Hamilton and Gifford (1976) provide basic empirical coverage of outgroup homogeneity and illusory correlation effects, respectively. Extensive conventional analysis of these phenomena and their implications can also be found in a large number of book chapters.

For a different perspective, Simon's (1992) chapter in the *European Review of Social Psychology* and Schaller and Maass' (1989) paper are worth reading as they demonstrate how principles from social identity work can inform and enrich analysis of both topics. Self-categorization theory's treatment of the two phenomena is covered in more detail in papers by Haslam et al. (1993b) and McGarty et al. (1993).

Hamilton, D. L. and Gifford, R. K. (1976) Illusory correlation in intergroup perception: A cognitive basis of stereotypic judgments. *Journal of Experimental Social Psychology*, 12, 392–407.

Haslam, S. A., Oakes, P. J., Turner, J. C. and McGarty, C. (1993b) *Social categorization and group homogeneity: Changes in the perceived applicability of stereotype content as a function of comparative context and trait favourableness*. Unpublished manuscript, The Australian National University.

McGarty, C., Haslam, S. A., Turner, J. C. and Oakes, P. J. (1993) Illusory correlation as accentuation of actual intercategory difference: Evidence for the effect with minimal stimulus information. *European Journal of Social Psychology*, 23, 391–410.

Park, B. and Rothbart, M. (1982) Perception of out-group homogeneity and levels of social categorization: Memory for the subordinate attributes of in-group and out-group members. *Journal of Personality and Social Psychology*, 42, 1051–1068.

Schaller, M. and Maass, A. (1989) Illusory correlation and social categorization: Toward an integration of motivational and cognitive factors in stereotype formation. *Journal of Personality and Social Psychology, 56,* 709–721.

Simon, B. (1992) The perception of ingroup and outgroup homogeneity: Reintroducing the social context. In W. Stroebe and M. Hewstone (Eds) *European Review of Social Psychology,* vol. 3. Chichester: Wiley.

8

Politics, Prejudice and Myth in the Study of Stereotypes

Over the last four chapters we have developed an analysis of stereotyping based on self-categorization theory. In chapter 4 we argued for the reality and distinctiveness of group-level phenomena and presented the idea that social categorical perception is the basic cognitive process underlying group interaction. In chapter 5 we addressed the 'why' and 'when' of categorization, emphasizing social categorization, and chapter 6 elaborated detailed links between the antecedents of categorization and patterns of stereotypic accentuation. The analysis was applied to the outgroup homogeneity and illusory correlation effects in chapter 7. In this final chapter we shall confront directly the issue of stereotype validity and seek to draw together the major points of the self-categorization perspective. We shall also broaden the argument, considering validity not merely in its cognitive aspect but also from the point of view of the social and ideological content of stereotypes.

The dominant view of stereotypes from the 1920s has been that they represent prejudiced, invalid cognition. They are identified with 'nearly all that is deficient in popular thinking' (Asch, 1952, p. 232). They are fixed, rigid, distorting images, insensitive to individual differences and social change. They reflect and promote social prejudice. Even proponents of the kernel of truth idea (chapter 2) implicitly concede that the kernel is adulterated by exaggeration and over-simplification.

In current thinking the dominant view takes a special cognitive form. Whilst accepting the normality of the cognitive processes which underlie stereotyping, it nevertheless traces the inevitability of prejudice to these same processes. In the cognitive analysis that was first developed by G. Allport and Tajfel, stereotyping is seen fundamentally as the product of social categorization and the perceptual accentuation of intragroup similarities and intergroup differences. Like categorization, therefore, it is seen as basic, normal and necessary. It is efficient, adaptive and useful, but *it is not, strictly speaking, accurate*. It is useful and efficient because it serves cognitive economy, not because it provides a valid representation of people. It conserves limited information-processing capacity by glossing over real differences between unique individuals, by assimilating complex, novel information to simple, ready-made schemata, by building on a range of cognitive shortcuts that sacrifice strict truth for fast, tolerable approximation or worse. Despite, or because of, its usefulness, therefore, stereotyping is inaccurate, over-simplifying, overgeneralizing, rigid, fixed, insensitive to the evidence of reality. In content, too, the picture remains the same. Stereotypic content is suffused by prejudices reflecting the motivational and social needs of the perceiver.

Only a handful of researchers (Asch, Sherif and Vinacke) have mounted serious arguments for stereotype validity (see chapter 2). One or two others have remained agnostic, arguing that we can never really assess validity, that inferiority in process does not necessarily imply inaccuracy in content (Fishman), or that stereotypes are indispensable and may not be as prejudicial to truth as we had supposed (R. Brown, 1986). Similarly agnostic, Leyens et al. (in press) argue that we should substitute pragmatics or usefulness for representational accuracy as the criterion of validity (cf. Fiske, 1993). The validity of stereotyping in their 'social judgeability' approach is a matter of the degree to which it serves the perceiver's purposes and goals and gives meaning to social interaction. The approach assumes that people make stereotypic judgements only when they believe they have normatively appropriate information.

There is no doubt about the value of the cognitive analysis. Tajfel's (1959, 1969) categorization-accentuation analysis, in particular, was a major step forward and is the basis of our own perspective. Nevertheless, we intend in this chapter to argue that the mainstream view is wrong, that stereotyping is psychologically rational, valid and reasonable, that it provides veridical social perception (i.e., it reflects reality accurately). This is not to say that all stereotypes are valid. This is the central puzzle that we wish to address: how can a veridical cognitive process give rise to false images? Even this question is too crude and is rooted in the categories of conventional thought on the issue. The validity problem is complex and subtle, with several different aspects. The question is better phrased as: how can a veridical cognitive process produce psychologically valid images, some of which, nevertheless, society is *entitled* to reject as false? We shall try to show in what follows that the question is not paradoxical but reflects the interdependence of social life and psychological functioning.

We shall begin by looking at cognitive aspects of validity. The cognitive aspects of stereotyping form the major subject of this book and have dominated social psychological enquiry. Then we turn to the social aspects of validity. The latter are almost never considered in their own right. If it is taken for granted that the cognitive aspects of stereotyping are deficient, then how much more the social content! If stereotype content rationalizes and justifies the treatment of the outgroup by the ingroup (as we assume), if it is self-interested and partisan, then naturally it is prejudiced and what is there to discuss? Nevertheless there are broad themes of theory in social psychology which allow us to provide a social perspective consistent with the cognitive argument. We present it as a preliminary answer to the questions of social validity that the cognitive analysis will inevitably provoke. It is still speculative, not confirmed by data, but not disconfirmed by any we know, and at least as plausible as the conventional view (which actually also rests on implicit theory more than distinctive evidence).

Cognitive Aspects of Stereotype Validity

The idea that stereotyping is rational and valid grew from our elaboration and development of self-categorization theory as it was applied to stereotyping. This section will summarize some of the key points of the analysis made in previous chapters relevant to cognitive aspects of validity.

Salience, Fit and the Reality of the Group

Self-categorization theory follows Tajfel in assuming that stereotypes are the outcome of social categorical perception. They are in form (accentuation) and content (group-level attributes) the product of categorizing at the ingroup–outgroup level. The theory explains the salience of social categories as a function of an interaction between relative accessibility (perceiver readiness) and comparative and normative fit (chapter 5). Salient social categories lead to the stereotypic perception (depersonalization) of ingroup and outgroup members and transform interpersonal into intergroup behaviour (chapter 4).

Through the concept of fit, the theory takes for granted that there is some social reality that is distinctively represented by social categorical perception. It assumes that individuals can and do act as both individual persons and social groups under different conditions. Since both individuals and social groups exist objectively, both personal and social categorizations are necessary for the veridical representation of social life. There is an objective variation in the unitariness of social behaviour, from interpersonal to intergroup and through all possible conflicts and compromises, which variation in the inclusiveness of self-categorization both reflects and underlies. *It is therefore in principle possible for social categorical perception to be valid.* There is a reality for it to represent and there is a governing principle of cognition that ties categorization to that reality. Given that groups are real, not to represent them would be inaccurate. It is no more wrong to categorize people as groups than it is to categorize them as individuals.

It is important to note that the theory not only asserts the reality of the group and the possibility of veridical group perception, but that it also asserts that the personal level of perception is also categorical. *Both person and group perception are categorization.* The issue of validity, therefore, is not a matter of opposing unreal, categorized groups to real, uncategorized individuals, of seeing either groups or individuals, of one or the other level of perception always being more real or valid than the other, but of doing both or either when appropriate. We suggest that this is precisely what people do. They define people as individuals in one context and as groups in another. There is context-dependent variation in behaviour and context-dependent variation in level of categorization. Leaving content aside for the moment, the issue is when do we categorize at the individual or group level? What is the principle governing variation? Does it guarantee the appropriateness of ingroup–outgroup categorization under normal circumstances?

We have suggested that the principles of comparative and normative fit are rational and reasonable ways of tying categorization to reality. It makes sense, for example, that we cannot explain a person's attitudes in terms of his being a male when we see other males disagreeing, but that we might when other males agree and only females disagree (Hogg and Turner, 1987). It makes sense that we would want to talk about a group of arts students not as 'students' or as 'individuals' but as 'arts students' when they agree with each other, but disagree with science students, on an issue that we know separates arts and science students and in a direction that we know is normative for arts students but not students in general (Oakes et al., 1991).

The Variability and Context-Dependence of
Stereotyping

If fit ties categorization to reality appropriately, then it follows that stereotyping must vary with the social context. When reality changes, stereotyping must change. The fit principle hypothesizes that self-categorization is inherently comparative, that it does not reflect the fixed, absolute properties of self and others but comparative, relational properties. It predicts, therefore, that social categorizing will be fluid, variable and relative to the social context. More specifically, our work has produced evidence for four major forms of stereotypic variation which are predicted by the fit principle as a function of changes in the social context. It has been shown that social categorizations, and their products, stereotypes, vary appropriately in level of inclusiveness, kind, content and prototypical meaning (chapters 4–7).

A number of studies (reviewed in chapters 5–7) have shown that the level at which people categorize and stereotype varies with the available meta-contrast of inter-class to intra-class differences. Whether people are seen as individuals or group members (or at other levels of identity) is a function of the perceived differences between self and others within the social context as a whole. It has been possible to explain the effects of a number of variables on stereotypic assimilation and contrast in these terms: the extent and/or extremity of the frame of reference, the effect of differences in own position and between extremists and moderates, and the effect of intragroup vs. intergroup comparison.

The general point is that meta-contrast can only find category identity for a group of stimuli by differentiating a contrasting category within the same context. A person cannot be defined as ingroup in contrast to outgroup where only ingroup members are available for comparison: a less inclusive level of (personal) self-categorization which contrasts the person with ingroup members must be found. Conversely, a person cannot easily be defined as an individual in contrast to ingroup members where the context provides a stronger contrast with outgroup members.

In chapter 7, for example, we applied the idea that level of self-categorization varies with context to the outgroup homogeneity effect. It was argued that perceived group homogeneity follows from category salience and stereotypic accentuation. Category membership will be more salient in intergroup than intragroup contexts. Therefore the tendency to perceive outgroups as more homogeneous than ingroups reflects, amongst other things, the fact that judgements of outgroup members tend to be made on the basis of intergroup comparisons, whereas judgements of ingroup members will often be made on the basis of intragroup comparisons. The same principle of comparative fit underlies both ingroup heterogeneity and outgroup homogeneity: they both reflect the level of self-other categorization which fits the context in terms of meta-contrast. No assumptions need be made about relative familiarity with ingroup members or prejudice against outgroup members, nor about the number of exemplars or type of information stored in memory. Perception of varying group homogeneity is a product of a dynamic process of comparison, categorization and stereotypic accentuation.

At any given level of social categorization, the specific category that becomes salient, its defining stereotypical dimensions and its prototypical meaning will also all vary with the social context being represented. The ingroup–outgroup categories selected must meaningfully interpret the content of people's attributes and actions in terms of the perceiver's background theories and knowledge. At the same time, the particular dimensions of intergroup comparison that define the categories and the internal structure (of the relative prototypicality of members) will vary flexibly with the intra- and intergroup differences observed. A person wearing the right uniform has to be called a 'policewoman' not a 'nurse' (under most circumstances); compared to policemen, policewomen may be seen as 'feminine', compared to scientists, they may be seen as 'uneducated'; in contrast to nurses they may be seen as 'masculine', in contrast to petty criminals they may be seen as 'highly educated'. Stereotypes are selected and constructed to represent meaningfully the observed relations between ingroup and outgroup on specific content dimensions and also vary in content as a function of these represented relations.

We have shown in sum that stereotyping is characterized by variability and context-dependence. A stereotype of the *same people* may vary in level, defining category, content dimensions and prototypical meaning as a function of changes in the social context. It will be shaped by intra- and intergroup relations in interaction with the implicit social theories the perceiver brings to the interpretation of behaviour. Several inferences can be drawn:

1. It appears that stereotyping does vary with the social context as predicted by the fit principle. Stereotypic variation is not arbitrary or based on subjective prejudice in the above examples, but lawfully follows fit. Moreover, the fit principle enables us to see how stereotyping normally assumed to be prejudiced can in fact be seen as quite appropriate and reasonable. Two good examples are provided by the reinterpretation of the outgroup homogeneity effect (chapter 7) and of the classic perceptual differences between extremists and moder-

ates (chapter 6). It is not after all that perception of outgroups and perception by extremists are prejudiced whereas perception of ingroups and perception by moderates are accurate. The same principle – but operating upon different realities and from different perspectives – underlies both sets of outcomes.

2. Stereotypes can be thought of as representations of the *group-in-context* in that they change with the context, not just with attributes of the group. They do not seem to be representations of fixed, absolute group properties somehow adjusted for or displaced by context. It may be more accurate to say that they are contextual definitions, definitions of the group in terms of its contextual, relational properties (always recognizing that relational properties imply specific dimensions of comparison which imply the content of social interaction). In a real sense, the group gains categorical identity from the context within which it is defined. The constraints upon category variation (apart from reality) are provided by the body of social knowledge and theory the perceiver brings to interpretation.

3. Stereotypes can be properly described as veridical in that their variation is systematically related to changes in social reality. Variability does not imply that the true identity of the group is being distorted by external circumstances. On the contrary, variability is necessary *if* social categorizing is to be veridical, if it is to get right the changing contextual properties of people. If reality changes, then on the assumption of validity, stereotypes must change. We shall return to this issue presently.

The Myth of Stereotype Rigidity

It now seems clear that the standard picture of stereotypes as fixed, rigid and insensitive to reality is mythical. Far from being rigid and unaccommodating, stereotypes appear to be fluid and variable and to change with the social context. Both traditional and contemporary evidence seems consistent with notions of stereotype variability (see chapters 2–7). It is time to jettison the idea that stereotypes reflect 'hardwired' biases – as we saw in chapter 7, even illusory correlations vary with intergroup relations (Haslam et al., 1993a).

One important source of relevant evidence is research on intergroup relations. Both realistic conflict theory (Sherif, 1967) and social identity theory (chapter 4) predict and find that intergroup stereotypes reflect and follow intergroup relations. Social identity theory is often misinterpreted as suggesting that ingroup bias is a universal, fixed feature of intergroup perceptions. This is quite false. The message of the theory is the variability of ingroup bias as a function of a variety of social and psychological factors which impinge on group identification and intergroup relations, and it is this variability which has proved to be the rule. Early research on the effects of social change (chapter 2) also show that real intergroup stereotypes change as a function of real social events which modify intergroup relations. But in line with the idea that variation 'fits' reality, stereotype change is not indiscriminate – stereotypes change on relevant dimensions when intergroup relations change. If intergroup relations do not change, then neither do the stereotypes. We demonstrated in our Iraq study (Haslam et al., 1992) how the stereotype of Americans varied significantly over a short period of time, in interaction with the frame of reference. Stereotypes vary with the level and content of social categorizations that become salient to represent and fit the comparative intergroup relations.

The myth of fixedness comes from looking for change in the wrong place. The general, usually implicit assumption has been that social categories should match the personality characteristics of individual members, that a correct category should reflect the 'true' properties of individuals (see Leyens et al., in press). Thus, the failure of stereotypes to change as a function of personal information about individual group members is taken as evidence of rigidity. In fact, of course, stereotypes represent *group*-level realities (as defined in the context of intergroup relations) and reflect the emergent properties of the social category as a whole, *not* the personal characteristics of individual members (cf. Lott and Lott, 1965).

It was a misconstrual of the representational object of stereotypes that created and then plagued the 'contact' hypothesis, the idea that personal contact with outgroup members would (inevitably) disconfirm negative outgroup stereotypes, reduce prejudice and improve intergroup relations. More recently, with the re-invigoration of Sherif's (e.g., 1967) intergroup perspective on social prejudice in the form of social identity theory, the many qualifications to the simple contact hypothesis have been put into a less reductionist perspective (R. J. Brown and Turner, 1981; Hewstone and R. J. Brown, 1986). As R. J. Brown and Turner (1981) conclude in their critique of the hypothesis, where social contact reduces prejudice, it is not because

it permits and encourages interpersonal friendships between members of different groups, but rather because it changes the nature and structure of the intergroup relationship ... prejudice and discrimination between groups are likely to be reduced more effectively by policies addressed directly to changing people's social identifications and intergroup relations (pp. 63–4).

Without an intergroup perspective, an appreciation that stereotypes are held by the members of one social group (or society or culture) about the members of another group with whom they stand in a definite intergroup relationship, irreducible to the level of *interpersonal* behaviour or contacts (R. J. Brown and Turner, 1981; Sherif, 1967; Tajfel, 1981a), analysis will remain implicitly individualistic and will tend to misconstrue, or simply continue to ignore, the problem of validity. Even purely cognitively, validity is not about whether social categories match the fixed, objective attributes of individual members; this is a reductionist view of group life and social category meaning (Turner and Oakes, 1986). Validity is about the match between social categories and intergroup realities.

It is a failure to appreciate this point about the emergent, distinctive reality of the group which underlies the kernel of truth argument for validity, with its assumption that stereotypes contain at least a part of the truth about group members, the part which summarizes their 'real' *individual* characteristics. Again, this ignores the fact that the group is irreducible to the individual. We saw in chapter 2 the immense difficulty researchers encountered when they actually brought stereotype content and individual people together in their attempt to identify valid, justifiable 'kernels'. In contemporary research, some researchers see the truth in a perceptual balance or compromise between social categorical and individuating information (see Leyens et al., in press), but this approach maintains the view that the ideal is to see the objectively fixed individual correctly. It suggests that group membership information should be employed only where it is accurately and rationally likely to indicate the true attributes of the single individual person. The pervasive theme is that reality is objectively individual and that individual attributes are fixed in personality (Judd and Park, 1993). In contrast, we have argued that the group is also real, and that it is *group* attributes that are represented in stereotypes.

The evidence for variation, that stereotyping is context-dependent, implies that stereotypes are not enduring, rigid distortions of a fluid reality, but are contextual representations of people. They define people in terms of their social comparative properties. A discussion of the veridicality of stereotypic accentuation will illustrate what we mean by this idea. We shall then argue that it is inconsistent with the notion of stereotypes as stored, fixed constructs.

The Veridicality of Stereotypic Accentuation

We have argued that variation in stereotyping is veridical in the sense that stereotypes change to match changes in reality. A problem with this argument is immediately apparent. The effect of a salient social categorization is the perceptual accentuation of intragroup similarities and intergroup differences (i.e., stereotypic assimilation and contrast). Even if social categorizations become salient when they fit, surely their perceptual effects are distorting, not reflecting the true character of the stimulus? This point is central to the classic condemnation of stereotypes as *over*generalization, the perception of outgroup members, for example, as more similar to each other and more different from us *than they really are*.

For example, when, solely as a function of context, as in the Haslam and Turner (1992) studies, another person who differs from you by some constant amount is categorized as similar and assimilated to self in one extended context and as different and contrasted away from self in a restricted context, isn't this distortion? Your own position has not changed, the other's position has not changed and yet the target other is categorized as either ingroup or outgroup, resulting in differential perception of the other. Reality has not changed, but perception has.

Casting these findings in this way misconstrues the nature of the match between categories and reality and ignores the relational character of both (Asch, 1952; see chapter 4). Reality *has* changed in terms of contextual properties and categories are contextual representations. The 'distortion' only appears as such if we begin with the assumption that social categories reflect isolated, fixed, absolute properties of the perceived. In contrast, we have argued that all perception is relative. All perception reflects categorization (Bruner, 1957) and categorization, we have argued, is intrinsically comparative and relational. When one changes the context of comparison, then, by definition, the relationship of the self and target other to the context must change. The social contextual, relational, comparative properties of the self and other must therefore change, and it is this *relative* reality that ingroup–outgroup categories embody. In the example from Haslam and Turner (1992), it is *not true* that social and self-categorization is varying independently of reality – which would be distortion. In our research we never find that self-categories vary without some corresponding, lawful change in the self, other or context.

From this perspective, stereotypic accentuation does not reflect distortion but appropriate variation in the level of self-categorization. As the level of categorization shifts from the personal to the social, intrapersonal similarities and interpersonal differences are replaced by intragroup similarities and intergroup differences. Similarly, as the level of categorization shifts from the social to the individual, intragroup similarities and intergroup differences are replaced by intrapersonal similarities and interpersonal differences. It is these shifts in the level of similarity and difference that we refer to as 'accentuation'. They reflect the salience of varying levels of category identity and express the rational selectivity of perception in which it is more appropriate to categorize at one level in some contexts and at a different level in others. Ingroup–outgroup differences are no more a distortion than individual differences (which are also lower-level accentuations). We accentuate the differences between persons in categorizing them at the individual level just as we accentuate differences between groups in categorizing at the ingroup–outgroup level. As we have argued, variation in level of categorization reflects real variation in the relational properties of people. Hence such contextual selectivity is inherently veridical.

Accentuation effects are measured against some baseline level of perception and indicate change away from that baseline. The idea that they are distortions implies a number of questionable assumptions and it is useful to summarize them:

1. That variation in the level of self–other categorization does not reflect changes in people's objective characteristics. We have argued, in contrast, that categorizing varies with people's comparative properties, which must vary with the context of comparison, and that their relational properties are real. The sensitivity of category level to the context of comparison was discussed above.
2. That only group perception is categorical; that the individual level is not categorical and does not involve accentuation effects relative to other levels. We reject this idea in point of theory and fact (see chapter 5). Moving to the individual level is not decategorizing but recategorizing (Gaertner et al., 1989).
3. That one level (the individual) is more real than the others (particularly the group and more superordinate levels) or, similarly, that the group level is appropriately reduced to the individual level (the reductionist view). Thus to move away from the individual level is by definition to move away from reality. This is a matter of individualism versus the reality of the group, a topic of long-standing controversy in social psychology and other social sciences (see chapters 4 and 5). Suffice to say, social identity and self-categorization theories

have presented detailed arguments against the theoretical and empirical validity of the individualistic thesis and for the alternative view.

4. That, lastly, the principle governing variation between levels (e.g. between individual and ingroup–outgroup perception) is not rational or reasonable or directed to representing reality appropriately. We have already touched on this claim, commenting that comparative and normative fit are quite reasonable ways of deciding to group stimuli together in a given context. Certainly, it is unclear that they are in any sense irrational. What is clear is that we see no problems with categorizing nonsocial objects or individuals on the basis of these or similar principles. We are happy to describe 'chairs' and 'tables' as 'furniture' in some contexts and act in terms of their perceived superordinate equivalence and we know that such variation in the categorization of nonsocial objects is also associated with accentuation (McGarty, 1990). Yet, apparently, it is only the grouping of people that disturbs us. In effect the argument about the principle of categorizing is not about process at all, but merely an objection to one outcome: it is a further version of the individualistic prejudice against group perception. It could be argued that relative accessibility based on irrational theories distorts the operation of fit. This issue will be dealt with presently.

Far from being solid evidence for distortion, therefore, accentuation is important evidence for the sensitivity of perception to changes in reality. It is evidence for perceptual change between levels as a function of social context. If we reject individualism and reductionism and acknowledge the emergent reality of the group, if we acknowledge the complexities and subtleties of human social behaviour – that it is not a matter of individuality or groupness, but of both according to circumstances – then the absence of accentuation would imply rigidity. What sense would it make to see people as groups when they were behaving as individuals or as individuals when they were behaving as groups? There are a variety of levels of categorization; shifts between them in any direction involve categorical accentuation (note the accentuation between individual stimuli as well as classes in table 3.1), the expression of perceptual selectivity dictated by reality.

Stereotypes as Stored Constructs

It has been assumed since Lippman (1922) that stereotypes are in some sense 'pictures in our heads', relatively enduring cognitive constructs, stored in memory and organized around, for example, beliefs, attitudes, social categories, or schemata, depending on one's theoretical preference. If stereotypes are contextual definitions of people, a direct inference is that this view may be inappropriate. The idea of stereotypes as relatively fixed mental structures, as stored concepts waiting-to-be-activated, may be neither meaningful nor necessary (cf. Smith and Zarate, 1992).

If stereotypes are contextual representations, how can they be stored or exist prior to their use? How can they be stored as pre-formed givens independent of the context in which they are used? Social contexts are infinitely variable, as are our relationships to them, which means that, in principle, there is no limit to the stereotypes we can generate. It is very unlikely, for example, that social psychologists have preformed representations of themselves as compared with circus performers, held in reserve against the slim possibility that they should be asked to make this comparison. Nevertheless, they could make it and provide an appropriate self-stereotype. Similarly, subjects in some of our own experiments have been asked to make stereotypical judgements in terms of their home town (Canberra) as compared to Detroit (USA), an unlikely comparison but one they based their judgements on without difficulty. It could be argued that we have a stored set of stereotypes which are adjusted in some way for new contexts. The requirement in that case is an explanation of how the adjustment occurs, a principle of the generation of the concepts used. However, once we have developed such a principle (as in the fit hypothesis, for example), it is not clear that the notion of prior-concepts-waiting-to-be-activated plays any further heuristic or explanatory role.

The stored-concept view may not be necessary since we can assume that varying stereotypic judgements are produced by general principles of categorization functioning at a given time to represent particular intergroup realities in interaction with background knowledge and perceiver readiness. We can think of stereotyping as a flexible, constructive process of judgement and meaningful inference in which any and all cognitive resources are used as and when necessary to create the appropriate social categories. Rather than activated concepts whose meaning is defined prior to their application, stereotypes can be seen as the varying outcomes of a dynamic process of social judgement. This notion of stereotypes as products of flexible, on-the-spot categorical judgements is in line with conclusions recently drawn about categories in cognitive psychology (see Neisser, 1987a; especially Barsalou, 1987) and about the self-process as a whole in self-categorization theory (Turner et al., in press).

There is of course stability as well as fluidity, continuity as well as discontinuity. Stability in stereotypic judgement arises from the stability of intergroup relationships, the higher-order knowledge frameworks used to give coherence to varying instances of group behaviour, the social groups, subcultures and social institutions which provide perceivers with long-term norms, values, and motives, and social influence and communication processes which translate particular conceptions of groups into social norms and validate the broader elaborative ideologies used in their construction.

Overview

In sum, the salience of ingroup–outgroup categorization, its variability, context-dependence and effects all indicate that it is psychologically rational and valid. Stereotypes are deployed when they fit group realities and content varies to provide relevant appropriate meaning. Stereotypic accentuation indicates not bias nor distortion but selective veridical perception of the varying contextual properties of people. However, when it comes to the validity of stereotyping, this is only the cognitive part of the story. It is evident that stereotypes serve political, social and ideological functions and that we reject and condemn some stereotypes at the same time as we advance our own. We are not saying that all stereotypes are valid. This is patently untrue. We are saying that when they are wrong, it is not because of cognitive or psychological deficit, or because there is something inherently wrong with the process of ingroup–outgroup categorization. It is, we suggest, a matter of political and ideological judgement.

Social Aspects of Stereotype Validity: The Political Dimension

Even if it is granted that the cognitive aspects of the stereotyping process appear reasonable and appropriate, the argument so far has been premised completely on fit. What of the influence of perceiver readiness, the tendency for certain ways of categorizing to be more accessible as a function of the perceiver's expectations, motives, values and goals? What of stereotypes which serve self-interest, which rationalize, ideologize and justify exploitative intergroup relations, which serve the goals, needs, values of the perceiver's group? At the extreme, many stereotypes are just self-serving propaganda, political and ideological weapons in a struggle between conflicting groups (Wetherell and Potter, 1992). Stereotypes do not merely describe group realities, they serve motivational and social functions. Surely these functions prejudice their content?

Is stereotyping a rational cognitive process whose content is none-theless distorted by the needs of group members to construct pictures of their own and other groups which protect their values and partisan interests, glorify the ingroup, justify the treatment of the outgroup and rationalize arrangements to the ingroup's advantage? This is one view and in many respects it is credible. It is probably close to what many social psychologists believe. Some have argued from a pragmatic perspec-tive that the validity of stereotyping (or cognition as a whole) is best defined in terms of the degree to which it serves the perceiver's goals. We cannot agree. Such a solution leads straight to *relativism*, the idea that all groups' stereotypes are equally valid. We shall argue in contrast that the interactive influence of perceiver readiness does not prejudice psychologi-cally the validity of the stereotyping process, but that what is *psychologi-cally* valid as a representation of reality is not necessarily socially and politically valid.

Perceiver Readiness and the Relativity of Perception

The role of perceiver readiness* in categorization and stereotyping is well established. The first point to make, however, is that *all perception* is influenced by the expectations, goals, needs and values of the perceiver (Bruner, 1957, 1983). All human perception is active, constructive, mo-tivated, purposeful, interpretative and elaborative. There are two basic ideas here which are widely shared in social and cognitive psychology: (1) that perception follows cognition, that it is an active, sense-making, hypothesis-testing process, in which what is seen is not passively received from the external world but selectively and constructively mediated by internal cognitive structures (e.g., schemata, categories, implicit theories, attitudes and beliefs, social representations); (2) that perception is moti-vated, purposeful, goal-driven, that we are primed to see what matters to us whilst we ignore what does not matter, to see what is relevant, useful

---

*   From here onwards the term 'perceiver readiness' (to use a category) is preferred to the 'relative accessibility' (of a category) both (a) because of the discussion above implying that the notion of 'stored-constructs-waiting-to-be-activated' is probably misleading and (b) because we wish to emphasize the contribution of the perceiver to what is perceived in a sense more general than merely cognitive.

and important in terms of our particular interaction with the world (chapter 5).

The evidence for these propositions is overwhelming – almost all the data of social psychology could be cited in one way or another as support (from the study of attitudes, through the New Look in perception to current studies in social cognition). They indicate that the influence of perceiver readiness is not a small aspect of selected stereotyping phenomena but a fundamental property of all human perception. The accessibility × fit hypothesis is a way of conceptualizing the idea that what a person perceives is a function of an interaction between the person doing the perceiving and the object being perceived. In this sense, the concept of perceiver readiness embodies the idea that perception is always relative to the perceiver, which means it is relative to self. It functions to ensure that we see the world veridically but in a way that is useful and relevant to our goals and needs and stamped by our values and theories. Stereotyping serves the perceiver and is therefore *constrained by* the perceiver in that it must represent reality from the singular vantage point of the perceiving person.

We tend to think in social psychology of this constraint the self puts upon perception as a filtering-out process in which information is lost, but the metaphor is wrong: it is more like a design feature of the cognitive system which tunes us in to information which we would otherwise not have. Perceiver readiness does not constrict, reduce, or limit human experience; it facilitates, elaborates, selects, and hence serves rather than compromises veridicality. If we summarize its basic effects this point becomes clearer:

1 Through the influence of perceiver readiness stimuli are *elaborated* in terms of categories provided by one's own past experience and the body of ideas, theories and knowledge acquired from one's culture (a perceiver not primed in this way is one who has literally learnt nothing and categorizes in ignorance).
2 Perceiver readiness leads to the *selective* categorization of the world in a way that is *meaningful, relevant and useful* in terms of the needs, goals and purposes of the perceiver.
3 It ensures that the categories used by the perceiver *evaluate* reality from the perspective of his or her own standards, norms and values.
4 It represents and judges reality *from the vantage point of one's own place in it*, from the perspective provided by one's own particular position.

To be influenced in categorizing by one's past experience or the cognitive gains of one's social community must improve rather than compromise the veridicality of perception. And it would make little sense for human perceivers to choose to categorize the physical or social world in the many ways available that have no human relevance. Selectivity is not invalidity and pointless selectivity is not to be preferred to useful selectivity. These two points are reasonably easy to grasp, but our third and fourth points about perceiver readiness are more difficult.

What about the influence of values on stereotype content? What if a right-wing politician who believes in unfettered, laissez-faire capitalism (who, like a recent British prime minster, rejects the reality of 'society' and affirms that there are only individuals making their own way) derogates the unemployed as 'lazy' and 'stupid', because as individuals they have failed to find work? This is a stereotypical judgement made from a set of political values and we might well react immediately with accusations of prejudice. But what if I disagree about the causes of unemployment and from a different set of values describe such politicians as 'callous' and 'stupid'? Is this also prejudice? It is easy to write off the impact of values we reject as prejudice, but what of our own evaluative judgements? Is my judgement false in this instance because it reflects my own political values and a specific political analysis of the contemporary unemployment problem? In fact, I take it for granted that my judgement is political (just as is the politician's) and it is the political analysis underlying my judgement that gives me confidence in its validity (e.g., I believe I understand the self-serving intentions and lousy economic theory behind the politician's slur). How could a political (or social or religious or economic) judgement be value-free, or be any more 'accurate' for being value-free? Without values I would make no judgement in the first place, there could be no political analysis, the politician would never have needed to derogate the unemployed (to *justify* a set of policies).

Political and social life is about values and clashes of values. To argue that a political judgement should not be evaluative (i.e., reflect the relevant values, standards, normative goals of the perceiver) or that it would be more accurate without evaluation is absurd: values are part of political reality and at the heart of the political process is the assertion of one's own values in contrast to others. One cannot state that a value of, say, 'community' is *objectively* false or correct, any more than is a value of 'selfishness'. But *as premises*, they do allow correct, if relative, judgement. Given that we have such values and judge events in terms of them, the evaluative connotations of such judgements can be either veridical or false from the perspective of the value which functions as the standard. If I am politically right-wing, I may well share the values of the politician who described the unemployed as 'lazy' and judge the epithet accurate. Others with contrasting values will see it as false and substitute their own version of truth. To choose not to apply values in social judgements in the interests of accuracy would imply much worse than a restricted form of social perception, it would require a diminution of human social life. We cannot, as Bogardus (1950) hoped, rescue stereotypes from invalidity by replacing them with scientifically neutral, value-free conceptions of groups (chapter 2). Such an intention misconceives the problem of validity and the social purpose of perception.

Judgements of social reality reflect one's own perspective, an evaluative and motivated point of view. The perceiver after all is not neutral or passive, but objectively involved in society. No judgement of society (or nature) is possible but from a human perspective stamped by values and ideologies. Reality is apprehended not merely through our ideas, cognitive schemata etc., but also through our values, and the validity of the evaluative aspects of stereotypes is also relative to the perceiver. Psychologically, it is as reasonable for political conservatives to construct a stereotype stamped with their own political values as it is for their opponents to do likewise. *There is no difference in the psychological process.* The difference is in the political values applied and therefore the outcome of judgement. Veridicality is not in opposition to values, therefore, but is relative to the specific values applied.

The fourth point was that perception is relative to one's social and psychological 'place'. We have already argued and shown experimentally that, depending on the comparative context and one's own position, self and others are categorized differently. We have argued that this is reasonable and appropriate, because categories are defined comparatively and people's relational properties are real. The relational properties of the social world vary *objectively* not only with the frame of reference but also *with one's own position.*

Probably the best example is provided by Haslam and Turner's (1993) research on the categorical differences between extremists and moderates (chapter 6). We have long known that extremists and moderates see the world differently. Extremists tend to categorize people into us and them more sharply and polarize in their judgements more than moderates (they see the social world as more black and white than grey, and more black than white). What is novel in the Haslam and Turner studies is the demonstration that the *same principle* (i.e., meta-contrast) underlies the differential categorization by extremists and moderates and that it is directed to veridicality. Extremists categorize the world differently from moderates not because they are odd, but because relatively speaking they are in different worlds. Extremists accentuate more than do moderates because their difference from outgroup members compared to their difference from ingroup members is larger than for moderates. The world for extremists compared to moderates *is* comprised of people who are relatively *more similar* or relatively *more different*, (i.e., more polarized). The point is not just that society is categorized differently, depending on where one is, but also that the categorizing is veridical because the reality is actually different.

Depending on who one is and where one is in society, reality not only looks different, it is different. Reality is not homogeneous, but varies with the perceivers who cognitively represent and interact with it, because psychologically they occupy different locations. This is most clear in social life. In the conflict between police and poll tax demonstrators (see the photograph in chapter 6), for example, each group, we can surmise, categorizes and evaluates itself and the other group differently (seeing the ingroup as more positive than the outgroup), interprets the interaction in terms of different social and political ideologies ('citizens exercising democratic freedoms' vs. 'maintaining law and order'), understands their own and the other groups' intentions differently ('peaceful protest' or 'violent troublemaking', 'doing a job' or 'brutal repression'), suffers different apprehensions and fears, has different emotions, hopes, expectations, and so on.

If a demonstrator finds the police aggressive and frightening, expects the worse and acts in kind, or a policewoman complains of the unrelenting hostility of the crowd, can we offer them the other group's judgement of itself (e.g. the police say, 'as far as we're concerned we're just here to maintain law and order') as disconfirmation of their own experience? Hardly. Nor can we provide the viewpoint of a third party such as government or media (or social scientists; see Reicher, 1987, and the discussion in chapter 2) as the objective, neutral definition of events. The parties involved and the parties on the sidelines each have their definite social relationship to each other and to the events taking place, their own definite interests, goals, values and beliefs. Third parties also judge from their own perspective and via the same psychological process as police or demonstrators. It is a commonplace of social psychology that the psychological situation *is* experienced differently depending on how one defines it. Each group naturally experiences the 'same' social event differently, but we cannot say that one group's experience is psychologically more valid than the other's. Each group's experience is valid from its own perspective, relative to its own psychological attributes.

Moreover, reality only exists for people as it is apprehended, cognized, judged, liked, feared, valued. The mental representations through which a concrete social interaction is apprehended are experienced as representations of the objective event, not as unreal epiphenomena. These experiences are part of the event and shape the event. Fear is part of war and

love part of marriage – we should have to leave out the human participants for this not to be true. If social reality only exists for perceivers as
psychologically apprehended and in part comprises their psychological
reactions (Asch, 1952), then social reality not only looks different but is
different for different perceivers. We are not suggesting that reality only
exists if it is perceived or that it is created by the mind; we are saying that
reality is *heterogeneous*, not uniform, and that different perceivers are
objectively interacting with different parts/ aspects/ features of it.

The relativity of perception means that it is selective, relevant, interpretative and evaluative, but it does not imply that it must be invalid.
Given our own goals, needs, values, perspectives, perceiver readiness
provides perception that is valid from one's own premises rather than
someone else's. Perception that was not relative to self would be pointless, futile, unimaginable and meaningless. It would not be human. The
ideal of human perception is not that of an omniscient being who sees all
things at all times from all perspectives, nor of a neutral computer that
analyses exhaustively and mechanically with no social purpose or emotional investment. What would be the point of stereotyping from another's point of view? Why would one want stereotypes that evaluated and
described groups from the standpoint of others' values and self-interest?
It is hard to imagine how or why any biological (or other) system would
evolve a capacity for perception unaffected by the functions, aims, properties and location of the perceiver.

None of the points that we have made about the effects of perceiver
readiness contradict the role of fit; it is just that fitting is active and interpretative and is informed by one's own perspective, values and goals.
They are interactive and work together, not in opposition or conflict. The
political, ideological and social contents of stereotypes are selective, relative and partisan but not psychologically inaccurate. They are appraisals
from a partial set of premises and their validity is partial and relative to
those premises, but they still have a form of validity. Others making
judgements from different premises will produce different judgements,
also psychologically valid. As Sherif noted in 1967, it is the very fact that
stereotypes represent groups from a 'singular point of view' which
renders the search for some absolute validity 'unrewarding' (p. 37).

Social Conflict and the Political Dimension

Why do we have so much trouble with the idea that stereotypes produced
by different groups can be equally valid? The obvious answer is that we
can all think of stereotypes that we reject, that we are convinced are false,

immoral and objectionable. There is an important empirical observation to be made here, however, which is nearly always overlooked. When we condemn stereotypes, it is always other people's, almost never our own! We are happy to assume that our own stereotypes are valid even as we reject others' stereotypes as false. They stereotype and are therefore in error; our views, being accurate, are not stereotypes. It is this asymmetry in the judgement of own and other's views, the fact that *people disagree*, that is the key point.

A rational process of social cognition, the same for all perceivers, that represents reality from the standpoint of varying social groups (as we have argued in terms of both comparative fit and perceiver readiness), must produce different views of society, must produce disagreement and conflicting stereotypes. This is not evidence of psychological deficit, however, of the fact that 'their' stereotype is produced by an irrational psychological process, but of the political dimension of stereotypes, of the political and social conflicts between human social groups.

Human beings are socially, culturally and historically heterogeneous. We belong to different social classes, sexes, ethnicities, nationalities, states, political and social systems, follow different religions, speak different languages, and work in different occupations. We occupy different geographic regions and different parts of the economic and political structures of our societies. The simple, obvious fact is that we belong to an endless variety of social groups which have different interests, values, needs and beliefs. This is not new or unusual. As Campbell (1967) pointed out, if such differences between human groups did not exist, the academic disciplines of anthropology, sociology and history would be largely if not wholly redundant. Social conflict of every kind is a pervasive feature of human history and society. It is hardly, surprising, therefore, in terms of the relativity of social perception, that we disagree about the content of stereotypes. What is valid for the ingroup is false for the outgroup; what is truth for 'us' is a lie for 'them'. We can all think of examples of current social antagonisms where this is true (e.g., Bar-Tal, 1990a, 1990b). This must be so for all the reasons stated. The disagreement reflects a process that works for all, but operates upon different premises for each.

When we reject stereotypes, therefore, this is a political act, not a judgement as to the rationality of the psychological process underlying their production. When we condemn stereotypes of the unemployed, women, minority groups, we are implicitly rejecting the premises from which the stereotype is derived, the economic ideology of right-wing politicians, the self-interest of men, the values of majorities. Stereotypes contain political analyses and are political weapons (we are using the term 'political' in this chapter in the broad sense in which political ideas exist not only in an explicit ideological form but can also be embedded in everyday culture and thought; e.g., Reicher, 1987); they embody particular views and advance particular causes. Argument about stereotypes, therefore, is a matter of political conflict and is consistent with the psychological rationality of the process. Rose-tinted notions that all political and social conflict is a matter of misunderstanding, a problem of psychology, are implausible and, at base, deeply pessimistic.

The ad hominem argument – that the groups we disagree with hold their views because they are irrational, crazy and abnormal has alway been part of the armoury of political rhetoric (see chapter 4 in Turner, 1991). It is a cheap and easy way to discredit an opponent and invalidate their views without having to present or discuss them. It is a notion that has made its way into social psychology in research on authoritarianism, dogmatism, etc., but it is still an idea with no empirical support or theoretical plausibility (Billig, 1976; R. Brown, 1965; Sherif, 1967). Why do Fascists have their ugly views? Because they are crazy. It is satisfying, but it is nonsense. We may justify our rejection of certain stereotypes in this way (and the rejection of stereotyping as a whole is in fact only ever a rejection of certain stereotypes, those we do not hold), but the rejection really reflects a clash of perspectives, of premises, of 'us' versus 'them'. Moreover, the clash is perfectly proper. If our stereotypes are cognitively rational, why should we not assert them? Why should we not affirm stereotypes which make sense from our vantage point, which advance our own interests as participants in the social process? When we propound some stereotypes and reject others, it is not that we are sane and our opponents crazy; we are psychologically equal, but different social beings with different social purposes and perspectives.

Has this discussion now brought us to relativism pure and simple? Is the validity of stereotypes socially as well as psychologically relative? Is there no *absolute* sense in which the racist stereotypes of Fascists and others can be rejected as factually wrong? Surely their point of view has allowed them to be *misled*? Is ultimate validity just a matter of who wins the political contest and who gets to write the history books? There is a sense in which power does control the story, but *influence* is more important. To understand how human groups move towards a higher social validity for their stereotypic views than that inherent in their own partisan perspective, we must understand that stereotypes are not only cognitive products, they are also social norms, arising from processes of social influence.

The Social Validation of Stereotypes

So far in this chapter and in this book we have talked as if the validity of stereotyping and other forms of cognition were simply a function of the veridicality of the individual psychological processes involved, of the degree to which they function appropriately to reflect features of reality. This is a common way of thinking about the matter but it ignores a major insight into cognition which social psychology has achieved. Seventy years' research on social influence (see Turner, 1991) has established that human beings do not seek validity solely through mental processes of representation, through what is called in the jargon of influence research 'physical reality testing' (the direct individual perceptual or cognitive testing of a belief against reality). They also engage in 'social reality testing' (consensual validation, social comparison with similar others). They seek subjective validity for a belief in the agreement of other group members.

In other words, people do not simply rest content with what they cognize and assume its validity. They check it out in discussion, argument and exchange of views with like-minded others: where similar others agree, they become more confident of the validity of their opinions (stereotypes); where similar others disagree, they become uncertain of the correctness of their stand and take action to reduce uncertainty by, for example, accepting influence from others or seeking to persuade others to change their stand (McGarty, Turner, Oakes and Haslam, 1993).

Self-categorization theory (see Turner, 1991) argues that it is the depersonalization of the self which makes it possible to produce socially validated knowledge (i.e., shared beliefs about ways of perceiving, thinking and doing which we assume to be appropriate in terms of objective reality). The theory explains influence processes as arising from the social categorization of others as similar to self in relevant respects. One only expects to agree with people categorized as similar to self and it is only disagreement with similar people that produces uncertainty. To reduce such uncertainty one can recategorize self and others (as different in relevant respects), redefine the objective stimulus situation as one that is not shared (i.e., as one that varies with the perceiver) or engage in influence activity.

Where one disagrees with people categorized as outgroup members, their perceived difference from self explains and justifies the disagreement, no uncertainty arises and there is no psychological pressure for mutual influence. No cognitive pressures for uniformity arise with different people, since their very difference explains why they are wrong and why one should not be persuaded. Why, for example, woul[...] need to agree about politics with people whose political [...] fundamentally opposed to one's own or about social psy[...] people who rejected the value of science? The theory is expl[...] persuasion can only be effected by people who are psychological ingroup members by some relevant criterion.

An important point argued by the theory is that physical and social reality testing are not alternative ways of validating one's cognitions, as traditionally assumed, but are interdependent phases of social cognition. Individual perception and cognition rest upon socially validated knowledge, theories, methods and categories, just as the power of social consensus to define reality for group members only makes sense if the individual views which make up the consensus have been independently tested. Social reality testing is therefore a basic extension of human cognitive activity. The knowledge, theories, understandings embodied in the meanings of categories, schemata, cognitive structures (including stereotypes) are collectively produced and validated. Categories are not only cognitive representations, they are also implicit social norms (McGarty and Turner, 1992; Turner et al., in press).

The relevance to stereotyping is fourfold:

1 Stereotypes are social norms. They are held in common by the members of one group about another and are anchored in particular group memberships. Their character as shared, consensual beliefs is regarded by many as a defining quality (e.g., Leyens et al., in press; Tajfel, 1981a). Certainly, stereotypes which are not shared are likely to be of little significance for intergroup relations.

2 Their subjective validity (people's confidence in the degree to which they match reality) is a function of both individual reality testing and social consensus.

3 Subjective validity is a matter of the agreement of similar others, but the similarity of others will vary with the level of self-categorization. At one level, ingroup and outgroup may disagree about stereotypes without uncertainty, but at the higher level of a superordinate social identity (as members of 'civilized society', 'Western culture', 'humanity'), even ingroup and outgroup will feel the need to reach agreement and reduce the uncertainty which arises from conflict. Our desire, despite being members of different social groups, to assert one stereotype over another as true for all, our belief that a level of validity higher than purely relativistic judgement is possible, can be derived from the hierarchical character of self- and social identity. When we argue for the validity of one stereotype over another, we are working

to create a higher-order societal norm. It is the fact that we share higher-order identities that makes it possible to define validity at a level higher than the judgement of a single group.

4 The psychological processes of relative perception and the social processes of collective discussion and conflict are interdependent means of achieving valid social stereotypes, each building on and correcting for the limitations of the other.

It is worth developing the last point. The problem with relativity occurs when perception starts from the wrong perspective, when a perceiver is in the wrong place at the wrong time. Certain social locations almost guarantee social invalidity. Would we expect slave-owners to form accurate stereotypes of slaves, for example? Given contemporary views on slavery, we are much more likely to agree with the slaves' stereotypes of the slave-owners. The problem for human perception is how to bootstrap itself out of its own relativity. The solution is a social mechanism. Relativity at the level of individual perception is corrected by social validation at the level of the group; relativity at the level of the group is corrected by argument at the level of society and beyond. Relativity is never eliminated – as we have argued, it would be meaningless for cognition to be otherwise – but at each level it can be transcended by a shift to a higher-level identity which coordinates multiple viewpoints. Social influence corrects for relativity, for any limitations in a singular point of view, by seeking agreement across individual or group perspectives. On the other hand, if relativity did not provide cognitively valid knowledge of reality, social consensus would be worthless, the group, society, could never be challenged by a perceiver with a novel perspective. Argument and controversy would be pointless and achieve nothing if all human views were nothing but prejudice.

The human search for truth, therefore, is not simply psychological, but also social, historical and political. The disagreements and conflicts over stereotypes are part of the social process of validation and invalidation. We argue, persuade, discuss and suppress. We seek to persuade others to accept our stereotypes and to reject the stereotypes held by outgroups. For want of better, for lack of understanding of the social relativity of cognition, we may use the ad hominem argument: they stereotype, we don't; their cognition is defective, we are rational. In reality, however, the clash of views, the ideological and political struggles, are part of a larger societal process of social influence and social change. Conflict over stereotypes is part of the historical process through which societies change stereotypes, intending to replace the false by the valid. Each group provides its own vision and the multiplicity of visions ensures societal development or movement through conflict and argument.

There is no guarantee of progress. There is no way we can escape current social and historical limitations, the inadequacies of contemporary common sense, science, culture. We cannot step outside of ourselves to pronounce on where the future is headed. But we are fully entitled to assert our own point of view, our own values and convictions, and we can take part in the social and political process. We can also look back and see where progress has occurred. We (Western, English-speaking social scientists) do not stereotype blacks, women, the Chinese, the working class, gays, Jews, Australians, etc., as once some did just a short century ago. Certain stereotypes have lost and others have won and the process of social change continues.

In sum, veridical perception is relative to self, just as reality is. But we can argue and make progress at a higher level of identity. Disagreements are part of the social process of correcting for insufficient information and limitations of perspective, not evidence of a defective psychological process. Political arguments play the role of achieving valid stereotypes, not merely psychologically valid ones but societally and culturally valid ones. Such arguments will change stereotypes but they will never eliminate them.

Overview and Conclusion

We have argued in this book that stereotypes are social categorical judgements, perceptions of people in terms of their group memberships. They represent categorizations at the level of social identity, in which people are defined in terms of the characteristics of the group as a whole in the context of intra- and intergroup relations. They are fluid, variable and context-dependent. A stereotype of the same people may vary in categorical level, kind, content, and prototypical meaning as a function of the relationship between self and others, the frame of reference, the dimensions of comparison, and the background knowledge, expectations, needs, values and goals of the perceiver.

Contrary to popular wisdom, we suggest that stereotypes are not rigid or fixed, but vary with intergroup relations, the context of judgement and the perspective of the perceiver. They are probably not stored in the head as enduring cognitive structures, but are better seen as the product of a dynamic process of social judgement and meaningful inference. We do not impose fixed mental images, but construct stereotypes flexibly to explain, describe and justify intergroup relations. The myth of rigidity arises from looking for stereotype change in the wrong place, from the assumption that stereotypes should change with information about the individual-level characteristics of group members.

Nor can stereotypes be seen as irrational, invalid cognitive prejudices. Social groups and collective relationships exist as much as do individual personalities and individual differences. Social categorizations become salient to fit group realities and provide veridical contextual representations of people's group relationships. Stereotypic accentuation reflects the rational selectivity of perception in which it is more appropriate to see people in some contexts at the level of social category identity than at the level of personal identity. It is no more a distortion to see people in terms of their social identity than in terms of their personal identity. Both are products of the same categorization processes. It is not true that individual differences are real but that social similarities are fictions. It is unjustifiable to assume that one level of categorization is inherently more real than another.

Stereotypes reflect fit in interaction with perceiver readiness. They are selective, constructive, evaluative and motivated. Like all perception, they vary with the expectations, needs, values and purposes of the perceiver. Their psychological validity is relative to the perspective of the perceiver. Psychological validity, however, is not the same as social validity. As social beings, human perceivers engage in social reality testing to validate or invalidate their judgements. Social and political conflict over stereotypes is not evidence of underlying psychological deficit, but of the political dimension of stereotype validity. Disagreement, argument and conflict between individuals and groups over the correctness of specific stereotypes is part of the social, political, historical process through which society moves (or tries to move) towards stereotypes which are valid from the perspective of the whole community. Individual cognition and social influence are interdependent processes for producing valid stereotypes.

At any given time, a stereotype may be produced which is wrong in the sense that it will be rejected later. At any given time, we may as a matter of fact be in error. But our conclusion is that there is nothing in the functioning of stereotyping as a *psychological* process which in principle works to promulgate error. We think it plausible that there are *social* processes which systematically distort the images which some groups form of certain other groups, but this issue falls outside of psychology proper and the scope of this book.

There are several conclusions which can be drawn from the perspective on stereotyping we have presented in this book. Perhaps the most important are, first, that the general cognitive model of stereotyping implicit in the field for so long is in need of revision. It may not be meaningful to think of stereotypes as fixed mental representations, stored in memory. This picture is consistent with rigidity but awkward if social categorizations are fluid, contextual judgements. Second, social categorical perception is a basic, normal and adaptive process of group life. It defines people in terms of their group relationships and underlies group formation and collective behaviour (Turner et al., in press). Group life is not based on cognitive distortion of the self and prejudice: it is in Asch's words one of 'the two permanent poles of all social processes' (1952, p. 251) and is an authentic expression of self. Third, much of the plausibility of the cognitive miser metaphor of social cognition has rested on the dominant view of categorizing and stereotyping as over-simplification. We have argued that this view is false. It is not necessary to assume that people have limited information-processing capacity to explain why people stereotype. It seems time to lay this metaphor to rest. Consistent with this message, we note that the heyday of research on cognitive biases, errors and illusions is already past. Researchers are once again talking of social perception as flexible, adaptive, complex, meaningful and purposeful (but are still hedging on veridical). Fourth, much of the difficulty researchers have had in understanding the rationality of stereotyping arises from a failure to put the analysis of cognition into a social context. Categorization processes do not function in a social vacuum, in the minds of isolated, asocial perceivers; human cognition is not purely individual, private, asocial, unaffected by group memberships, social norms and values. We believe that individual cognitive activity is always mediated by the social context within which it takes place, and that our research on stereotyping shows the need for a fully social psychological perspective on cognition.

Do we now need a new metaphor for social cognition and stereotyping? We think not. No metaphor will ever adequately match the complexities and subtleties of the interaction between the psychological and the social at work in social cognition. At best any metaphor will mislead just where theory needs to advance creatively. More than another partial model, incorporating various implicit and untested assumptions, we need to rediscover the interactionist metatheory of social psychology in all its richness and frame our theories and research accordingly. We believe that a *social* psychological metatheory of cognition will do much to advance the prospects for a productive integration of theories of the cognitive form and the social content of stereotypes and it is this integration that is surely the next major task for stereotyping researchers.

References

Abate, M. and Berrien, F. K. (1967) Validation of stereotypes: Japanese versus American students. *Journal of Personality and Social Psychology*, 7, 435–438.

Abrams, D. (1985) Focus of attention in minimal intergroup discrimination. *British Journal of Social Psychology*, 24, 65–74.

Abrams, D. and Hogg, M. A. (1987) Language attitudes, frames of reference, and social identity: A Scottish dimension. *Journal of Language and Social Psychology*, 6, 201–213.

Abrams, D. and Hogg, M. A. (Eds) (1990) *Social Identity Theory: Constructive and critical advances*. Hemel Hempstead: Harvester Wheatsheaf.

Abrams, D., Thomas, J. and Hogg, M. A. (1990) Numerical distinctiveness, social identity, and gender salience. *British Journal of Social Psychology*, 29, 87–92.

Acorn, D. A., Hamilton, D. L. and Sherman, S. J. (1988) Generalization of biased perceptions of groups based on illusory correlations. *Social Cognition*, 6, 345–372

Adorno, T. W., Frenkel-Brunswik, E., Levinson, D. J. and Sanford, R. N. (1950) *The Authoritarian Personality*. New York: Harper.

Allen, V. L. and Wilder, D. A. (1979) Group categorization and attribution of belief similarity. *Small Group Behaviour*, 10, 73–80.

Allport, F. H. (1924) *Social Psychology*. New York: Houghton, Mifflin.

Allport, F. H. (1933) *Institutional Behaviour*. Chapel Hill: University of North Carolina Press.

Allport, F. H. (1962) A structuronomic conception of behaviour: Individual and collective. *Journal of Abnormal and Social Psychology*, 64, 3–30.

Allport, G. W. (1954) *The Nature of Prejudice*. Cambridge, MA: Addison Wesley.

Allport, G. W. and Postman, L. J. (1947) *The psychology of rumour*. New York: Holt, Rinehart and Winston.

Amir, Y. (1969) Contact hypothesis in ethnic relations. *Psychological Bulletin*, 71, 319–342.

Amir, Y. (1976) The role of intergroup contact in change of prejudice and ethnic relations. In P. A. Katz (Ed.) *Toward the elimination of racism* (pp. 245–308). New York: Pergamon Press.

Andersen, S. M. and Klatzky, R. L. (1987) Traits and social stereotypes: Levels of categorization in person perception. *Journal of Personality and Social Psychology*, 53, 235–246.

Andersen, S. M., Klatzky, R. L. and Murray, J. (1990) Traits and social stereotypes: Efficiency differences in social information processing. *Journal of Personality and Social Psychology*, 59, 192–201.

Aronson, E. (1972) *The Social Animal*. San Francisco: W. H. Freeman and Company.

Asch, S. E. (1952) *Social Psychology*. New York: Prentice-Hall.

Ashmore, R. D. and Del Boca, F. K. (1981) Conceptual approaches to stereotypes and stereotyping. In D. L. Hamilton (Ed.) *Cognitive processes in stereotyping and intergroup behaviour*. Hillsdale, NJ: Erlbaum, pp. 1–35.

Bargh, J. A., Bond, R. N., Lombardi, W. L. and Tota, M. E. (1986) The additive nature of chronic and temporary sources of construct accessibility. *Journal of Personality and Social Psychology*, 50, 869–879.

Barsalou, L. W. (1987) The instability of graded structure: Implications for the nature of concepts. In U. Neisser (Ed.) *Concepts and conceptual development: Ecological and intellectual factors in categorization*. Cambridge: Cambridge University Press.

Bar-Tal, D. (1990) *Group Beliefs*. New York: Springer Verlag. (a)

Bar-Tal, D. (1990) Israeli-Palestinian conflict: a cognitive analysis. *International Journal of Intercultural Relations*, 14, 7–29. (b)

Bayton, J. A. (1941) The racial stereotypes of Negro college students. *Journal of Abnormal and Social Psychology*, 36, 97–102.

Beck, L., McCauley, C., Segal, M. and Hershey, L. (1988) Individual differences in prototypicality judgements about trait categories. *Journal of Personality and Social Psychology*, 55, 286–292.

Biernat, M., Manis, M. and Nelson, T. E. (1991) Stereotypes and standards of judgment. *Journal of Personality and Social Psychology*, 60, 485–499.

Biko, B. S. (1988) *I write what I like*. London: Penguin (first published in 1978).

Billig, M. (1976) *Social psychology and intergroup relations*. London: Academic Press.

Billig, M. (1978) *Fascists: A social psychological view of the National Front*. London: Academic Press.

Billig, M. (1985) Prejudice, categorization, and particularization: From a perceptual to a rhetorical approach. *European Journal of Social Psychology*, 15, 79–103.

Billig, M. and Tajfel, H. (1973) Social categorization and similarity in intergroup behaviour. *European Journal of Social Psychology*, 3, 27–52.

Bodenhausen, G. V. (1988) Stereotypic biases in social decision making and memory: Testing process models of stereotype use. *Journal of Personality and Social Psychology*, 55, 726–737.

Bodenhausen, G. V. (1990) Stereotypes as judgemental heuristics: Evidence of circadian variations in discrimination. *Psychological Science*, 1, 319–322.

Bodenhausen, G. V. and Lichtenstein, M. (1987) Social stereotypes and informa-tion-processing strategies: The impact of task complexity. *Journal of Personality and Social Psychology*, 52, 871–880.

Bodenhausen, G. V. and Wyer, R. S. (1985) Effects of stereotypes on decision making and information-processing strategies. *Journal of Personality and Social Psychology*, 48, 267–282.

Bogardus, E. S. (1933) A social distance scale. *Sociology and Social Science Research*, 17, 265–271.

Bogardus, E. S. (1950) Stereotypes versus sociotypes. *Sociology and Social Science Research*, 34, 286–291.

Borgida, E., Locksley, A. and Brekke, N. (1981) Social stereotypes and social judgement. In N. Cantor and J. F. Kihlstrom (Eds) *Personality, cognition and social interaction*. Hillsdale, NJ: Erlbaum.

Bornstein, G., Crum, L., Wittenbraker, J., Harring, K., Insko, C. A. and Thibaut, J. (1983) On the measurement of social orientations in the minimal group paradigm. *European Journal of Social Psychology*, 13, 321–350. (a)

Bornstein, G., Crum, L., Wittenbraker, J., Harring, K., Insko, C. A. and Thibaut, J. (1983) Reply to Turner's comments. *European Journal of Social Psychology*, 13, 369–382. (b)

Boyanowsky, E. O. and Allen, V. L. (1973) Ingroup norms and self-identity as determinants of discriminatory behaviour. *Journal of Personality and Social Psychology*, 25, 408–418.

Branthwaite, A., Doyle, S. and Lightbown, N. (1979) The balance between fairness and discrimination. *European Journal of Social Psychology*, 9, 149–163.

Brewer, M. B. (1979) Ingroup bias in the minimal intergroup situation: a cogni-tive-motivational analysis. *Psychological Bulletin*, 86, 307–324.

Brewer, M. B. (1988) A dual process model of impression formation. In T. K. Srull and R. S. Wyer (Eds) *Advances in social cognition* (vol. 1, pp. 1–36). Hillsdale, NJ: Erlbaum.

Brewer, M. B., Dull, V. and Lui, L. (1981) Perceptions of the elderly: Stereotypes as prototypes. *Journal of Personality and Social Psychology*, 41, 656–670.

Brewer, M. B. and Kramer, R. M. (1985) The psychology of intergroup attitudes and behaviour. *Annual Review of Psychology*, 36, 219–243.

Brewer, M. B. and Lui, L. (1984) Categorization of the elderly by the elderly: Effects of perceiver's category membership. *Personality and Social Psychology Bulletin*, 10, 585–595.

Brewer, M. B. and Lui, L. (1989) The primacy of age and sex in the structure of person categories. *Social Cognition*, 7, 262–274.

Brewer, M. B. and Miller, N. (1984) Beyond the contact hypothesis: theoretical perspectives on desegregation. In N. Miller and M. B. Brewer (Eds) *Groups in contact: the psychology of desegregation*. New York: Academic Press.

Brewer, M. B. and Silver, M. (1978) Ingroup bias as a function of task character-istics. *European Journal of Social Psychology*, 8, 393–400.

Brigham, J. C. (1971) Ethnic stereotypes. *Psychological Bulletin*, 76, 15–38.

Brigham, J. C. (1973) Ethnic stereotypes and attitudes: A different mode of analysis. *Journal of Personality, 41,* 206–233.

Brim, O. G. and Hoff, D. B. (1957) Individual and situational differences in desire for certainty. *Journal of Abnormal and Social Psychology, 54,* 225–279.

Brown, R. (1965) *Social psychology.* New York: Free Press.

Brown, R. (1986) *Social psychology: the second edition.* New York: Free Press.

Brown, R. J. and Turner, J. C. (1981) Interpersonal and intergroup behaviour. In J. C. Turner and H. Giles (Eds) *Intergroup behaviour.* Oxford: Blackwell; Chicago: University of Chicago Press.

Bruner, J. S. (1957) On perceptual readiness. *Psychological Review, 64,* 123–152.

Bruner, J. S. (1958) Social psychology and perception. In E. E. Maccoby, T. M. Newcomb and E. L. Hartley (Eds) *Readings in social psychology.* New York: Holt, Rinehart and Winston.

Bruner, J. S. (1983) *In search of mind: Essays in autobiography.* New York: Harper and Row.

Bruner, J. S. and Goodman, C. C. (1947) Value and need as organizing factors in perception. *Journal of Abnormal and Social Psychology, 42,* 33–44.

Bruner, J. S., Goodnow, J. J. and Austin, G. (1956) *A study of thinking.* New York: Wiley.

Buchanan, W. (1951) Stereotypes and tensions as revealed by the UNESCO International Poll. *International Social Science Bulletin, 3,* 515–528.

Campbell, D. T. (1958) Common fate, similarity, and other indices of the status of aggregates of persons as social entities. *Behavioural Science, 3,* 14–25.

Campbell, D. T. (1967) Stereotypes and the perception of group differences. *American Psychologist, 22,* 817–829.

Cantor, N. and Mischel, W. (1979) Prototypes in person perception. In L. Berkowitz (Ed.) *Advances in Experimental Social Psychology* (vol. 12, pp. 3–52). New York: Academic Press.

Caporael, L. R., Dawes, R. M., Orbell, J. M. and van de Kragt, A. J. C. (1989) Selfishness examined: cooperation in the absence of egoistic incentives. *Behavioural and Brain Sciences, 12,* 683–699.

Capozza, D. and Nanni, R. (1986) Differentiation processes for social stimuli with different degrees of category representativeness. *European Journal of Social Psychology, 16,* 399–412.

Cartwright, D. (1979) Contemporary social psychology in historical perspective. *Social Psychology Quarterly, 42,* 82–93.

Cartwright, D. and Zander, A. (1968) *Group Dynamics.* London: Tavistock.

Cauthen, N. R., Robinson, I. E. and Krauss, H. H. (1971) Stereotypes: A review of the literature 1926–1968. *Journal of Social Psychology, 84,* 103–125.

Chapman, L. J. and Chapman, J. P. (1967). Genesis of popular but erroneous psychodiagnostic signs. *Journal of Abnormal Psychology, 72,* 193–204.

Cheyne, W. M. (1970) Stereotyped reactions to speakers with Scottish and English regional accents. *British Journal of Social and Clinical Psychology, 9,* 77–79.

Chin, M. G. and McClintock, C. G. (1993) The effects of intergroup discrimination and social values on level of self-esteem in the minimal group paradigm. *European Journal of Social Psychology*, 23, 63–75.

Codol, J-P. (1975) On the so-called 'superior conformity of the self' behaviour: Twenty experimental investigations. *European Journal of Social Psychology*, 5, 457–501.

Cohen, C. E. (1981) Person categories and social perception: Testing some boundaries of the processing effects of prior knowledge. *Journal of Personality and Social Psychology*, 40, 441–452.

Collins, A. M. and Loftus, E. F. (1975) A spreading-activation theory of semantic processing. *Psychological Review*, 82, 407–428.

Condor, S. G. (1990) Social stereotypes and social identity. In D. Abrams and M. A. Hogg (Eds) *Social identity theory: Constructive and critical advances*. Hemel Hempstead: Harvester Wheatsheaf.

Cook, S. W. (1969) Motives in a conceptual analysis of attitude-related behaviour. In W. J. Arnold and D. Levine (Eds) *Nebraska Symposium on Motivation* (vol. 17, pp. 179–235). Lincoln: University of Nebraska Press.

Crocker, J., Hannah, D. B. and Weber, R. (1983) Person memory and causal attribution. *Journal of Personality and Social Psychology*, 44, 55–66.

David, B. and Turner, J. C. (1992) *Studies in self-categorization and minority conversion*. Paper presented at the joint EAESP/SESP Meeting, Leuven/Louvain-la-Neuve, Belgium, 15–18 July.

Dawes, R. M., Singer, D. and Lemons, F. (1972) An experimental analysis of the contrast effect and its implications for intergroup communication and the indirect assessment of attitude. *Journal of Personality and Social Psychology*, 21, 281–295.

Deaux, K. and Lewis, L. L. (1984) Structure of gender stereotypes: Interrelationships among components and gender label. *Journal of Personality and Social Psychology*, 46, 991–1004.

Deaux, K., Winton, W., Crowley, M. and Lewis, L. L. (1985) Level of categorization and content of gender stereotypes. *Social Cognition*, 3, 145–167.

Deschamps, J-C. (1984) The social psychology of intergroup relations and categorical differentiation. In H. Tajfel (Ed.) *The social dimension* (vol. 2). Cambridge: Cambridge University Press; Paris: Éditions de la Maison des Sciences de l'Homme.

Devine, P. G. (1989) Stereotypes and prejudice: Their automatic and controlled components. *Journal of Personality and Social Psychology*, 56, 5–18.

Diab, L. N. (1962) National stereotypes and the 'reference group' concept. *Journal of Social Psychology*, 57, 339–351.

Diab, L. N. (1963) Factors affecting studies of National stereotypes. *Journal of Social Psychology*, 59, 29–40. (a)

Diab, L. N. (1963) Factors determining group stereotypes. *Journal of Social Psychology*, 61, 3–10. (b)

Dion, K. L. (1979) Intergroup conflict and intragroup cohesiveness. In W. G. Austin and S. Worchel (Eds) *The social psychology of intergroup relations*. Monterey, California: Brooks/Cole.

Dion, K. L., Earn, B. M. and Yee, P. H. N. (1978) The experience of being a victim of prejudice: an experimental approach. *International Journal of Psychology, 13*, 197–214.

Doise, W. (1978) *Individuals and groups: Explanations in social psychology.* Cambridge: Cambridge University Press.

Doise, W. (1988) Individual and social identities in intergroup relations. *European Journal of Social Psychology, 18*, 99–111.

Doise, W., Csepeli, G., Dann, H. D., Gouge, C., Larsen, K. and Ostell, A. (1972) An experimental investigation into the formation of intergroup representations. *European Journal of Social Psychology, 2*, 202–204.

Doise, W., Deschamps, J-C. and Meyer, G. (1978) The accentuation of intracategory similarities. In H. Tajfel (Ed.) *Differentiation between social groups.* London: Academic Press.

Doise, W. and Sinclair, A. (1973) The categorization process in intergroup relations. *European Journal of Social Psychology, 3*, 145–157.

Dollard, J., Doob, L. W., Miller, N. E., Mowrer, O. H. and Sears, R. R. (1939) *Frustration and aggression.* New Haven, CT: Yale University Press.

Dudycha, G. Y. (1942) The attitudes of college students toward war and the Germans before and during the Second World War. *Journal of Social Psychology, 15*, 317–324.

Duijker, H. C. J. and Frijda, N. H. (1960) *National character and National stereotypes: A trend report for the International Union of Scientific Psychology.* Amsterdam: North-Holland Publishing Company.

Duncan, B. L. (1976) Differential social perception and attribution of intergroup violence: Testing the lower limits of stereotyping of blacks. *Journal of Personality and Social Psychology, 34*, 590–598.

Dunning, D., Perie, M. and Story, A. L. (1991) Self-serving prototypes of social categories. *Journal of Personality and Social Psychology, 61*, 957–968.

Dustin, D. S. and Davis, H. P. (1970) Evaluative bias in group and individual competition. *Journal of Social Psychology, 80*, 103–108.

Dutta, S., Kanungo, R. N. and Freibergs, V. (1972) Retention of affective material: Effects of intensity of affect on recall. *Journal of Personality and Social Psychology, 23*, 64–80.

Eagly, A. H. and Kite, M. E. (1987) Are stereotypes of nationalities applied to both men and women? *Journal of Personality and Social Psychology, 53*, 451–462.

Eagly, A. H. and Steffen, V. J. (1984) Gender stereotypes stem from the distribution of men and women into social roles. *Journal of Personality and Social Psychology, 46*, 735–754.

Eagly, A. H. and Wood, W. (1982) Inferred sex differences in status as a determinant of gender stereotypes about social influence. *Journal of Personality and Social Psychology, 43*, 915–928.

Ehrlich, H. J. (1962) Stereotyping and Negro-Jewish stereotypes. *Social Forces, 41*, 171–176.

Ehrlich, H. J. and Rinehart, J. W. (1965) A brief report on the methodology of stereotype research. *Social Forces, 43*, 564–575.

Eiser, J. R. (1971) Enhancement of contrast in the absolute judgement of attitude statements. *Journal of Personality and Social Psychology, 17,* 1–10.

Eiser, J. R. (1973) Judgement of attitude statements as a function of judges' attitudes and the judgemental dimension. *British Journal of Social and Clinical Psychology, 12,* 231–240.

Eiser, J. R. (Ed.) (1984) *Attitudinal judgement.* New York: Springer Verlag.

Eiser, J. R. (1990) *Social judgement.* Pacific Grove CA: Brooks/Cole.

Eiser, J. R. and Mower White, C. J. (1975) Categorization and congruity in attitudinal judgement. *Journal of Personality and Social Psychology, 31,* 769–775.

Eiser, J. R. and Stroebe, W. (1972) *Categorization and social judgement.* European Monographs in Social Psychology, no. 3; London: Academic Press.

Eiser, J. R. and van der Pligt, J. (1982) Accentuation and perspective in attitudinal judgement. *Journal of Personality and Social Psychology, 42,* 224–238.

Eiser, J. R. and van der Pligt, J. (1984) Attitudes in a social context. In H. Tajfel (Ed.) *The social dimension* (vol. 2). Cambridge: Cambridge University Press; Paris: Éditions de la Maison des Sciences de l'Homme. (a)

Eiser, J. R. and van der Pligt, J. (1984) Accentuation theory, polarization, and the judgement of attitude statements. In J. R. Eiser (Ed.) *Attitudinal judgement.* New York: Springer Verlag. (b)

English, H. B. and English, A. C. (1959) *A comprehensive dictionary of psychological and psychoanalytic terms.* New York: Longmans, Green.

Erber, R. and Fiske, S. T. (1984) Outcome dependency and attention to inconsistent information. *Journal of Personality and Social Psychology, 47,* 709–726.

Eysenck, H. J. and Crown, S. (1948) National stereotypes: An experimental and methodological study. *International Journal of Opinion and Attitude Research, 2,* 26–39.

Fehrer, E. (1952) Shifts in scale values of attitude statements as a function of the composition of the scale. *Journal of Experimental Psychology, 44,* 179–188.

Feldman, J. M. and Hilterman, R. J. (1975) Stereotype attribution revisited: The role of stimulus characteristics, racial attitude, and cognitive differentiation. *Journal of Personality and Social Psychology, 31,* 1177–1188.

Fernberger, S. W. (1948) Persistence of stereotypes concerning sex differences. *Journal of Abnormal and Social Psychology, 43,* 97–101.

Festinger, L. (1947) The role of group belongingness in a voting situation. *Human Relations, 1,* 154–180.

Festinger, L. (1954) A theory of social comparison processes. *Human Relations, 7,* 117–140.

Fiedler, K. (1991) The tricky nature of skewed frequency tables: An information loss account of distinctiveness-based illusory correlations. *Journal of Personality and Social Psychology, 60,* 26–36.

Fishman, J. A. (1956) An examination of the process and function of social stereotyping. *Journal of Social Psychology, 43,* 27–64.

Fiske, S. T. (1988) Compare and contrast: Brewer's dual process model and Fiske et al.'s continuum model. In T. K. Srull and R. S. Wyer (Eds) *Advances in*

Social Cognition (vol. 1, pp. 65–76). Hillsdale, NJ: Erlbaum.

Fiske, S. T. (1989) Examining the role of intent: Toward understanding its role in stereotyping and prejudice. In J. S. Uleman and J. A. Bargh (Eds) *Unintended Thought*. New York: The Guilford Press.

Fiske, S. T. (1993) Social cognition and social perception. *Annual Review of Psychology, 44,* 155–194.

Fiske, S. T. and Neuberg, S. L. (1989) Category-based and individuating processes as a function of information and motivation: Evidence from our laboratory. In D. Bar-Tal, C. F. Graumann, A. W. Kruglanski and W. Stroebe (Eds) *Stereotyping and prejudice: Changing conceptions.* (pp. 83–104) New York and London: Springer Verlag.

Fiske, S. T. and Neuberg, S. L. (1990) A continuum of impression formation, from category-based to individuating processes: Influences of information and motivation on attention and interpretation. In M. P. Zanna (Ed.) *Advances in Experimental Social Psychology* (vol. 23, pp. 1–73). New York: Random House.

Fiske, S. T., Neuberg, S. L., Beattie, A. E. and Milberg, S. J. (1987) Category-based and attribute-based reactions to others: Some informational conditions of stereotyping and individuating processes. *Journal of Experimental Social Psychology, 23,* 399–427.

Fiske, S. T. and Taylor, S. E. (1991) *Social cognition.* NY: McGraw-Hill Inc.

Ford, T. E. and Stangor, C. (1992) The role of diagnosticity in stereotype formation: Perceiving group means and variances. *Journal of Personality and Social Psychology, 63,* 356–367.

Forgas, J. P. (1983) The effects of prototypicality and cultural salience on perceptions of people. *Journal of Research in Personality, 17,* 153–173.

Frable, D. E. S. and Bem, S. L. (1985) If you're gender-schematic, all members of the opposite sex look alike. *Journal of Personality and Social Psychology, 49,* 459–468.

Frenkel-Brunswik, E. (1948) A study of prejudice in children. *Human Relations, 1,* 295–306.

Freud, S. (1921) *Group psychology and the analysis of the ego.* London: Hogarth Press.

Gaertner, S. L., Mann, J., Murrell, A. and Dovidio, J. F. (1989) Reducing intergroup bias: The benefits of recategorization. *Journal of Personality and Social Psychology, 57,* 239–249.

Gardner, R. C. (1973) Ethnic stereotypes: The traditional approach, a new look. *The Canadian Psychologist, 14,* 133–148.

Gardner, R. C. (1991) *Stereotypes as Consensual Beliefs: Their Behavioral Consequences.* Paper presented at the 7th Ontario Symposium on the Psychology of Prejudice, University of Waterloo, June 22–23.

Gilbert, D. T. and Hixon, J. G. (1991) The trouble of thinking: Activation and application of stereotypic beliefs. *Journal of Personality and Social Psychology, 60,* 509–517

Gilbert, G. M. (1951) Stereotype persistence and change among college students. *Journal of Abnormal and Social Psychology, 46,* 245–54.

Goethals, G. R. and Darley, J. M. (1977) Social comparison theory: An attributional approach. In J. M. Suls and R. L. Miller (Eds) *Social comparison processes*. Washington, DC: Hemisphere.

Grant, P. R. and Holmes, J. G. (1981) The integration of implicit personality theory schemas and stereotypic images. *Social Psychology Quarterly*, 44, 107–115.

Gurin, P. and Markus, H. (1988) Group identity; The psychological mechanisms of durable salience. *Revue Internationale de Psychologie Sociale*, 1, 257–274.

Gurwitz, S. B. and Dodge, K. A. (1977) Effects of confirmations and disconfirmations of stereotype-based attributions. *Journal of Personality and Social Psychology*, 35, 495–500.

Hamilton, D. L. (1968) Personality attributes associated with extreme response style. *Psychological Bulletin*, 69, 193–203.

Hamilton, D. L. (1979) A cognitive-attributional analysis of stereotyping. In L. Berkowitz (Ed.) *Advances in experimental social psychology* (vol. 12). New York: Academic Press.

Hamilton, D. L. (Ed.) (1981) *Cognitive processes in stereotyping and intergroup behaviour*. Hillsdale, NJ: Erlbaum. (a)

Hamilton, D. L. (1981) Illusory correlation as a basis for stereotyping. In D. L. Hamilton (Ed.) *Cognitive processes in stereotyping and intergroup behaviour*. Hillsdale, NJ: Erlbaum. (b)

Hamilton, D. L. (1981) Stereotyping and intergroup behaviour: Some thoughts on the cognitive approach. In D. L. Hamilton (Ed.) *Cognitive processes in stereotyping and intergroup behaviour*. Hillsdale, NJ: Erlbaum, pp. 333–353. (c)

Hamilton, D. L., Dugan, P. M. and Trolier, T. K. (1985) The formation of stereotypic beliefs: Further evidence for distinctiveness-based illusory correlations. *Journal of Personality and Social Psychology*, 48, 5–17.

Hamilton, D. L. and Gifford, R. K. (1976) Illusory correlation in intergroup perception: A cognitive basis of stereotypic judgments. *Journal of Experimental Social Psychology*, 12, 392–407.

Hamilton, D. L. and Rose, T. L. (1980) Illusory correlation and the maintenance of stereotypic beliefs. *Journal of Personality and Social Psychology*, 39, 832–845.

Hamilton, D. L. and Sherman, S. J. (1989) Illusory correlations: Implications for stereotype theory and research. In D. Bar-Tal, C. F. Graumann, A. W. Kruglanski and W. Stroebe (Eds) *Stereotyping and prejudice: Changing conceptions*. New York and London: Springer Verlag.

Hamilton, D. L. and Trolier, T. K. (1986) Stereotypes and stereotyping: An overview of the cognitive approach. In J. F. Dovidio and S. L. Gaertner (Eds) *Prejudice, discrimination, and racism*. New York and Orlando, FL: Academic Press, pp. 127–163.

Harding, J., Kutner, B., Proshansky, H. and Chein, I. (1954) Prejudice and ethnic relations. In G. Lindzey (Ed.) *Handbook of social psychology* (vol. 2). Cambridge, MA: Addison-Wesley.

Hartley, E. L. (1946) *Problems in prejudice*. New York: King's Crown Press.

Hartsough, W. F. and Fontana, A. F. (1970) Persistence of ethnic stereotypes and the relative importance of positive and negative stereotyping for associative prejudices. *Psychological Reports, 27*, 723–731.

Haslam, S. A. (1990) *Social comparative context, self-categorization, and stereotyping.* Unpublished Ph.D. thesis. Macquarie University.

Haslam, S. A., Brooks, L. and Oakes, P. J. (1993) *Stereotype validity: A question of content or context?* Paper presented at the General Meeting of the European Association of Experimental Social Psychology, Lisbon, Sept. 15–20.

Haslam, S. A., McGarty, C., Oakes, P. J. and Turner, J. C. (1993a) Social comparative context and illusory correlation: Testing between ingroup bias and social identity models of stereotype formation. *Australian Journal of Psychology, 45*, 97–101.

Haslam, S. A., Oakes, P. J. Turner, J. C. and McGarty, C. (1993b) *Social categorization and group homogeneity: Changes in the perceived applicability of stereotype content as a function of comparative context and trait favourableness.* Unpublished manuscript, The Australian National University.

Haslam, S. A. and Turner, J. C. (1992) Context-dependent variation in social stereotyping 2: The relationship between frame of reference, self-categorization and accentuation. *European Journal of Social Psychology, 22*, 251–278.

Haslam, S. A. and Turner, J. C. (1993) *Context-dependent variation in social stereotyping 3: Extremism as a self-categorical basis for polarized judgment.* Unpublished manuscript, The Australian National University.

Haslam, S. A., Turner, J. C, Oakes, P. J., McGarty, C. and Hayes, B. K. (1992) Context-dependent variation in social stereotyping 1: The effects of intergroup relations as mediated by social change and frame of reference. *European Journal of Social Psychology, 22*, 3–20.

Hastie, R. (1981) Schematic principles in human memory. In E. T. Higgins, C. P. Herman and M. P. Zanna (Eds) *Social cognition: The Ontario Symposium* (vol. 1, pp. 39–88). Hillsdale, NJ: Erlbaum.

Hastie, R. and Kumar, P. A. (1979) Person memory: Personality traits as organizing principles in memory for behaviours. *Journal of Personality and Social Psychology, 37*, 25–38.

Hayakawa, S. I. (1950) Recognizing stereotypes as a substitute for thought. *Etc.; A Review of General Semantics, 7*, 208–210.

Helson, H. (1948) Adaptation-level as a basis for a quantitative theory of frames of reference. *Psychological Review, 55*, 297–313.

Hemsley, G. D. and Marmurek, H. H. C. (1982) Person memory: The processing of consistent and inconsistent person information. *Personality and Social Psychology Bulletin, 8*, 433–438.

Hensley, V. and Duval, S. (1976) Some perceptual determinants of perceived similarity, liking, and correctness. *Journal of Personality and Social Psychology, 34*, 159–168.

Herman, S. and Schild, E. (1960) Ethnic role conflict in a cross-cultural situation. *Human Relations, 13*, 215–228.

Herr, P. M., Sherman, S. J. and Fazio, R. H. (1983) On the consequences of priming: Assimilation and contrast effects. *Journal of Experimental Social*

Psychology, 19, 323–340.

Hewstone, M. (1989) *Causal Attribution: From cognitive processes to collective beliefs.* Oxford: Basil Blackwell. (a)

Hewstone, M. (1989) Changing stereotypes with disconfirming evidence. In D. Bar-Tal, C. F. Graumann, A. W. Kruglanski and W. Stroebe (Eds) *Stereotyping and prejudice: Changing conceptions.* New York and London: Springer Verlag. (b)

Hewstone, M. and Brown, R. J. (Eds) (1986) *Contact and conflict in intergroup encounters.* Oxford: Basil Blackwell.

Hewstone, M., Hantzi, A. and Johnston, L. (1991) Social categorization and person memory: The pervasiveness of race as an organising principle. *European Journal of Social Psychology, 21,* 517–528.

Hewstone, M., Hopkins, N. and Routh, D. A. (1992) Cognitive models of stereotype change: (1) Generalization and subtyping in young people's views of the police. *European Journal of Social Psychology, 22,* 219–234.

Hewstone, M. and Jaspars, J. M. F. (1984) Social Dimensions of Attribution. In H. Tajfel (Ed.) *The social dimension* (vol. 2). Cambridge: Cambridge University Press; Paris: Éditions de la Maison des Sciences de l'Homme.

Hewstone, M., Johnston, L. and Aird, P. (1992) Cognitive models of stereotype change: (2) Perceptions of homogeneous and heterogeneous groups. *European Journal of Social Psychology, 22,* 235–249.

Hewstone, M., Johnston, L., Frankish, C. and Macrae, N. (1990) *Cognitive models of stereotype change: (4) Evidence of subtyping from person-memory paradigms.* Paper presented at the General Meeting of the European Association of Experimental Social Psychology, Budapest.

Higgins, E. T. and Bargh, J. A. (1987) Social cognition and social perception. *Annual Review of Psychology, 38,* 369–425.

Higgins, E. T., Bargh, J. A. and Lombardi, W. (1985) The nature of priming effects on categorization. *Journal of Experimental Psychology: Learning, Memory, and Cognition, 11,* 59–69.

Higgins, E. T. and King, G. A. (1981) Accessibility of social constructs: Information-processing consequences of individual and contextual variability. In N. Cantor and J. S. Kihlstrom (Eds) *Personality, cognition, and social interaction* (pp. 69–122). Hillsdale, NJ: Erlbaum.

Hilton, J. L. and Darley, J. M. (1991) The effects of interaction goals on person perception. In M. P. Zanna (Ed.) *Advances in Experimental Social Psychology* (vol. 24, pp. 235–267). San Diego, CA: Academic Press.

Hintzman, D. L. (1986) 'Schema abstraction' in a multiple-trace memory model. *Psychological Review, 93,* 411–428.

Hoffman, C. and Hurst, N. (1990) Gender stereotypes: Perception or rationalization? *Journal of Personality and Social Psychology, 58,* 197–208.

Hogg, M. A. (1992) *The social psychology of group cohesiveness.* Hemel Hempstead: Harvester Wheatsheaf.

Hogg, M. A. and Abrams, D. (1988) *Social identifications: A social psychology of intergroup relations and group processes.* London: Routledge.

Hogg, M. A. and Abrams, D. (1990) Social motivation, self-esteem and social identity. In D. Abrams and M. A. Hogg (Eds) *Social Identity Theory: Constructive and critical advances* (pp. 28–47). Hemel Hempstead: Harvester Wheatsheaf.

Hogg, M. A. and Turner, J. C. (1985) Interpersonal attraction, social identification and psychological group formation. *European Journal of Social Psychology, 15*, 51–66. (a)

Hogg, M. A. and Turner, J. C. (1985) When liking begets solidarity: an experiment on the role of interpersonal attraction in psychological group formation. *British Journal of Social Psychology, 24*, 267–281. (b)

Hogg, M. A. and Turner, J. C. (1987) Intergroup behaviour, self-stereotyping and the salience of social categories. *British Journal of Social Psychology, 26*, 325–340.

Hogg, M. A., Turner, J. C. and Davidson, B. (1990) Polarized norms and social frames of reference: A test of the self-categorization theory of group polarization. *Basic and Applied Social Psychology, 11*, 77–100

Hovland, C. I. and Sherif, M. (1952) Judgemental phenomena and scales of attitude measurement: Item displacement in Thurstone scales. *Journal of Abnormal and Social Psychology, 47*, 822–832.

Hovland, C. I., Harvey, O. J. and Sherif, M. (1957) Assimilation and contrast effects in reactions to communication and attitude change. *Journal of Abnormal and Social Psychology, 55*, 244–252.

Howard, J. W. and Rothbart, M. (1980) Social categorization and memory for in-group and out-group behaviour. *Journal of Personality and Social Psychology, 38*, 301–310.

Huici, C. (1984) The individual and social functions of sex role stereotypes. In H. Tajfel (Ed.) *The social dimension: European developments in social psychology* (vol. 2). Cambridge: Cambridge University Press.

Hymes, R. W. (1986) Political attitudes as social categories: A new look at selective memory. *Journal of Personality and Social Psychology, 51*, 233–241.

Ichheiser, G. (1947) Projection and the mote-beam mechanism. *Journal of Abnormal and Social Psychology, 42*, 131–133.

Ickes, W. J., Patterson, M. L., Rajecki, D. W. and Tanford, S. (1982) Behavioural and cognitive consequences of reciprocal versus compensatory responses to preinteraction expectancies. *Social Cognition, 1*, 160–190.

Jackson, L. A. and Hymes, R. W. (1985) Gender and social categorization: Familiarity and ingroup polarization in recall and evaluation. *Journal of Social Psychology, 125*, 81–88.

James, K. (1986) Priming and social categorizational factors: Impact on awareness of emergency situations. *Personality and Social Psychology Bulletin, 12*, 462–467.

Johnston, L. and Hewstone, M. (1992) Cognitive models of stereotype change: (3) Subtyping and the perceived typicality of disconfirming group members. *Journal of Experimental Social Psychology,*

Jones, E. E., Wood, G. C. and Quattrone, G. A. (1981) Perceived variability of personal characteristics in ingroups and outgroups: The role of knowledge and evaluation. *Personality and Social Psychology Bulletin, 7*, 523–528.

Jones, R. A. (1982) Perceiving other people: Stereotyping as a process of social cognition. In A. G. Miller (Ed.) *In the eye of the beholder: Contemporary issues in stereotyping*. New York: Praeger.

Jones, R. A., Scott, J., Solernou, J., Noble, A., Fiala, J. and Miller, K. (1977) Availability and formation of stereotypes. *Perceptual and Motor Skills, 44*, 631–638.

Judd, C. M. and Harackiewicz, J. M. (1980) Contrast effects in attitude judgement: An examination of the accentuation hypothesis. *Journal of Personality and Social Psychology, 38*, 390–398.

Judd, C. M. and Krosnick, J. A. (1982) Attitude centrality, organization, and measurement. *Journal of Personality and Social Psychology, 42*, 436–447.

Judd, C. M. and Park, B. (1988) Out-group homogeneity: Judgements of variability at the individual and group levels. *Journal of Personality and Social Psychology, 54*, 778–788.

Judd, C. M. and Park, B. (1993) Definition and assessment of accuracy in social stereotypes. *Psychological Review, 100*, 109–128.

Judd, C. M., Ryan, C. S. and Park, B. (1991) Accuracy in the judgement of in-group and out-group variability. *Journal of Personality and Social Psychology, 61*, 366–379.

Jussim, L. (1986) Self-fulfilling prophecies: A theoretical and integrative review. *Psychological Review, 93*, 429–445.

Jussim, L. (1991) Social perception and social reality: A reflection-construction model. *Psychological Review, 98*, 54–73.

Jussim, L., Coleman, L. M. and Lerch, L. (1987) The nature of stereotypes: A comparison and integration of three theories. *Journal of Personality and Social Psychology, 52*, 536–546.

Kahneman, D. and Miller, D. T. (1986) Norm theory: Comparing reality to its alternatives. *Psychological Review, 93*, 136–153.

Kahneman, D. and Tversky, A. (1973) On the psychology of prediction. *Psychological Review, 80*, 237–251.

Kanungo, R. N. and Dutta, S. (1966) Retention of affective material: Frame of reference or intensity? *Journal of Personality and Social Psychology, 4*, 27–35.

Karlins, M., Coffman, T. L. and Walters, G. (1969) On the fading of social stereotypes: Studies in three generations of college students. *Journal of Personality and Social Psychology, 13*, 1–16.

Katz, D. and Braly, K. (1933) Racial stereotypes of one hundred college students. *Journal of Abnormal and Social Psychology, 28*, 280–290.

Katz, D. and Braly, K. (1935) Racial prejudice and racial stereotypes. *Journal of Abnormal and Social Psychology, 30*, 175–193.

Katz, D. and Schanck, R. L. (1938) *Social psychology*. New York: Wiley.

Kelley, H. H. (1955) Salience of membership and resistance to change of group-anchored attitudes. *Human Relations, 8*, 275–289.

Kelly, C. (1989) Political identity and perceived intragroup homogeneity. *British Journal of Social Psychology, 28*, 239–250.

Kerr, M. (1943) An experimental investigation of national stereotypes. *Sociological Review, 35*, 37–43.

Kim, H-S. and Baron, R. S. (1988) Exercise and the illusory correlation: Does arousal heighten stereotypic processing? *Journal of Experimental Social Psychology, 24,* 366–380.

Klineberg, O. (1950) Tensions affecting international understanding. *Social Science Research Council Bulletin* (vol. 62). New York.

Klineberg, O. (1951) The scientific study of national stereotypes. *International Social Science Bulletin, 3,* 505–515.

Krueger, J. (1992) On the Overestimation of Between-Group Differences. In W. Stroebe and M. Hewstone (Eds) *European Review of Social Psychology* (vol. 3). Chichester, UK: Wiley, pp. 31–56.

Krueger, J. and Rothbart, M. (1988) Use of categorical and individuating information in making inferences about personality. *Journal of Personality and Social Psychology, 55,* 187–195.

Krueger, J. and Rothbart, M. (1990) Contrast and accentuation effects in category learning. *Journal of Personality and Social Psychology, 59,* 651–663.

Lambert, W. E., Hodgson, R. C., Gardner, R. C. and Fillenbaum, S. (1960) Evaluational reactions to spoken languages. *Journal of Abnormal and Social Psychology, 60,* 44–51.

Langer, E. J. (1978) Rethinking the role of thought in social interaction. In J. H. Harvey, W. Ickes and R. F. Kidd (Eds) *New directions in attribution research* (vol. 2, pp. 35–58). Hillsdale, NJ: Erlbaum.

LaPiere, R. T. (1936) Type-rationalizations and group antipathy. *Social Forces, 15,* 232–237.

Larsen, K. S. (1971) Affectivity, cognitive style and social judgement. *Journal of Personality and Social Psychology, 19,* 119–123.

Laviolette, F. and Silvert, K. H. (1951) A theory of stereotypes. *Social Forces, 29,* 257–262.

LeBon, G. (1895, translated 1947) *The crowd: A study of the popular mind.* London: Ernest Benn (also London: Unwin, 1896).

Lemyre, L. and Smith, P. M. (1985) Intergroup discrimination and self-esteem in the minimal group paradigm. *Journal of Personality and Social Psychology, 49,* 660–670.

Lent, J. R. (1970) Binocular resolution and the perception of race in the United States. *British Journal of Psychology, 61,* 521–533.

Leyens, J-P., Yzerbyt, V. and Schadron, G. (in press) *Stereotypes, social cognition, and social explanation.* London: Sage.

Linville, P. W. (1982) The complexity-extremity effect and age-based stereotyping. *Journal of Personality and Social Psychology, 42,* 193–211.

Linville, P. W. and Jones, E. E. (1980) Polarized appraisals of outgroup members. *Journal of Personality and Social Psychology, 38,* 689–703.

Linville, P. W., Fischer, G. W. and Salovey, P. (1989) Perceived distributions of the characteristics of in-group and out-group members: Empirical evidence and a computer simulation. *Journal of Personality and Social Psychology, 57,* 165–188.

Linville, P. W., Salovey, P. and Fischer, G. W. (1986) Stereotyping and perceived distributions of social characteristics: An application to ingroup-outgroup perception. In J. F. Dovidio and S. L. Gaertner (Eds) *Prejudice, discrimination and racism*. New York and Orlando, FL: Academic Press.

Lippman, W. (1922) *Public opinion*. New York: Harcourt Brace.

Litterer, O. F. (1933) Stereotypes. *Journal of Social Psychology*, 4, 59–69.

Locksley, A., Borgida, E., Brekke, N. and Hepburn, C. (1980) Sex stereotypes and social judgement. *Journal of Personality and Social Psychology*, 39, 821–831.

Locksley, A., Hepburn, C. and Ortiz, V. (1982) Social stereotypes and judgement of individuals: An instance of the base-rate fallacy. *Journal of Experimental Social Psychology*, 18, 23–42.

Lott, A. J. and Lott, B. E. (1965) Group cohesiveness as interpersonal attraction: A review of relationships with antecedent and consequent variables. *Psychological Bulletin*, 64, 259–309.

Lui, L. and Brewer, M. B. (1983) Recognition accuracy as evidence of category consistency effects in person memory. *Social Cognition*, 2, 89–107.

McArthur, L. Z. and Friedman, S. A. (1980) Illusory correlation in impression formation: Variations in the shared distinctiveness effect as a function of the distinctive person's age, race, and sex. *Journal of Personality and Social Psychology*, 39, 615–624.

McArthur, L. Z. and Post, D. L. (1977) Figural emphasis in person perception. *Journal of Experimental Social Psychology*, 13, 520–535.

McCauley, C. (1988) The content of awareness and top-down versus bottom-up processing. In T. K. Srull and R. S. Wyer (Eds) *Advances in social cognition* (vol. 1, pp. 119–126). Hillsdale, NJ: Erlbaum.

McCauley, C. and Stitt, C. L. (1978) An individual and quantitative measure of stereotypes. *Journal of Personality and Social Psychology*, 36, 929–940.

McCauley, C., Stitt, C. L. and Segal, M. (1980) Stereotyping: From prejudice to prediction. *Psychological Bulletin*, 87, 195–208.

McCauley, R. N. (1987) The role of theories in a theory of concepts. In U. Neisser (Ed.) *Concepts and conceptual development: Ecological and intellectual factors in categorization*. Cambridge: Cambridge University Press.

McDougall, W. (1921) *The group mind*. Cambridge: Cambridge University Press.

Mace, C. A. (1943) National stereotypes: Their nature and function. *Sociological Review*, 35, 29–36.

McGarty, C. (1990) *Categorization and the Social Psychology of Judgement*, Unpublished PhD thesis, Macquarie University.

McGarty, C. and Penny, R. E. C. (1988) Categorization, accentuation and social judgement. *British Journal of Social Psychology*, 27, 147–157.

McGarty, C., Haslam, S. A., Turner, J. C. and Oakes, P. J. (1993) Illusory correlation as accentuation of actual intercategory difference: Evidence for the effect with minimal stimulus information. *European Journal of Social Psychology*, 23, 391–410.

McGarty, C. and Turner, J. C. (1992) The effects of categorization on social judgement. *British Journal of Social Psychology*, 31, 147–157.

McGarty, C., Turner, J. C., Oakes, P. J. and Haslam, S. A. (1993) The creation of uncertainty in the influence process: The roles of stimulus information and disagreement with similar others. *European Journal of Social Psychology*, 23, 17–38.

McGuire, W. J. and McGuire, C. V. (1981) The spontaneous self concept as affected by seasonal distinctiveness. In M. D. Lynch, A. Norem-Hebeisen and K. J. Gergen (Eds) *Self-concept: Advances in theory and research*. Cambridge, MA: Ballinger.

McGuire, W. J., McGuire, C. V., Child, P. and Fujioka, T. (1978) Salience of ethnicity in the spontaneous self-concept as a function of one's ethnic distinctiveness in the social environment. *Journal of Personality and Social Psychology*, 36, 511–20.

McGuire, W. J., McGuire, C. V. and Winton, W. (1979) Effects of household sex composition on the salience of one's gender in the spontaneous self-concept. *Journal of Experimental Social Psychology*, 15, 77–90.

Mackie, D. M. and Allison, S. T. (1987) Group attribution errors and the illusion of group attitude change. *Journal of Experimental Social Psychology*, 23, 460–480.

Mackie, D. M., Allison, S. T. and Worth, L. T. (1988) *The impact of outcome-biased influences and illusory change on stereotype modification*. Paper presented at the XXIV International Congress of Psychology, Sydney, Australia. August 28–September 3.

Mackie, M. (1973) Arriving at 'truth' by definition: The case of stereotype inaccuracy. *Social Problems*, 20, 431–447.

Macrae, N., Hewstone, M. and Griffiths, R. J. (1993) Processing load and memory for stereotype-based information. *European Journal of Social Psychology*, 23, 77–87.

Major, B., Cozzarelli, C., Testa, M. and McFarlin, D. B. (1988) Self-verification versus expectancy confirmation in social interaction: The impact of self-focus. *Personality and Social Psychology Bulletin*, 14, 346–359.

Malhotra, N. K., Jain, A. K. and Pinson, C. (1983) Extremity of judgement and personality variables: Two empirical investigations. *Journal of Social Psychology*, 120, 111–118.

Malpass, R. and Kravitz, L. (1969) Recognition for faces of own and other race. *Journal of Personality and Social Psychology*, 13, 330–334.

Manis, M. (1960) The interpretation of opinion statements as a function of recipient attitude. *Journal of Abnormal and Social Psychology*, 60, 340–344.

Manis, M. (1961) The interpretation of opinion statements as a function of message ambiguity and recipient attitude. *Journal of Abnormal and Social Psychology*, 63, 76–81.

Manis, M. (1964) Comment on Upshaw's 'Own attitude as an anchor in equal-appearing intervals'. *Journal of Abnormal and Social Psychology*, 68, 689–691.

Manis, M., Nelson, T. E. and Shedler, J. (1988) Stereotypes and social judgement: Extremity, assimilation, and contrast. *Journal of Personality and Social Psychology*, 55, 28–36.

Mansbridge, J. J. (Ed.) (1990) *Beyond self-interest*. Chicago and London: University of Chicago Press.

Marques, J. M. (1990) The black-sheep effect: Outgroup homogeneity in social comparison settings. In D. Abrams and M. A. Hogg (Eds) *Social identity theory: Constructive and critical advances*. Hemel Hempstead: Harvester Wheatsheaf.

Marques, J. M., Yzerbyt, V. Y. (1988) The black sheep effect: Judgemental extremity towards ingroup members in inter- and intra-group situations. *European Journal of Social Psychology*, 18, 287–292.

Marques, J. M., Yzerbyt, V. Y. and Leyens, J-P. (1988) The 'Black Sheep Effect': Extremity of judgements towards ingroup members as a function of group identification. *European Journal of Social Psychology*, 18, 1–16.

Mascaro, G. F. and Graves, W. (1973) Contrast effects of background factors on the similarity attraction relationship. *Journal of Personality and Social Psychology*, 25, 346–350.

Medin, D. L. (1988) Social categorization: Structures, processes and purposes. In T. K. Srull and R. S. Wyer (Eds) *Advances in social cognition* (vol. 1, pp. 119–126). Hillsdale, NJ: Erlbaum.

Medin, D. L. (1989) Concepts and conceptual structure. *American Psychologist*, 44, 1469–1481.

Medin, D. L. and Wattenmaker, W. D. (1987) Category cohesiveness, theories, and cognitive archeology. In U. Neisser (Ed.) *Concepts and Conceptual Development: Ecological and Intellectual Factors in Categorization*. Cambridge: Cambridge University Press.

Meenes, M. (1943) A comparison of racial stereotypes of 1935 and 1942. *Journal of Social Psychology*, 17, 327–336.

Mervis, C. B. and Rosch, E. (1981) Categorization of natural objects. In M. R. Rosenzweig and L. W. Porter (Eds) *Annual Review of Psychology* (vol. 32, pp. 89–115). Palo Alto. CA: Annual Reviews.

Messick, D. M. and Mackie, D. M. (1989) Intergroup Relations. In M. R. Rosenzweig and L. W. Porter (Eds) *Annual Review of Psychology* (vol. 40, pp. 45–81). Palo Alto. CA: Annual Reviews.

Miller, C. T. (1986) Categorization and stereotypes about men and women. *Personality and Social Psychology Bulletin*, 12, 502–512.

Milner, D. (1981) Racial prejudice. In J. C. Turner and H. Giles (Eds) *Intergroup behaviour*. Oxford: Blackwell; Chicago: University of Chicago Press.

Mischel, W. (1977) The interaction of person and situation. In D. Magnusson and N. S. Endler (Eds) *Personality at the crossroads: Current issues in interactional psychology*. Hillsdale, NJ: Erlbaum.

Mischel, W. (1981) *Introduction to personality* (3rd ed.) New York: Holt, Rinehart and Winston.

Mullen, B. and Hu, L. (1989) Perceptions of ingroup and outgroup variability: A meta-analytic integration. *Basic and Applied Social Psychology*, 10, 233–252.

Mullen, B. and Johnson, C. (1990) Distinctiveness-based illusory correlations and stereotyping: A meta-analytic integration. *British Journal of Social Psychology*, 29, 11–28.

Mummendey, A. and Schreiber, H. J. (1983) Better or just different?: Positive social identity by discrimination against or differentiation from outgroups. *European Journal of Social Psychology, 13,* 389–397.

Mummendey, A. and Simon, B. (1989) Better or just different? III: The impact of comparison dimension and relative group size upon intergroup discrimination. *British Journal of Social Psychology, 28,* 1–16.

Murphy, G. L. and Medin, D. L. (1985) The role of theories in conceptual coherence. *Psychological Review, 92,* 289–316.

Mussen, P. H. (1950) Some personality and social factors related to changes in children's attitudes towards Negroes. *Journal of Abnormal and Social Psychology, 45,* 423–441.

Neisser, U. (1976) *Cognition and Reality.* San Francisco: W. H. Freeman and Co.

Neisser, U. (Ed.) (1987) *Concepts and Conceptual Development: Ecological and Intellectual Factors in Categorization.* Cambridge: Cambridge University Press. (a)

Neisser, U. (1987) Introduction: The ecological and intellectual bases of categorization. In U. Neisser (Ed.) *Concepts and Conceptual Development: Ecological and Intellectual Factors in Categorization.* Cambridge: Cambridge University Press. (b)

Neisser, U. (1987) From direct perception to conceptual structure. In U. Neisser (Ed.) *Concepts and Conceptual Development: Ecological and Intellectual Factors in Categorization.* Cambridge: Cambridge University Press. (c)

Nelson, T. E., Biernat, M. R. and Manis, M. (1990) Everyday base rates (sex stereotypes): Potent and resilient. *Journal of Personality and Social Psychology, 59,* 664–675.

Nesdale, A. R., Dharmalingam, S. and Kerr, G. K. (1987) Effect of subgroup ratio on stereotyping. *European Journal of Social Psychology, 17,* 353–356.

Nettler, G. (1961) Good men, bad men, and the perception of reality. *Sociometry, 24,* 279–294.

Neuberg, S. L. (in press) Stereotypes, prejudice, and expectancy confirmation. In M. P. Zanna and J. M. Olson (Eds) *Psychology of prejudice: The seventh Ontario Symposium on personality and social psychology.* NJ: Lawrence Erlbaum.

Neuberg, S. L. and Fiske, S. T. (1987) Motivational influences on impression formation: Outcome dependency, accuracy-driven attention, and individuating processes. *Journal of Personality and Social Psychology, 53,* 431–444.

Nisbett, R. E. and Ross, L. (1980) *Human Inference: Strategies and shortcomings of social judgement.* Englewood Cliffs, NJ: Prentice-Hall.

Nisbett, R. E., Zukier, H. and Lemley, R. E. (1981) The dilution effect: Non-diagnostic information weakens the implications of diagnostic information. *Cognitive Psychology, 13,* 248–277.

Oakes, P. J. (1987) The salience of social categories. In J. C. Turner, M. A. Hogg, P. J. Oakes, S. D. Reicher and M. S. Wetherell *Rediscovering the Social Group: A self-categorization theory.* Oxford: Blackwell.

Oakes, P. J. and Haslam, S. A. (1993) *Social influence as a determinant of stereotype content and perceived homogeneity.* Unpublished M.S., Australian National University.

Oakes, P. J. and Turner, J. C. (1980) Social categorization and intergroup behaviour: Does minimal intergroup behaviour make social identity more positive? *European Journal of Social Psychology, 10*, 295–301.

Oakes, P. J. and Turner, J. C. (1986) Distinctiveness and the salience of social category memberships: Is there a perceptual bias towards novelty? *European Journal of Social Psychology, 16*, 325–344. (a)

Oakes, P. J. and Turner, J. C. (1986) Authors' rejoinder to Jahoda and Tetlock. *British Journal of Social Psychology, 25*, 257–258. (b)

Oakes, P. J. and Turner, J. C. (1990) Is limited information processing capacity the cause of social stereotyping? In W. Stroebe and M. Hewstone (Eds) *European Review of Social Psychology* (vol. 1). Chichester, UK: Wiley.

Oakes, P. J., Turner, J. C. and Haslam, S. A. (1991) Perceiving people as group members: The role of fit in the salience of social categorizations. *British Journal of Social Psychology, 30*, 125–144.

O'Donovan, D. (1965) Rating extremity: Pathology or meaningfulness? *Psychological Review, 72*, 358–372.

Ostrom, T. M. and Sedikides, C. (1988) *Outgroup homogeneity effects in natural and minimal groups.* Unpublished MS, Ohio State University.

Parducci, A. (1963) Range-frequency compromise in judgement. *Psychological Monographs, 77* (2, whole no. 565).

Park, B. and Hastie, R. (1987) The perception of variability in category development: Instance-versus abstraction-based stereotypes. *Journal of Personality and Social Psychology, 53*, 621–635.

Park, B. and Judd, C. M. (1990) Measures and models of perceived group variability. *Journal of Personality and Social Psychology, 59*, 173–191.

Park, B., Judd, C. M. and Ryan, C. S. (1991) Social categorization and the representation of variability information. In W. Stroebe and M. Hewstone (Eds) *European Review of Social Psychology*, vol. 2. Chichester: Wiley.

Park, B. and Rothbart, M. (1982) Perception of out-group homogeneity and levels of social categorization: Memory for the subordinate attributes of in-group and out-group members. *Journal of Personality and Social Psychology, 42*, 1051–1068.

Park, B., Ryan, C. S. and Judd, C. M. (1992) Role of meaningful subgroups in explaining differences in perceived variability for ingroups and outgroups. *Journal of Personality and Social Psychology, 63*, 553–567.

Pepitone, A. (1981) Lessons from the history of social psychology. *American Psychologist, 36*, 972–985.

Perdue, C. W., Dovidio, J. F., Gurtman, M. B. and Tyler, R. B. (1990) Us and them: Social categorization and the process of intergroup bias. *Journal of Personality and Social Psychology, 59*, 475–486.

Perkins, T. E. (1979) Rethinking stereotypes. In M. Barrett, P. Corrigan, A. Kuhn and J. Wolff (Eds) *Ideology and cultural production.* London: Croon-Helm.

Pettigrew, T. F. (1969) Racially separate or together? *Journal of Social Issues, 25*, 43–69.

Pettigrew, T. F. (1981) Extending the stereotype concept. In D. L. Hamilton (Ed.) *Cognitive processes in stereotyping and intergroup behaviour* (pp. 303–332).

Hillsdale, NJ: Erlbaum.

Pettigrew, T. F., Allport, G. W. and Barnett, E. O. (1958) Binocular resolution and perception of race in South Africa. *British Journal of Psychology, 49*, 265–278.

Poulton, E. C. (1968) The new psychophysics: Six models for magnitude estimation. *Psychological Bulletin, 69*, 1–19.

Pratto, F. and Bargh, J. A. (1991) Stereotyping based on apparently individuating information: Trait and global components of sex stereotypes under attention overload. *Journal of Experiemntal Social Psychology, 27*, 26–47.

Prothro, E. T. (1955) The effect of strong personal involvement on the placement of items in a Thurstone Scale. *Journal of Social Psychology, 41*, 11–17.

Prothro, E. T. (1957) Personal involvement and item displacement on Thurstone scales. *Journal of Social Psychology, 45*, 191–196.

Prothro, E. T. and Melikian, L. H. (1955) Studies in stereotypes: V. Familiarity and the kernel of truth hypothesis. *Journal of Social Psychology, 41*, 3–10.

Pryor, J. B. (1986) The influence of different encoding sets upon the formation of illusory correlations and group impressions. *Personality and Social Psychology Bulletin, 12*, 216–226.

Quattrone, G. A. (1986) On the perception of a group's variability. In S. Worchel and G. Austin (Eds) *Psychology of intergroup relations*. Chicago: Nelson Hall.

Quattrone, G. A. and Jones, E. E. (1980) The perception of variability within ingroups and outgroups: Implications for the law of small numbers. *Journal of Personality and Social Psychology, 38*, 141–152.

Rabbie, J. M., Schot, J. and Visser, L. (1989) Social identity theory: A conceptual and empirical critique from the perspective of a behavioural interaction model. *European Journal of Social Psychology, 19*, 171–202.

Razran, G. (1950) Ethnic dislikes and prejudice: A laboratory study. *Journal of Abnormal and Social Psychology, 45*, 7–27.

Reicher, S. D. (1987) Crowd behaviour as social action. In J. C. Turner, M. A. Hogg, P. J. Oakes, S. D. Reicher and M. S. Wetherell, *Rediscovering the social group: A self-categorization theory*. Oxford: Blackwell.

Rice, S. A. (1926–7) 'Stereotypes': A source of error in judging human character. *Journal of Personnel Research, 5*, 267–276.

Richter, M. N. (1956) The conceptual mechanism of stereotyping. *American Sociological Review, 21*, 568–571.

Rokeach, M. (1948) Generalized mental rigidity as a factor in ethnocentrism. *Journal of Abnormal and Social Psychology, 43*, 259–278.

Romer, D. (1983) Effects of own attitude on polarization of judgement. *Journal of Personality and Social Psychology, 44*, 273–284.

Rosch, E. (1978) Principles of categorization. In E. Rosch and B. B. Lloyd (Eds) *Cognition and Categorization*. Hillsdale, NJ: Erlbaum.

Rosch, E., Mervis, C. B., Gray, W. D., Johnson, D. M. and Boyes-Braem, P. (1976) Basic objects in natural categorization. *Cognitive Psychology, 8*, 382–439.

Rosenthal, R. (1974) *On the social psychology of the self-fulfilling prophecy: Further evidence for the Pygmalion effects and their mediating mechanisms.*

New York: MSS Modular Publications (Module 53).

Rothbart, M. (1981) Memory processes and social beliefs. In D. L. Hamilton (Ed.) *Cognitive processes in stereotyping and intergroup behaviour*. Hillsdale, NJ: Erlbaum, pp. 145–182.

Rothbart, M., Evans, M., and Fulero, S. (1979) Recall for confirming events: Memory processes and the maintenance of social stereotypes. *Journal of Experimental Social Psychology*, 15, 343–355.

Rothbart, M., Fulero, S., Jensen, C., Howard, J. and Birrell, P. (1978) From individual to group impressions: Availability heuristics in stereotype formation. *Journal of Experimental Social Psychology*, 14, 237–255.

Rothbart, M. and John, O. P. (1985) Social categorization and behavioural episodes: A cognitive analysis of the effects of intergroup contact. *Journal of Social Issues*, 41, 81–104.

Rothbart, M. and Lewis, S. (1988) Inferring category attributes from exemplar attributes: Geometric shapes and social categories. *Journal of Personality and Social Psychology*, 55, 861–872.

Sachdev, I. and Bourhis, R. Y. (1984) Minimal minorities and majorities. *European Journal of Social Psychology*, 14, 35–52.

Sachdev, I. and Bourhis, R. Y. (1987) Status differentials and intergroup behaviour. *European Journal of Social Psychology*, 17, 277–293.

Sachdev, I. and Bourhis, R. Y. (1991) Power and status differentials in minority and majority group relations. *European Journal of Social Psychology*, 21, 1–24.

Saenger, G. and Flowerman, S. (1954) Stereotypes and prejudicial attitudes. *Human Relations*, 7, 217–238.

Sagar, H. A. and Schofield, J. W. (1980) Racial and behavioural cues in black and white children's perceptions of ambiguously aggressive acts. *Journal of Personality and Social Psychology*, 39, 590–598.

St. Claire, L. and Turner, J. C. (1982) The role of demand characteristics in the social categorization paradigm. *European Journal of Social Psychology*, 12, 307–314.

Sampson, E. E. (1977) Psychology and the American ideal. *Journal of Personality and Social Psychology*, 35, 767–782.

Sanbonmatsu, D. M., Shavitt, S., Sherman, S. J. and Roskos-Ewoldsen, D. R. (1987) Illusory correlation in the perception of performance by self or a salient other. *Journal of Experimental Social Psychology*, 23, 518–543.

Sanbonmatsu, D. M., Sherman, S. J. and Hamilton, D. L. (1987) Illusory correlation in the perception of individuals and groups. *Social Cognition*, 5, 1–25.

Schaller, M. and Maass, A. (1989) Illusory correlation and social categorization: Toward an integration of motivational and cognitive factors in stereotype formation. *Journal of Personality and Social Psychology*, 56, 709–721.

Schneider, D. J. (1991) Social cognition. *Annual Review of Psychology*, 42, 527–561.

Schoenfeld, N. (1942) An experimental study of some problems relating to stereotypes. *Archives of Psychology*, no. 270.

Schuman, H. (1966) Social change and the validity of regional stereotypes in East

Pakistan. *Sociometry, 29,* 428–440.

Seago, D. W. (1947) Stereotypes: Before Pearl Harbour and after. *Journal of Social Psychology, 23,* 55–63.

Secord, P. F. (1959) Stereotyping and favourableness in the perception of Negro faces. *Journal of Abnormal and Social Psychology, 59,* 309–314.

Secord, P. F., Bevan, W. and Katz, B. (1956) The Negro stereotype and perceptual accentuation. *Journal of Abnormal and Social Psychology, 53,* 78–83.

Seeleman, V. (1940) The influence of attitude upon the remembering of pictorial material. *Archives of Psychology,* no. 258.

Sellitz, C., Edrich, H. and Cook, S. W. (1965) Ratings of favourableness of statements about a social group as an indicator of attitude toward the group. *Journal of Personality and Social Psychology, 2,* 408–415.

Shaw, M. E. (1976) *Group dynamics: The psychology of small group behaviour.* New Delhi: Tata McGraw-Hill.

Sherif, M. (1935) An experimental study of stereotypes. *Journal of Abnormal and Social Psychology, 29,* 371–375.

Sherif, M. (1936) *The psychology of social norms.* New York: Harper.

Sherif, M. (1967) *Group conflict and co-operation: Their social psychology.* London: Routledge and Kegan Paul.

Sherif, M. and Hovland, C. I. (1961) *Social judgement: Assimilation and contrast effects in communication and attitude change.* New Haven, CT and London: Yale University Press.

Sherif, C. W., Sherif, M. and Nebergall, R. E. (1965) *Attitude and attitude change: The social judgement-involvement approach.* Philadelphia and London: W. B. Saunders Co.

Shrieke, B. J. O. (1936) *Alien Americans.* New York: Viking.

Sidanius, J. (1988) Political sophistication and political deviance: A structural equation examination of context theory. *Journal of Personality and Social Psychology, 55,* 37–51.

Sigall, H. and Page, R. (1971) Current stereotypes: A little fading, a little faking. *Journal of Personality and Social Psychology, 18,* 247–255.

Simon, B. (1992) The perception of ingroup and outgroup homogeneity: Re-introducing the social context. In W. Stroebe and M. Hewstone (Eds) *European Review of Social Psychology,* vol. 3. Chichester: Wiley.

Simon, B. (1993) On the asymmetry in the cognitive construal of ingroup and outgroup: A model of egocentric social categorization. *European Journal of Social Psychology, 23,* 131–147.

Simon, B. and Brown, R. J. (1987) Perceived intragroup homogeneity in minority–majority contexts. *Journal of Personality and Social Psychology, 53,* 703–711.

Simon, B., Glassner-Bayerl, B. and Stratenwerth, I. (1991) Stereotyping and self-stereotyping in a natural intergroup context: The case of heterosexual and homosexual men. *Social Psychology Quarterly, 54,* 252–266.

Simon, B. and Mummendey, A. (1991) Perceptions of relative group size and group homogeneity: We are the majority and they are all the same. *European Journal of Social Psychology, 20,* 351–356.

Simon, B. and Pettigrew, T. F. (1990) Social identity and perceived group homogeneity. *European Journal of Social Psychology, 20,* 269–286.

Sinha, A. K. P. and Upadhyaya, O. P. (1960) Change and persistence in the stereotypes of university students toward different ethnic groups during Sino-Indian border dispute. *Journal of Social Psychology, 52,* 31–39.

Slusher, M. P. and Anderson, C. A. (1987) When reality monitoring fails: The role of imagination in stereotype maintenance. *Journal of Personality and Social Psychology, 52,* 653–662.

Smith, E. E. (1989) Concepts and induction. In M. I. Posner (Ed.) *Foundations of cognitive science.* Cambridge, MA: MIT Press.

Smith, E. E. and Medin, D. L. (1981) *Categories and Concepts.* Cambridge, MA: Harvard University Press.

Smith, E. R. (1991) Illusory correlation in a simulated exemplar-based memory. *Journal of Experimental Social Psychology, 27,* 107–123.

Smith, E. R. and Zarate, M. A. (1992) Exemplar-based model of social judgement. *Psychological Review, 99,* 3–21.

Snyder, M. (1981) On the self-perpetuating nature of social stereotypes. In D. L. Hamilton (Ed.) *Cognitive processes in stereotyping and intergroup behaviour.* Hillsdale, NJ: Erlbaum. (a)

Snyder, M. (1981) Seek and ye shall find: Testing hypotheses about other people. In E. T. Higgins, C. P. Herman and M. P. Zanna (Eds) *Social cognition: The Ontario Symposium* (vol. 1). Hillsdale, NJ: Erlbaum. (b)

Snyder, M. (1984) When belief creates reality. In L. Berkowitz (Ed.) *Advances in experimental social psychology* (vol. 18). New York: Academic Press.

Snyder, M. (in press) Motivational foundations of behavioural confirmation. In M. P. Zanna (Ed.) *Advances in experimental social psychology* (vol. 25). San Diego, CA: Academic Press.

Snyder, M. and Swann, W. B. (1978) Hypothesis-testing processes in social interaction. *Journal of Personality and Social Psychology, 36,* 1202–1212.

Snyder, M., Tanke, E. D. and Berscheid, E. (1977) Social perception and interpersonal behaviour: On the self-fulfilling nature of social stereotypes. *Journal of Personality and Social Psychology, 35,* 656–666.

Snyder, M. and Uranowitz, S. W. (1978) Reconstructing the past: Some cognitive consequences of person perception. *Journal of Personality and Social Psychology, 36,* 941–950.

Spears, R. and Manstead, A. S. R. (1989) The social context of stereotyping and differentiation. *European Journal of Social Psychology, 19,* 101–121.

Spears, R., van der Pligt, J. and Eiser, J. R. (1985) Illusory correlation in the perception of group attitudes. *Journal of Personality and Social Psychology, 48,* 863–875.

Spears, R., van der Pligt, J. and Eiser, J. R. (1986) Generalizing the illusory correlation effect. *Journal of Personality and Social Psychology, 51,* 1127–1134.

Srull, T. K. (1981) Person memory: some tests of associative storage and retrieval models. *Journal of Experimental Psychology: Human Learning and Memory, 7,* 440–462.

Stangor, C. and Duan, C. (1991) Effects of multiple task demands upon memory for information about social groups. *Journal of Experimental Social Psychology, 27,* 357–378.

Stangor, C. and Ford, T. E. (1992) Accuracy and expectancy-confirming processing orientations and the development of stereotypes and prejudice. In W. Stroebe and M. Hewstone (Eds) *European Review of Social Psychology* (vol. 3, pp. 57–89). New York: Wiley.

Stangor, C., Lynch, L., Duan, C. and Glass, B. (1992) Categorization of individuals on the basis of multiple social features. *Journal of Personality and Social Psychology, 62,* 207–218.

Steiner, I. D. (1974) Whatever happened to the group in social psychology? *Journal of Experimental Social Psychology, 10,* 94–108.

Stephan, W. G. (1985) Intergroup relations. In G. Lindzey and E. Aronson (Eds) *Handbook of Social Psychology* (vol. 2). New York: Random House.

Stephan, W. G. (1989) A cognitive approach to stereotyping. In D. Bar-Tal, C. F. Graumann, A. W. Kruglanski and W. Stroebe (Eds) *Stereotyping and prejudice: Changing conceptions.* New York and London: Springer Verlag.

Stephan, W. G. and Rosenfield, D. (1982) Racial and ethnic stereotypes. In A. G. Miller (Ed.) *In the eye of the beholder: Contemporary issues in stereotyping.* New York: Praeger.

Stern, L.D., Marrs, S., Millar, M. G. and Cole, E. (1984) Processing time and the recall of inconsistent and consistent behaviours of individuals and groups. *Journal of Personality and Social Psychology, 47,* 253–262.

Stroebe, W. and Insko, C. A. (1989) Stereotype, prejudice, and discrimination: Changing conceptions in theory and research. In D. Bar-Tal, C. F. Graumann, A. W. Kruglanski and W. Stroebe (Eds) *Stereotyping and prejudice: Changing conceptions.* New York and London: Springer Verlag, pp. 3–34.

Tajfel, H. (1957) Value and the perceptual judgement of magnitude. *Psychological Review, 64,* 192–204.

Tajfel, H. (1959) Quantitative judgement in social perception. *British Journal of Psychology, 50,* 16–29.

Tajfel, H. (1969) Cognitive aspects of prejudice. *Journal of Social Issues, 25,* 79–97.

Tajfel, H. (1972) Social categorization. In S. Moscovici (Ed.) *Introduction a la psychologie sociale* (vol. 1). Paris: Larouse.

Tajfel, H. (1978) Introduction. In H. Tajfel (Ed.) *Differentiation between social groups: Studies in the social psychology of intergroup relations.* London: Academic Press. (a)

Tajfel, H. (1978) Interindividual behaviour and intergroup behaviour. In H. Tajfel (Ed.) *Differentiation between social groups: Studies in the social psychology of intergroup relations.* London: Academic Press. (b)

Tajfel, H. (1978) Social categorization, social identity and social comparison. In H. Tajfel (Ed.) *Differentiation between social groups: Studies in the social psychology of intergroup relations.* London: Academic Press. (c)

Tajfel. H. (1978) The achievement of group differentiation. In H. Tajfel (Ed.) *Differentiation between social groups: Studies in the social psychology of intergroup relations.* London: Academic Press. (d)

Tajfel, H. (Ed.) (1978) *Differentiation between social groups: Studies in the social psychology of intergroup relations.* London: Academic Press. (e)

Tajfel, H. (1979) Individuals and groups in social psychology. *British Journal of Social and Clinical Psychology, 18,* 183–190.

Tajfel, H. (1980) The 'New Look' and social differentiations: A semi-Brunerian perspective. In D. Olson (Ed.) *The social foundations of language and thought: Essays in honour of J. S. Bruner.* New York: Norton.

Tajfel, H. (1981) Social stereotypes and social groups. In J. C. Turner and H. Giles (Eds) *Intergroup behaviour.* Oxford: Blackwell; Chicago: University of Chicago Press, pp. 144–167. (a)

Tajfel, H. (1981) *Human groups and social categories.* Cambridge: Cambridge University Press. (b)

Tajfel, H., Flament, C., Billig, M. G. and Bundy, R. F. (1971) Social categorization and intergroup behaviour. *European Journal of Social Psychology, 1,* 149–177.

Tajfel, H., Sheikh, A. A. and Gardner, R. C. (1964) Content of stereotypes and the inference of similarity between members of stereotyped groups. *Acta Psychologica, 22,* 191–201.

Tajfel, H. and Turner, J. C. (1979) An integrative theory of intergroup conflict. In W. G. Austin and S. Worschel (Eds) *The social psychology of intergroup relations.* Monterey, CA: Brooks/Cole.

Tajfel, H. and Turner, J. C. (1986) The social identity theory of intergroup behaviour. In S. Worschel and W. G. Austin (Eds) *Psychology of intergroup relations* (2nd ed.). Chicago: Nelson-Hall.

Tajfel, H. and Wilkes, A. L. (1963) Classification and quantitative judgement. *British Journal of Psychology, 54,* 101–114. (a)

Tajfel, H. and Wilkes, A. L. (1963) Salience of attributes and commitment to extreme judgements in the perception of people. *British Journal of Social and Clinical Psychology, 2,* 40–49. (b)

Taylor, D. M. and Aboud, F. E. (1973) Ethnic stereotypes: Is the concept necessary? *Canadian Psychologist, 14,* 330–338.

Taylor, D. M. and Jaggi, V. (1974) Ethnocentrism and causal attribution in a S. Indian context. *Journal of Cross-Cultural Psychology, 5,* 162–171.

Taylor, S. E. (1981) A categorization approach to stereotyping. In D. L. Hamilton (Ed.) *Cognitive processes in stereotyping and intergroup behaviour.* Hillsdale, NJ: Erlbaum, pp. 88–114. (a)

Taylor, S. E. (1981) The interface of cognitive and social psychology. In J. Harvey (Ed.) *Cognition, social behaviour and the environment.* Hillsdale, NJ: Erlbaum, pp. 189–211. (b)

Taylor, S. E. and Falcone, H.-T. (1982) Cognitive bases of stereotyping: The relationship between categorization and prejudice. *Personality and Social Psychology Bulletin, 8,* 426–432.

Taylor, S. E. and Fiske, S. T. (1978) Salience, attention, and attribution: Top-of-the-head phenomena. In L. Berkowitz (Ed.) *Advances in experimental social psychology* (vol. 11). New York: Academic Press.

Taylor, S. E., Fiske, S. T., Etcoff, N. L. and Ruderman, A. J. (1978) Categorical and contextual bases of person memory and stereotyping. *Journal of Personality and Social Psychology*, 36, 778–793.

Tresselt, M. E. (1948) The effect of experience of contrast groups upon the formation of a new scale. *Journal of Social Psychology*, 27, 209–216.

Triandis, H. C. and Vassiliou, V. (1967) Frequency of contact and stereotyping. *Journal of Personality and Social Psychology*, 7, 316–328.

Turner, J. C. (1975) Social comparison and social identity: Some prospects for intergroup behaviour. *European Journal of Social Psychology*, 5, 149–178. (a)

Turner, J. C. (1975) *Social categorization and social comparison in intergroup relations*. Unpublished PhD thesis, University of Bristol. (b)

Turner, J. C. (1978) Social categorization and social discrimination in the minimal group paradigm. In H. Tajfel (Ed.) *Differentiation between social groups: Studies in the social psychology of intergroup relations*. London: Academic Press.

Turner, J. C. (1980) Fairness or discrimination in intergroup behaviour? A reply to Branthwaite, Doyle and Lightbown. *European Journal of Social Psychology*, 10, 131–147.

Turner, J. C. (1981) The experimental social psychology of intergroup behaviour. In J. C. Turner and H. Giles (Eds) *Intergroup behaviour*. Oxford: Blackwell; Chicago: University of Chicago Press.

Turner, J. C. (1982) Towards a cognitive redefinition of the social group. In H. Tajfel (Ed.) *Social Identity and Intergroup Relations*. Cambridge: Cambridge University Press.

Turner, J. C. (1983) Some comments on . . . 'the measurement of social orientations in the minimal group paradigm'. *European Journal of Social Psychology*, 13, 351–367. (a)

Turner, J. C. (1983) A second reply to Bornstein, Crum, Wittenbraker, Harring, Insko and Thibaut on the measurement of social orientations. *European Journal of Social Psychology*, 13, 383–387. (b)

Turner, J. C. (1984) Social identification and psychological group formation. In H. Tajfel (Ed.) *The social dimension: European developments in social psychology*. Cambridge: Cambridge University Press.

Turner, J. C. (1985) Social categorization and the self-concept: A social cognitive theory of group behaviour. In E. J. Lawler (Ed.) *Advances in Group Processes* (vol. 2). Greenwich, CT: JAI Press.

Turner, J. C. (1987) Introducing the problem: Individual and group. In J. C. Turner, M. A. Hogg, P. J. Oakes, S. D. Reicher and M. S. Wetherell, *Rediscovering the social group: A self-categorization theory*. Oxford: Blackwell. (a)

Turner, J. C. (1987) Rediscovering the social group. In J. C. Turner, M. A. Hogg, P. J. Oakes, S. D. Reicher and M. S. Wetherell, *Rediscovering the social group: A self-categorization theory*. Oxford: Blackwell. (b)

Turner, J. C. (1987) The analysis of social influence. In J. C. Turner, M. A. Hogg, P. J. Oakes, S. D. Reicher and M. S. Wetherell, *Rediscovering the social group: A self-categorization theory*. Oxford: Blackwell. (c)

Turner, J. C. (1988) Comments on Doise's 'Individual and social identities in intergroup relations'. *European Journal of Social Psychology*, *18*, 113–116.

Turner, J. C. (1991) *Social Influence*. Milton Keynes: Open University Press.

Turner, J. C., Brown, R. J. and Tajfel, H. (1979) Social comparison and group interest in ingroup favouritism. *European Journal of Social Psychology*, *9*, 187–204.

Turner, J. C. and Giles, H. (Eds) (1981) *Intergroup behaviour*. Oxford: Blackwell; Chicago: University of Chicago Press. (a)

Turner, J. C. and Giles, H. (1981) Introduction: The social psychology of intergroup behaviour. In J. C. Turner and H. Giles (Eds) *Intergroup behaviour*. Oxford: Blackwell; Chicago: University of Chicago Press. (b)

Turner, J. C., Hogg, M. A., Oakes, P. J., Reicher, S. D. and Wetherell, M. S. (1987) *Rediscovering the social group: A self-categorization theory*. Oxford: Blackwell.

Turner, J. C. and Oakes, P. J. (1986) The significance of the social identity concept for social psychology with reference to individualism, interactionism, and social influence. *British Journal of Social Psychology*, *25*, 237–252.

Turner, J. C. and Oakes, P. J. (1989) Self-categorization theory and social influence. In P. B. Paulus (Ed.) *The psychology of group influence*. Hillsdale, NJ: Erlbaum.

Turner, J. C., Oakes, P. J., Haslam, S. A. and McGarty, C. A. (in press) Self and collective: cognition and social context. *Personality and Social Psychology Bulletin*.

Turner, J. C., Sachdev, I. and Hogg, M. A. (1983) Social categorization, interpersonal attraction and group formation. *British Journal of Social Psychology*, *22*, 227–239.

Tversky, A. (1977) Features of similarity. *Psychological Review*, *84*, 327–352.

Upshaw, H. S. (1962) Own attitude as an anchor in equal-appearing intervals. *Journal of Abnormal and Social Psychology*, *64*, 85–96.

van der Pligt, J. and van Dijk, J. A. (1979) Polarization of judgement and preference for judgemental labels. *European Journal of Social Psychology*, *9*, 233–242.

van der Pligt, J., Eiser, J. R. and Spears, R. (1987) Comparative judgements and preferences: The influence of the number of response alternatives. *British Journal of Social Psychology*, *26*, 269–280.

van Knippenberg, A. F. M. (1984) Intergroup differences in group perceptions. In H. Tajfel (Ed.) *The social dimension* (vol. 2). Cambridge: Cambridge University Press; Paris: Éditions de la Maison des Sciences de l'Homme.

van Knippenberg, A. F. M. and Ellemers, N. (1990) Social identity and intergroup differentiation processes. In W. Stroebe and M. Hewstone (Eds) *European Review of Social Psychology* (vol. 1). Chichester, UK: Wiley.

Vinacke, W. E. (1949) Stereotypes among national-racial groups in Hawaii: A study in ethnocentrism. *Journal of Social Psychology*, *30*, 265–291.

Vinacke, W. E. (1956) Explorations in the dynamic process of stereotyping. *Journal of Social Psychology*, *43*, 105–132.

Vinacke, W. E. (1957) Stereotypes as social concepts. *Journal of Social Psychology*, *46*, 229–243.

Volkmann, J. (1951) Scales of judgement and their implications for social psychology. In J. H. Rohrer and M. Sherif (Eds) *Social psychology at the crossroads*. New York: Harper and Row.

Walker, P. and Antaki, C. (1986) Sexual orientation as a basis for categorization in recall. *British Journal of Social Psychology*, 25, 337–339.

Ward, C. D. (1965) Ego involvement and the absolute judgement of attitude statements. *Journal of Personality and Social Psychology*, 2, 202–208.

Warr, P. B. and Coffman, T. L. (1970) Personality, involvement and extremity of judgement. *British Journal of Social and Clinical Psychology*, 9, 108–121.

Weber, R. and Crocker, J. (1983) Cognitive processes in the revision of stereotypic beliefs. *Journal of Personality and Social Psychology*, 45, 961–977.

Weiss, W. (1959) The effects on opinions of a change in scale judgements. *Journal of Abnormal and Social Psychology*, 58, 329–334.

Wetherell, M. S. and Potter, J. (1992) *Mapping the language of racism: Discourse and the legitimation of exploitation*. Hemel Hempstead: Harvester Wheatsheaf.

White, B. J. and Harvey, O. J. (1965) Effects of personality and own stand on judgement and production of statements about a central issue. *Journal of Experimental Social Psychology*, 1, 334–347.

Wilder, D. A. (1978) Perceiving persons as a group: Effects on attributions of causality and beliefs. *Social Psychology*, 1, 13–23. (a)

Wilder, D. A. (1978) Reduction of intergroup discrimination through individuation of the outgroup. *Journal of Personality and Social Psychology*, 36, 1361–1374. (b)

Wilder, D. A. (1981) Perceiving persons as a group: Categorization and intergroup relations. In D. L. Hamilton (Ed.) *Cognitive processes in stereotyping and intergroup behaviour*. Hillsdale, NJ: Erlbaum.

Wilder, D. A. (1984) Predictions of belief homogeneity and similarity following social categorization. *British Journal of Social Psychology*, 23, 323–333.

Wilder, D. A. (1986) Social categorization: Implications for creation and reduction of intergroup bias. In L. Berkowitz (Ed.) *Advances in experimental social psychology* (vol. 19). New York: Academic Press.

Wilder, D. A. and Allen, V. L. (1978) Group membership and preference for information about others. *Personality and Social Psychology Bulletin*, 4, 106–110.

Wilder, D. A. and Shapiro, P. N. (1984) Role of outgroup cues in determining social identity. *Journal of Personality and Social Psychology*, 47, 342–348.

Wilder, D. A. and Thompson, J. E. (1988) Assimilation and contrast effects in the judgements of groups. *Journal of Personality and Social Psychology*, 54, 62–73.

Williams, R. M., Jr. (1947) The reduction of intergroup tensions: A survey of research on problems of ethnic, racial, and religious group relations. *Social Science Research Council Bulletin*, 57, whole issue.

Worchel, S. (1979) Co-operation and the reduction of intergroup conflict: Some determining factors. In W. G. Austin and S. Worchel (Eds) *The social psychology of intergroup relations*. Monterey, California: Brooks/Cole.

Word, C. O., Zanna, M. P. and Cooper, J. (1974) The nonverbal mediation of self-fulfilling prophecies in interracial interaction. *Journal of Experimental Social Psychology, 10,* 109–120.

Wyer, R. S., Jr. and Gordon, S. (1982) The recall of information about persons and groups. *Journal of Experimental Social Psychology, 18,* 128–164.

Wyer, R. S. and Srull, T. K. (1981) Category accessibility: Some theoretical and empirical issues concerning the processing of social stimulus information. In E. T. Higgins, C. P. Hermans and M. P. Zanna (Eds) *Social cognition: The Ontario symposium* (vol. 1, pp. 161–198). Hillsdale, NJ: Erlbaum.

Yates, J. (1985) The content of awareness is a model of the world. *Psychological Review, 92,* 249–284.

Zadny, J. and Gerard, H. B. (1974) Attributed intentions and informational selectivity. *Journal of Experimental Social Psychology, 10,* 34–52.

Zavalloni, M. and Cook, S. W. (1965) Influence of judge's attitudes on ratings of favourableness of statements about a social group. *Journal of Personality and Social Psychology, 1,* 43–54.

Zawadzki, B. (1942) Limitations of the scapegoat theory of prejudice. *Journal of Abnormal and Social Psychology, 43,* 127–141.

Zebrowitz-McArthur, L. (1988) Where is the stimulus person in impression formation? In T. K. Srull and R. S. Wyer (Eds) *Advances in Social Cognition* (vol. 1, pp. 103–109). Hillsdale, NJ: Erlbaum.

Author Index

Subject Index

*Compiled by Patricia Brown, Diana
Grace and Kate Reynolds.*